Pam Verner has written a fearless, honest memoir. She pulls no punches, frankly describing the ups and the sometimes-terrifying downs of her eventful private life. She also writes of her experiences in psychotherapy (as both patient and, eventually, therapist), and shares her unique and inspiring spiritual path. Come to this book with an open mind and an open heart and let Pam's voice speak to you as if you are her intimate friend. It's an unusual and compelling tale – one you'll not soon forget.

—Jack Lloyd
Fellow journeyer/contemplative/activist/
a retired guy with irons in many spiritual fires

In this page-turner of a memoir, Pam Verner reveals how perseverance, resiliency, and divine intervention result in personal transformation and healing during her inspirational journey. Ms. Verner's courage, faith and targeted guidance received by unseen Spirit helpers enable her to overcome a multitude of hurdles. The reader is inspired and left with a renewed appreciation for humanity's ability to prevail against the odds while being mystified and intrigued by the helpful interventions from the spirit realms. This is a well-crafted story that will keep the reader engaged and wanting more.

—Ana Reluzco
M.S. Ed. Educational Administrator

This book is a must-read for anyone who has ever struggled with thoughts of suicide or felt overwhelmed by the darkness of life. For this is a story of both darkness and light, death and rebirth, despair and hope as we follow the narrative so beautifully woven of Pam's life.

Her story provides both a "candle and a rose" lighting a way of hope thru the darkness, that only one who has been there could possibly provide.

Her journey is a testament to the transformation that is possible when one enters the dark and vulnerable places of the psyche with compassion and forgiveness, which is truly the doorway to the expansive space of unconditional Love.

The beauty of her words and her expertise as a therapist provide an extraordinary framework for anyone struggling in this process called life and open the possibility that yes! "It is worth every step of the journey."

—Cathy Haggerty
 – retired teacher, BA;
Ph.D. in Alternative Healing;
fellow journeyer.

In her intimate and vulnerable memoir, Pam Verner takes us into the experience of the universal struggle for one's sense of belonging in this life.

She invites us into the journey largely forgotten in Western culture of engaging the world hidden to many beyond the veil of ordinary five sensed reality.

The courage to trust her own experience allows Pam to be mentored by helpful spirit guides at critical moments in her life.

In unveiling this sacred thread for us, we see it universally woven through and available to our own lives, past and present.

—William J. McElroy DDS, MA; Spiritual Director;
Founding Convener of Illinois Illuman
Men As Learners and Elders; Retreat Director.

The author's beautifully written journey of self-discovery, emotional recovery, and eventual fulfillment was revealing, informative, mystical, and spiritually rich. I read it through in one day, then reread Part Three a week later. Part Three had me spellbound.

—Don Thomas,
retired after 40 years in police work,
retired Police Chief

Pam has carefully stitched each piece of a hauntingly difficult life, tracing it back to her early years when she felt terribly unwanted and uncared for to the point of wanting to end her life many times over, astonishingly weaving it into a tapestry of love.

Her story is one of tenacity and courage – to keep going no matter how tough the going. She does this from a deep faith in her soul's larger story underneath the everyday story. Listening to her dreams and letting them guide her, the mysterious voices that have spoken to her time and again that she intuitively knew were there to keep her safe, acknowledging the invisible guides that came to help her, and when her trust in others had been so violated, allowing individuals who showed up in her life with genuine concern for her wellbeing to assist her in the many ways they did.

Pam's story is inspiring because she has taken what fate dealt her and woven it into her destiny, paying close attention to the many mysterious events, memories, and ancestral voices, understanding they were attempting to tell her something. She could so easily have fallen through the cracks into addiction, the bitterness of betrayal, or depression, but step by step she instead found her true voice and the love that holds our world together. Bravo Pam!

—Annie Bloom, Vision Quest leader,
Ancestral Retreats, owner of Buffalo Dream Lodge

In her memoir, Pam weaves a story of how she regained her power by realizing that love is always with us. In her life struggles, obstructions, emotional despair and pain, Pam ultimately realizes that we are not alone and certainly never abandoned. It is a chronicle of how she awakens spiritually and how she opened to the metaphysical power of self-healing. Her story is one of courage, determination, self-awareness and the tenacity to keep going in the face of many difficult challenges. It is a must-read for those who feel disempowered by life and a must-read for those who feel thwarted on their spiritual journey. It is a book of hope, strength, and self-acceptance.

—Mel Doerr-
Intuitive Consultant and metaphysical teacher.

Pamela Verner's book is riveting. She expresses what happens when we open ourselves to the sacred spiritual parts of our lives (without any religious upbringing), and how she transformed trauma into love and forgiveness, even when it seemed impossible. The reader is captivated by the many synchronistic miracles, revelations, and sheer power of her will to survive. Enjoy!!

—Abigail Ehrhardt
LCSW
practitioner for 39 years

I am deeply grateful to Pamela for sharing her courageous and visionary Soul's journey memoir. As a holistic psychotherapist, I see many people who are highly intuitive and sensitive to "multi-dimensional" experiences as she describes. Her book will bring empathy, hope and reassurance for those people who feel so alone and are discounted by some in the mental health system. Pam's experience as a psychotherapist comes through in her descriptions of psycho-spiritual methods of treatment, such as past life regression, that acknowledge the evolution of the Soul. I look forward to passing this book on to my clients who wish to move through the "dark night of the Soul" to "Breathing into the Light".

—Susan Wisehart,
MS, LMFT, NCSP, holistic psychotherapist and
author of *Soul Visioning: Clear the Past, Create Your Future*

In her memoir, Pam reflects on a personal journey of self-discovery and finding long-searched-for love and peace. She masterfully intertwines the stories of her epiphanies and realizations throughout life, starting from childhood to adulthood, and shares her humility and vulnerability with the reader. Her work and words reflect her courage and deep strengths she never thought she had but ingeniously discovered through moments of personal enlightenment, "soldiering through a battlefield" of life with some help and advice from the spiritual realm. Pam's story gives hope to those who are lost and lonely. She teaches us, readers, that people don't need to look externally to find "true love" but search within, trust yourself, and believe in an infinite field of Love.

—Irina Zlatogorova, Ph.D.,
Adjunct Faculty at The Chicago School of Professional
Psychology and Southern New Hampshire University

In her compelling and inspiring memoir, Pam Verner chronicles the events of her life with fierce honesty from the emotional challenge of attempted suicide to the final moment when she awakens to a greater Love that embraces all life. She takes us along her desperate paths of survival to a growing awareness that she is never abandoned, even in the darkest times. She shows curiosity, fortitude and tremendous courage to face the questions that plague her and will open her to a conscious life.

—JoAnne McElroy, MA,
Spiritual Director, Enneagram Presenter

Everyone wants to find that place and that way of being that says "home". For some, the search seems easy, even with its inevitable difficulties. For others, it seems a dangerous quest, full of threats, fear, and pain. We're grateful to those brave enough to share their quest. They reassure us that we too may have a homecoming of our own.

Sometimes raw, sometimes comforting, frequently challenging, always inspiring, Pam Verner's account of the liminal spaces of her life is well worth the reading. Experiences of the non-rational and mysterious can be powerful guides in the journey into our deepest and healthiest selves. Pam shows us how that looks and feels to one woman struggling with issues of abuse, abandonment, self-harm, loneliness, despair, and the threat of a meaningless life.

Pam's story is not Everywoman's (nor Everyman's). We don't all receive such vibrant invitations into the realm of the inexplicable. Still, whether it's encountering beautiful synchronicity or meeting an ancestral spirit, Pam presents her experiences without apology, suggesting that the path is open to any with eyes to see and ears to hear the unexpected hints and whispers of realms of experience beyond the everyday happenings of mundane living. She writes matter-of-factly (although with her astonishment clearly on display) about metaphysical insights, inexplicable knowings, extraordinary encounters with not just her psyche, but also the spiritual truths that she argues belong to all of us. This is a book to approach with an open mind and open heart.

I found many of my favorite certainties challenged while others were affirmed. I ended with a longing for a less prosaic path of my own into a deeper self-understanding and continuing spiritual growth. I commend Pam's story to you. May it help guide you home.

—The Rev. Dr. Lindsay Bates
Minister Emerita
The Unitarian Universalist Society
of Geneva, Illinois

This memoir is a page-turner. Writing as if the reader is sitting next to her, the author courageously shares her journey of abandonment, betrayal and deep suicidal depression with grit, wisdom and grace. She has woven together her life experiences of suffering with brutal honesty, along with mystical happenings – which ultimately brought her to the universal truth: no matter what faith tradition, all are loved, and all belong. No exceptions.

The reader is richly blessed with her insights which become an invitation to go deeper into our own transformational journey, back to "the labyrinth of our soul" – back home.

—**Deborah Marqui LCSW**,
author of *From the Fire into the Garden:
A Healing Journey* and
Healing Gardens: Where the Soul Is Tended

Authentic, engaging, and uplifting are words describing this incredible journey. The author takes deep, sensitive topics and engages the reader in a real-life adventure. While many books like this can be a bit dark or insulting towards the villains in the story, this one surely is not.

The author narrates her story with incredible insight and care for all. This is a must-read if you are looking for a feel-good, dramatic, makes you wonder, kind of book!

—**Karen Love**
Master's Degree Candidate, Edgar Cayce's
Educational Foundation

In her book, *Breathing Into the Light,* Pamela Verner examines the arc of her own life, as well as the ancestral and cultural events that have shaped her and her family.

Weaving her encounters with the metaphysical realm into the physical and emotional experiences of her life – including trauma, sexual abuse, grief and recovery – Pam creates a narrative of triumph and integration.

As she traverses one challenge after another, she describes the physical and non-physical support systems helping to bring her forward to a place of self-knowing and peace. Through understanding Pam's fascinating journey, readers can learn how to better explore and navigate the seemingly unknowable trajectory of events in their own lives.

—Marianne Cirone,
MS, MFA, CYT500;
Co-author of *From Alignment to Enlightenment:*
using Props to Achieve Stability and Ease in Yoga Poses.

Pam shares a compelling account of her journey through painful life experiences and of the healing she went through to make peace, and to come home to her soul.

—Nevenka Radovic,
woman, mother, fellow journeyer

BREATHING INTO THE LIGHT

ONE WOMAN'S JOURNEY EMBRACING THE SACREDNESS OF ALL LIFE

PAMELA VERNER

Paperback ISBN: 979-8-9855448-9-3
EBook ISBN: 979-8-9855448-1-7
Audio: 979-8-9855448-2-4
First Printing, 2022
Breathing Into the Light Publishing House
St. Charles, IL

Editor: CSusanNunn.com
Book Cover Design: Pro_eBook Covers at Fiverr
Book Interior and E-book Design by Amit Dey | amitdey2528@gmail.com

TABLE OF CONTENTS

AUTHOR'S NOTE

I've made my living sitting in a comfortable chair listening to others tell me their stories. I've never told anyone my own. I've always kept my personal life private and separate from my professional life. That's a good thing. Clients do not come to a therapist to hear about another's life. They come to hear about their own. And their telling of it helps them hear themselves more fully.

Sharing my story is something I'd never planned on doing. Basically, I'm an introvert. A lot of therapists are. But an encounter with a cousin who died before I was even born inspired and emboldened me to tell my story. He helped me find my courage. He surely had plenty of his own.

You see, I've had what some may call a rather difficult life. But one that turned out amazingly well. It was only because others held hope for me when I couldn't hold it for myself. It was only because I've walked many paths and turned around and around many times. And then proceeded forward, again. Always looking for home. Believing in my "Mozart Street Experience."

My struggle and my path helped me hold the same for others. I do believe we all walk in similar shoes. We just have different stories. All of them leading us home. Eventually.

This is my story. And how I finally found home.

DEDICATION

I dedicate this book to my three daughters, Melanie, Caitlynn, and Sarah, who always held the light of love, and to my late husband, Jim, who convinced me from the beginning "all will be okay".

And to Ray, who held me solid at times when I could not hold myself. And to Mr. Raspiller, the first person to see my light, however dim it was.

And to Guy W. Iversen, a WWII hero.

INTRODUCTION TO THE ANCIENT GRANDMOTHER

As you read this book, you may wonder how I ever survived or came to the place of peace in which I did. It was because I had many helpers. Most of them walked in present time on this land in my life right alongside me. But some had been here long before me and were 'beyond the veil' in the unseen world of spirit.

We are all descendants from many healed ancient and indigenous peoples who came before us and are in the world of spirit, caring about us, our human condition on this earth, calling us home to greater truths. Tall Man, the Ancient Grandmother, and my cousin Guy were helpers from the world of spirit who held a candle guiding me through some of my darkest hours, lighting my path forward, holding for me the scent of the rose of unconditional love.

As my story unfolds, just know we never walk alone.

What follows is an introduction conveyed to me by the Ancient Grandmother, a helper I first experienced midway through my life.

PREFACE

As Told By
Ancient Grandmother

Instead of murdering herself, Pam decided to save her life. It seemed at the time it was one decision made in one moment. But it took her a lifetime. In the end, she learned to love. Not a selfish love, but a deep love grown through forgiving and through walking into darkness carrying a candle and a rose.

We witnessed every step. Every misstep. Every ending. Every beginning. And held her with love. As promised millenniums ago.

We sent her a series of invitations, many of them she found painful, but all leading her into knowing love. Choice made the difference between Grace and Hell. And everything in between.

We were there, holding her, as she danced with suicide and depression through a very long dark night of the soul. She thought she had lost us. She was sure innocence had died. Then, searching deeply inside her heart, walking backward through the darkness and the mystery of her life and our human lineage, she found a deeper, truer part of herself.

Finally, one morning, about 8:10 a.m., with a sip of coffee warming her tongue, she remembered. She realized she could love. And she could come home.

For her, the end was worth the walks into darkness; the struggles with slippery mud; the falling and the getting up. She came to know she is not who she thought she was. And neither are any of us who walk upon this earth. We are so much more.

She came to know her soul, a deeper, eternal part of herself, and to experience a timeless Universal Love underneath all life.

She wouldn't share this until now. Until she knew the ending. And remarkably, until she experienced the beginning.

And so we start with the moment she finally recognized a great shift was upon her, and she could deny her deeper self no longer.

CHAPTER ONE

AT GABRIEL'S INSISTENCE

"And now here is my secret, a very simple secret: It is only with the heart that one can see rightly; what is essential is invisible to the eye."

—The Little Prince

Awareness. God, how we strive for awareness. Just to be aware as we walk this path. For most of us, it comes gently, almost imperceptibly, barely without our knowing. But for me, it came disguised in a golden package of 1500 pounds of horseflesh who just couldn't resist the urge of wildness within him. His name was Gabriel.

The first thing I recall was the hardness of the ground beneath my body. As I slowly opened my eyes, I knew in my heart I was awakening into a new experience, a new world. The dust particles, caught in the glow of the powerful arena lights, swirled eerily above me. The light seemed a beacon, as I lay there struggling to make sense of where I was, what had happened. In the distance, I could hear kicking and snorting. Hear? Feel? Which is it, I wondered? It felt as if a jackhammer far away, yet somehow nearby, was reverberating throughout my body and the earth beneath me.

I took in a breath, becoming aware for the first time of the pain in my neck. Oh, my God, the pain. I wondered, am I dreaming? Or am I waking into the worst nightmare of my life? And then I remembered, I'd been riding Gabriel and he had bucked me off.

Not moving, just listening, feeling, and hearing, I realized he was bucking and galloping all over the indoor arena, the empty stirrups slapping against the sides of his now vacant saddle. I was lying on the ground, flat on my back, my arms outstretched. Wondering if I'd broken my neck, I wiggled my fingers and toes. Noticing I could move them, I figured my neck must be okay. In muddled awareness, I decided to get up and rein in Gabriel.

At just the moment I was to move, a feminine angelic presence hovered closely over me sharing an immense calm. Somehow she conveyed, "Do not move. Not one inch. You've broken your neck."

And so, with Gabriel wildly out of control, snorting, racing circles around me, posing a threat to me lying helpless on the ground, I laid there. Completely still.

My daughter, the only other person in the arena that cold February evening, came running to me, leaning over my left side, "Get up mom!!!" she cried. "Gabriel is running and bucking all over the place. He's gonna trample you!"

The angel's message was calming and unmistakably clear. "Do not move," she said again. "Your neck is broken."

"Get up mom!!!" Melanie yelled. "Now!! Gabriel's gonna trample you! He's wild!"

I continued to feel the calming presence of the angel telling me Gabriel would not trample me, I had broken my neck and must not move. Not one inch.

Melanie couldn't get Gabriel. She didn't have enough experience to rein in such a wild horse. Surely she could get hurt in the process. Yet there was no one else around.

"Melanie," I faintly but calmly said, "You have to leave me here to get help."

"I can't leave you alone. There's nobody else around. Gabriel's gonna trample you," she yelled into my ear again for what seemed to be the umpteenth time.

"Go. Get. Help," I said again, barely above a whisper. "Gabriel will not trample me. I cannot get up. I cannot move," I slowly but firmly said. "You have to leave me. Go. Now."

Wrapped in fear, Melanie ran for help, leaving me lying on the arena floor with Gabriel somewhere out of my view. I slowly took in the smell of wood shavings mixed with horse manure as I felt the calming presence of the angel. I listened to Gabriel's snorting and felt the vibrations of his hoofs stomping heavily on the ground beneath me.

I just laid there. There was nothing else I could do.

Animals have a way of inviting us into our own humanity. That's what Gabriel did for me. But it was a very deep invite, into a mystery I kept secret and denied as a child.

Gabriel taught me many things, but the most profound lesson was about love. Never buy a horse you cannot love. Horses require authenticity. They are a little different from most humans in that way. You cannot feign love to a horse like you can to a human. Horses always know. Always.

Gabriel insisted on a deeper authenticity and a deeper love than most horses. One I had forgotten. And one he and his kind had been deprived of long ago. One he was calling me to remember.

There is an ancient agreement between horse and man. One made when horses were first domesticated. One Gabriel was now rejecting. One perhaps he had never accepted. And one I hadn't even considered. It goes like this,

Horse: "I will carry you into battle and you will protect me."

Man: "I will protect you, but you must do everything I say."

In the days when I first met Gabriel, I hadn't considered the possibility horses have any sense of awareness or require authenticity, or perhaps they could reject dominance and control by us humans. Somehow horses, and all animals, I thought, were separate from humans. They were tools for competition. Tools to prove worth. Or skill. Our modern human version of 'battle'.

That's odd, given what I did for a living. I was a psychotherapist, quite familiar with authenticity, familiar with the need for all of us to consciously acknowledge the truth of our feelings, familiar with the need to let go of battle, both within and without, and work for a truth and a love beyond battle. It was something I practiced on a daily basis with my clients, and it was the cornerstone of my work. But that was with humans. And it was in a controlled environment, within the four walls of my office.

Somehow in the container of my office, it was possible for me to be aware of my own authenticity, and to practice unconditional caring for another. I had no need for games. No need to prove my worth. No need to secure another's love. And I had no fears to soothe. No battles to fight.

For me, the great privilege of being a therapist was my clients allowed me to experience myself feeling an unconditional acceptance of them and to grow that within and for myself, to challenge myself to carry it outside the walls of my office. They gave me the opportunity to experience a sense of a Higher Power, Spirit, or God, working within our lives in the practice of psychotherapy. In so many ways, my clients gave me more than I could ever give them. I was an addictions counselor familiar with a Higher Power and the Twelve Step Program of Alcoholics Anonymous.

But I often felt a separation from myself and others, both human and animal. It seems to be our shared human condition. My awareness at the time was there were three worlds, all separate—the world of earth and animals, the world of humans, and the world of a Higher Power, God or Spirit. And most of the understanding I honored was based upon a dualistic, materialistic, intellectual, linear understanding of life and time. That was the primary separation. We humans seem to do that—to honor our material intellect over any deeper experiential awareness. It's how we are all 'domesticated' in these modern times. But I was now being called into a fuller experience and a fuller understanding.

I lived authentically within a small bandwidth of awareness. But apparently, I had much deeper to go. I'd left parts of myself separate and secret from others, and parts of myself unknown and forgotten even to myself. Like a veil protecting me from imagined battles. Those were parts I shielded from myself, sort of like a porcelain mask separating my awareness of a fuller and deeper love and truth, a fuller bandwidth, a fuller humanity, so to speak. I had forgotten parts of myself I needed to welcome home, parts, like Gabriel, my humankind had domesticated out of me, depriving me of a deeper more authentic humanity.

Gabriel insisted on more from me than I insisted on from myself.

He was a huge golden chestnut gelding, about seventeen hands high, I bought for $7,000 from a trainer who brought him up from a barn in southern Illinois. He'd been 'owned' for three years by a ten-year-old girl, I had been told, who wanted a more challenging horse.

After riding him, two trainers at our barn told me he was 'bombproof'. The only one expressing some concern about this horse was my veterinarian, who, after checking him out, declared with a slight upward pitch of warning in his voice, "You might find this horse has an engine a little too big for you." Somehow, he must have noticed Gabriel's rejection of his human domesticators.

But I ignored the vet, thinking, well, what does this guy know anyway? He hasn't ridden him. He's only a vet. This horse had been owned by a ten-year-old, after all. How big could his 'engine' be?

I'd been riding other people's horses for several years by this time and desperately wanted my own horse. He was the first one to show up. Gabriel had an expansive smooth trot when trainers rode him. And Lyle, my trainer, was a well-respected nationally known trainer and judge of dressage competitions. So, I figured, he knew what he was talking about. Right?

After riding Gabriel around the arena several times, Lyle halted near where I was standing, and while leaning over the horse's shoulder, he said, "I could do a lot with this horse."

I decided Lyle meant he saw potential in Gabriel. In retrospect, I wish I had paid attention to the deeper meaning of what my intuition heard, even then, "This horse needs a lot of training and I can make a lot of money." But, of course, at the time, other than in sessions with clients, I was rarely honoring my own 'horse sense'. I decided to buy him anyway.

Lyle knew I was committed to proper training and to learning safely. Once a week Lyle would work individually with Gabriel, and once a week he would work with me while I was riding Gabriel. I'd be paying him about three hundred dollars a month.

Lyle worked with us, both together and separately each week for several months. Things seemed to be going fine. My one problem was I just didn't love Gabriel. Which was odd, I thought, given how much I love horses and given how much I already loved my daughter's horse. Why not Gabriel? This was different. I just didn't know or understand. But it was true. I didn't want to admit it fully, even to myself. And so I feigned love for him, being inauthentic, hoping it would grow. And Gabriel feigned an inauthentic acceptance of our 'training'.

Gabriel was a mirror to me as I was a mirror to him.

There was a part of him he was hiding—a deep part many of his kind had let slip away for the safety of domestication. And there was a deep part of me that I, and many of my kind, let slip away in order to be accepted by others, to feel safe in the imagined battle we see as our human life, our human form of domestication.

But I didn't know any of that then.

I focused on technique. Pulling the reins a certain way. Being light on the reins. Sitting in the saddle, holding my legs one way or another. Putting ever so slight pressure on one side or the other. I suppose we could say I saw Gabriel as a tool needing my 'refinement'. Lyle was providing instruction for 'refinement'. And we practiced and practiced.

And then, one morning I woke with a dream I had been bucked off Gabriel's right shoulder onto the arena floor. I was shocked. All of my life, long before becoming a psychotherapist, I've made a practice of noting my dreams. They have always provided me with profound guidance. I made a practice of discerning which dreams were advising me of deeper issues, which were processing unresolved feelings, and of particular interest and focus throughout my life have been dreams predicting the future. I've had many of those. They always have a specific feel to them.

This dream about Gabriel bucking me off definitely was predictive. Of that, I was entirely sure.

Then I had the dream again.

And then again.

Each time, I considered what I could do to make sure the dream didn't happen in real life. I talked with my trainer. I made sure he was working with Gabriel on the ground without me. I made sure I had a lesson with Lyle at least once a week. Gabriel never showed any indication of bucking. Never. And everyone continued to say this horse was "bomb proof".

Perhaps, I thought, I'm mistaken about this dream. Perhaps it isn't predictive. Perhaps it's symbolic and metaphoric, rather than predictive. I thought about what meanings could be associated with horse and rider. I denied my deeper knowing.

And now, here I was, lying motionless and helpless on the arena floor, an angel telling me my neck had been broken, with Gabriel wildly bucking and racing circles around me.

Melanie finally found the only other person around, a barn hand, in another part of the building. I was losing my peripheral vision and could barely see his face as he stood over me, asking me to get up.

"Don't let him talk you into moving," I heard the angel say. "Your neck is broken. Remain perfectly still."

"No, I can't," I said to the barn hand, just barely above a whisper. "I think my neck may be broken. Please get Gabriel."

Silently and without responding further, he turned and walked away, corralling Gabriel and taking him to his stall. Melanie called an ambulance.

I was amazingly calm, thanks to the presence of the angel leaning over me until the paramedics came.

"Thank you so much for coming," I said, beginning to cry for the first time.

They kneeled next to me, one at each side, for several minutes, speaking softly to each other, assessing what to do. The paramedic to my right touched my arm, calming me, then said "We're going to take off your helmet and put on a neck brace, but we need you to remain perfectly still. You must relax all your muscles and let us move each part of your body. We do not want you to use any of your muscles in an effort to help us in any way. Do you understand?"

So I had to surrender my body, in every sense of the word, to these two paramedics, and hope they would handle my body without injuring me further. I wasn't to move one muscle. Softly I whispered "Yes."

And then, ever so slowly, they worked together, in a sort of graceful and gentle dance, coordinating their four hands. They removed my helmet, brushing hair from my face making absolutely sure they did not move my neck or head in any way and placed a brace tightly around my neck, preventing me from moving my head up or down or from side to side.

They spoke gently and softly, reassuring me every step of the way.

Those two paramedics will always be my heroes.

Off and on I cried uncontrollably as the ambulance driver made our way to the hospital at an unbelievably slow crawl, sirens blaring and lights flashing. One of the paramedics stayed at my side, stroking my left arm, soothing me, keeping me engaged in small talk, frustrating my own inclinations to lapse into a sleep of unconsciousness.

I don't know how I got tied onto the board. Probably it was the paramedics who did it in the arena. But with the noise and the bright lights of the ER, I became aware for the first time my entire body was strapped with leather straps onto a board. My feet. My knees. My thighs. My stomach. My chest. Even my head. I could not move one inch.

I started screaming.

The two ER doctors attending me were stuttering, "P-p-please, please ma'am," one of them said, not yet knowing my name, "We n-n-need you to be perfectly still, the more you scream, the more you move. W-w-we've got to get you in for an x-ray and perhaps a cat scan."

The other one came over to me, placing his hand softly on my arm, also trying in vain to calm me, "Be patient, we need s-s-some time to see what's going on here."

As the doctor pleaded with me to be quiet, and as I was yelling, "Take me off this board!" a nurse walked into the room with my husband, Jim, at her side, his mouth gaping open, his eyebrows furled in near panic. He looked first at me and then at the doctor standing to my right as if to question what's happening. Given Jim has always been calm in just about every single experience I've ever had with him, I became even more frightened. The doctors, noticing this, asked him to sit outside in the waiting room. I screamed even more.

The doctors didn't care, they were focused on the crisis and not deterred. Which is probably a good thing. They took scissors and cut my new, and rather expensive, winter riding shirt right off me. "Don't tell me I'll never ride a horse again!" I continued to scream over and over.

The second doctor, who by this time knew my name, came over to my other side and said, while stuttering, "P-p-please Pam, we need you to be calm."

"I can't! I may never ride a horse again!" I yelled.

Somehow with all my screaming and crying, and their stuttering and pleading with me to be quiet and motionless, they were able to get me in for an x-ray and then a cat scan. They brought me back to the ER room while I continued to scream and cry. At least one of them stayed constantly at my side continuing to plead with me to be quiet and calm. But I just couldn't.

I begged them to remove all the straps. My body was hurting from being placed so flat and so firmly on my back.

"N-n-no, we can't P-p-pam," said the one doctor who stuttered more than the other. "If we take off the straps you could m-m-move. We can't allow you to move."

"Well then, give me something for the pain!" I screamed. This was an entirely unusual demand for me to make, given I don't like pain medication. And given I was an addictions counselor. But I was badly hurting.

"No m-m-medication either. We can't drug you. You might have a head injury," one of the doctors said, stuttering.

The other doctor was outside in the hallway talking and arguing with someone on the phone. Somehow through my own yelling and screaming, I could hear him say, without stuttering, to the person on the phone, "She was wearing a helmet. I have it right here. It's really beat up. You have to come here right now. We can't wait until tomorrow. Her neck is broken. She needs surgery! Now!"

There was quite a bit of discussion between the person on the other end of the line and both ER doctors pleading for him to come right away.

After several hours of apparent arguing and discussing with whoever it was on the other end of the phone and the stuttering ER doctors, they decided to secure my neck with another more stable brace and admit me, taking me upstairs to a hospital room.

I was finally able to see Jim, who had been patiently sitting in the waiting room just outside the ER all this time. He walked at my side, gently touching my arm, as they wheeled me to my room.

Somehow, someway, I don't recall, someone took me out of those leather straps and off the board. I don't know how they did it. Reassured I would be okay for the evening, Jim tenderly stroked my arm in a gentle goodbye, saying he would see me the next morning. And then nurses proceeded to check in on me, flashing bright lights into my eyes, every thirty minutes or so for the rest of the night.

The next morning, I found out what all the arguing and discussion was about between the ER doctors and the unnamed person on the other end of the phone. The unnamed person was the neurosurgeon, Dr. Jonah, the ER doctors had called in to take care of me. He visited me at first light.

"The doctors last night were freaked about your injury," Dr. Jonah said. "They'd never seen an injury like this where the patient survived."

He went on to say the ER doctors wanted him to come in to do surgery the night before and he had to explain to them surgery wouldn't help. The fracture had to be secured and my body would do the healing.

"Essentially," he said, "you broke your neck, C1. And fractured part of your brain stem also. But it was all fractured, not broken through. That's what saved your life. If it had been broken through, the nerve connection between your brain and heart and lungs would have been severed. You wouldn't have lived past the arena floor."

I don't know why, but for some reason, I just couldn't take in his words. I remembered them but couldn't take in the meaning of them until many days later. My head and neck hurt so badly I could hardly speak, the reverberation of my speech caused painful vibration inside my head. And I could hardly see. It was as if I had tunnel vision. No matter how much I tried to move my eyes and to see, my peripheral vision was gone.

At discharge, Dr. Jonah explained I would be in a brace for three months. Night and day. Even when I slept. I could not be without it. And then he pulled out a second brace. So I would have two.

"When you take a shower," he explained, "shower with the brace on. When you come out of the shower, have this other brace nearby and line your body up against the wall, being perfectly straight. Have your husband take off the wet brace and place the dry one on. All without you moving in any way."

Ok, now, so I began to realize this brace and I would be pretty close for three months. I would have to wear it as I showered and slept. And surely, I wouldn't be able to drive. Or ride. I wondered how I would get to my office to work. Would I be able to work? Would my eyesight improve?

When Jim came in to take me home, the nurse showed him the extra brace, how to work it, and then instructed him on how to remove it and place the new one on. She was very clear in outlining to him the importance of my need to wear the brace. Night and day. For three months.

When I took my first shower about a week later, the seriousness of the injury hit me. Jim stayed nearby as I showered. I came out and lined myself straight and immobile against a nearby wall, just as Dr. Jonah instructed, while Jim, breathing heavily with anxiety, slowly removed the brace and placed on the new one. After dressing, we began some serious talking.

"Jim," I started, "I had a dream I was going to get bucked off Gabriel before it happened."

By this time in our marriage, it was well understood between Jim and me I had predictive dreams. Even though neither of us understood how this happens, these things had been verified so many times we both accepted it.

"Why didn't you pay attention?" Jim asked, raising his voice with some irritation.

"I did," I responded. "I spoke with Lyle and made sure we were doing everything as we should. I was always careful. I don't understand why this happened."

"He was supposed to be 'bomb-proof,'" Jim responded.

Yeah, I thought but didn't say, horses are unpredictable, ultimately. They are huge creatures. But what about the warning? And what about that I just never loved Gabriel?

"Jim, I think this is about something much deeper," I said, tears welling in my eyes. "Something I have no awareness of— something I need to search for and explore. Something I need to know, something I need to find," I continued. "Think of this. I have a dream I get bucked off Gabriel. Then it happens. And I come within a tiny fraction of an inch from immediately dying. What's that about? What's the message?"

He rested his elbow on the arm of the chair he was sitting upon, put his hand up to his mouth, gulped in a breath, and held it as if trying to stop himself from speaking. Then shed a tear. An unusual event for Jim. Clearly, we were aware of what a close call this was and were both glad I had survived.

We each took a few deep breaths while sitting in silence for several minutes, facing each other, yet looking down at the floor. I knew we were avoiding something, and so I decided to go there, "Jim, what if, after all these years, I'm suicidal again, only unconscious about it?"

Jim flinched just a bit, likely remembering the long gut-wrenching walk we both went through many years before, when I stood on the razor's edge of suicide. Likely remembering the times when he made sure all our electrical outlets were grounded; when he removed all the knives from our house, and the time when he rushed me to the ER bleeding from a razor cut. All the close calls. All the psychotherapy sessions. All the work we had both done.

That was years before. I worked long and hard in my own psychotherapy to overcome trauma and depression. After all the work, I ended up pursuing a career in psychotherapy myself. My experiences on the 'other side of the desk' made me a more aware and empathic psychotherapist. But after all these years, I wondered, how could I be dealing with this again? Or was I? Could this be something else? What was this about?

After those dark times, Jim and I were now living our dreams. Our relationship was on solid ground. He loved being a science teacher. He was a recovering alcoholic, and I was a recovering codependent. I loved being a psychotherapist working with trauma, codependency, addictions, and doing Family Intervention Counseling. We had three daughters, all doing well. We had moved back to Jim's family farm and built our dream house. We'd overcome and grown through so much. What more could I want? How is it I could in any way be missing something?

But I was. And I needed to find out.

Oddly, the beginning of an answer came with the gift of a book.

A few days after my discharge from the hospital, our middle daughter, Caitlynn, who was attending college in Chicago, came home for a visit. She and her boyfriend, Mike, walked in the door as I was standing at the stove in the kitchen. Since I could not turn my head, I stiffly turned my entire body around to face them as they entered. Caitlynn winced a bit at noticing my stiffness and the brace on my neck, then smiled and greeted me with tears in her eyes and a gentle hug. Mike smiled as he reached out and handed me a book, The Holographic Universe, by Michael Talbot, saying, "Mrs. Verner, you're gonna love this book."

I hardly knew Mike. I had no idea why he thought I'd like this book. But obviously, in retrospect, he had tapped into some of his own deeper wisdom. The book invited me to remember a past I put aside and denied. It was a full-out invitation to open my 'bandwidth of awareness,' and ultimately open my deeper heart.

Talbot's book explores the frontiers of conceptual physics and combined the search with investigations into telepathy, dreams, past lives, out-of-body and near-death experiences. His book was endorsed by Fred Alan Wolf, Ph.D., and Larry Dossey, M.D., both well-respected leaders in their fields. Talbot put forth the idea, held by many physicists at the time but not yet accepted as mainstream, that everything is frequency and vibration, and our universe is a hologram. The implications of this theory are vast. It offers a pathway into a scientific understanding of mystical/spiritual experiences.

Predictive dreams, strong intuition, mental telepathy, and contact with the departed seemed to be family traditions among the women in my family. But they were things we kept quiet and spoke of only in whispers amongst ourselves. Humanity itself, after all, has quite a history of burning people at the stake for sharing such experiences.

Reading this book encouraged me to go beyond the hundreds of years of 'conventional domestication' of our culture, and to look deeper into my own spiritual experiences, and acknowledge them. Experiences I hid, even from Jim, under a porcelain mask of domestication which Gabriel insisted on cracking open that cold February evening.

I began by looking into my distant past to experiences I had as a young child, beginning when I wasn't quite five years old. Oddly, with all the psychotherapy I'd been through, we hadn't explored my childhood in any depth. At the time I was undergoing all the intense psychotherapy, I would have kept those experiences to myself anyway. We had to focus on my immediate situation, the suicidal crisis and trauma I was working through as a young adult, rather than dive deeply into my history. But with this 'accident,' I knew I had to proceed where I hadn't gone before.

Jim, as a recovering alcoholic, was well acquainted with the sense of a Higher Power. And the way he made sense of my predictive dreams was that the Higher Power was guiding me through dreams. He believed in the teachings of his Lutheran religion and saw the Higher Power within the Twelve Step Program as the God from his Lutheran upbringing. As for me, I was raised with absolutely no religion, yet I believed in a Higher Power, God, Universal Love, because of those deep spiritual experiences I had as a child, which I kept secret. My entrance into the addictions field as a therapist gave me the opportunity to be with colleagues who also believed in some other divine guidance or force working for healing within our lives. Because of the spiritual foundation of The Twelve Steps, I felt a sense of coming home. Apparently, however, I had further to go.

PART ONE

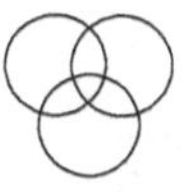

THE GRACE OF INNOCENCE LOST

CHAPTER TWO

IT ALL STARTED ON MOZART STREET

"The distinction between past, present, and future is only an illusion, however persistent."

—Einstein

A few days after my discussion with Jim, just after waking, I sat alone in our living room sipping a cup of freshly brewed hot coffee, my eyes and heart drawn to the wild and magnificent wetlands just beyond our front door. Since our house faced west, nearly every evening we were held by the red sky of the setting sun, and the huge expanse of an eighty-acre wetland just outside our door.

As I looked out at the open fields, the February morning sky blue and clear, memories of childhood experiences I'd kept to myself for decades began to surface. Somehow, at the time of those experiences, I knew I had to keep them to myself. But now, after Gabriel's buck and reading this new book, I began to consider I might need to share them and work with them.

Although I didn't know it all those years before, the day destined to be the touchstone of my life took place on one particular sunny summer afternoon on Mozart Street, in Humboldt Park, Chicago, in the early fifties. I wasn't quite five years old.

To me at the time, it was just an ordinary day. To a nearly five-year-old child, miraculous experiences are ordinary. They happen every day. But as years go on, and innocence is lost, they are generally forgotten. As I looked back from the distance of decades and the vista of the eighty-acre field, and recalled the event I committed to memory, I realized it put me on notice to pay close attention throughout my entire life, and to clearly remember what I've always called "The Mozart Street Experience."

In the early fifties, Humboldt Park was home to mostly working-class immigrants from Northern Europe. The smell of fish cooking and the sounds of Norwegian and Swedish accents filled the air. My dad's father, along with many others in our neighborhood, came to America around 1925. My grandmother, with my dad at her side, sailed across the Atlantic, joining him four years later. It was quite a journey for a nine-year-old to leave his small island home off the coast of Norway where he'd been born and come to live in a huge inland city far from the ocean he loved. In the middle of the American Depression, no less. While my dad didn't talk about it much, he always held a silent grief over leaving his childhood home on a small island with the North Atlantic licking at its edges.

After years of cleaning fish in local markets, washing floors, and laying bricks building the city of Chicago, by the late forties and after World War II, my dad's parents were finally able to buy a four flat apartment in Humboldt Park.

This was lucky for my mom and dad, because in the early fifties when I was three, they lost our home in a small farming town in Iowa. My dad, a WWII Navy veteran, wasn't able to make enough money painting houses to provide for our growing family. When they couldn't afford their house, they packed all four of us kids, with another one on the way, and moved us to Grandpa's apartment building on Mozart Street.

Silent grief, aided by poverty, was the foundational cornerstone experience for both my mom and dad. They worked hard. They did their best. Of that I am sure. But their grief was a silent, unspoken force running throughout their entire lives. And of course, our family as well.

We were poor. There was no doubt. But I didn't know what that meant then. I had one toy, a brown teddy bear I called Teddy. We had no books and no television. Our apartment was a small nearly empty three-bedroom on the second floor of Grandpa's four-flat. Wood floors. Huge high ceilings. Between the scarce furniture, the high ceilings and the wood floors, every sound echoed throughout our entire space.

On this one afternoon, Mom was busy washing dishes, getting ready to prepare dinner. My infant brother, the seventh member of our family, was taking a nap in a small room next to the kitchen. For some very odd reason, and to my good fortune that day, everyone else was gone, giving me an unusual chance for some alone moments with Mom. I quickly took the opportunity. While placing my teddy bear on the tile floor in the kitchen, I looked up at Mom's back, her wavy dark hair nearly brushing her shoulders, and decided she couldn't avoid answering my questions this time, as she'd always done in the past.

"Mom," I asked, never calling her 'mommy,' "Remember the old man with the horse and cart who came by selling fruit? Why wouldn't you let me get strawberries?"

"Pammie," Mom said, breathing out her typical sigh of boredom, "there never was a man who came by with a horse selling fruit. It never happened. I've told you this before."

Here we go again, I thought. I know there was. I remember. In detail. Huge brown and black horse. Old man. Dressed in dark baggy clothes with a small brown hat. White hair. White beard. Brown eyes. Missing teeth. Kind smile.

"Yes, there was Mom! I remember," I said.

"No, you don't Pammie," she responded, shifting her stance just a bit while continuing to face the sink, keeping her back to me, indicating a low level of irritation.

But this time I wasn't going to let it go. We were alone in the kitchen after all. There was no one to interrupt us.

"Ok, Mom," I continued. "So how about the thing I saw in the sky? What was that?"

"An airplane, Pammie," she quickly responded.

"No, Mom. It wasn't an airplane," I said. "Airplanes make a lot of noise. They have wings and fly fast. That wasn't what this thing did."

For some reason, even though I'd said all this before, she was interested. She went over to a drawer and pulled out a small piece of paper and a pencil. While placing it on the kitchen table, she said, "Draw it."

She'd never asked this before. Wow! I had her attention! I jumped up, leaving Teddy on the floor, ran over to the kitchen table and began to draw. I drew an oblong object with a cup-like piece in the middle at the bottom with a fan at one end. I put the pencil down and looked up at her. She squinted for a few moments in silent puzzlement at my very rudimentary drawing.

"Oh, that's a blimp," she finally said, with certainty. "But we don't have them here and you've never seen one." Then she walked away, again turning her back on me, returning to wash the dishes at the kitchen sink.

"Yes I did, Mom. I know I did," I said, in frustration. And so, this conversation ended the way all the others ended. With Mom denying what I know I remembered.

Leaving Mom there in the kitchen, I picked up Teddy and walked into our living room. Why is it she tells me these things didn't happen when I know they did, I wondered? This was very concerning to me. I was absolutely sure of my memory. There was only one other option. Mom was lying. But I couldn't figure out why she would lie to me about a man and a horse and a blimp, and all the other memories I'd asked her about before. Why would she lie? It made no sense. Then I wondered, with some concern, would she lie to me about other things?

I sat on the wood floor of our living room, telling Teddy of my frustration with Mom. And then suddenly I heard a voice, calling from outside.

"Yoohoo Pammie! Yoohoo Pammie!" was the call. That's how we kids invited others to play with us in those days. We just stood out on the sidewalk and called our friend's name. We didn't go to our friend's door and ring the doorbell. I became silent, turned my ear to the window, listening closely. Was this a call for me? I listened carefully to make sure the call ended with my name. "Yoohoo Pammie! Yoohoo Pammie," I heard again. I jumped onto our worn green couch and looked out the window at Mozart Street below. It was Eileen, calling for me.

As I looked at her standing on the street, her pretty blue dress with her new shoes, and her long blonde braids trailing down her chest, I noticed she had a bright red scooter next to her. A new toy! Maybe she would share it! Eileen always had new things and always dressed pretty. I wore dresses, too. But everything I wore was a hand-me-down and was a little faded and worn. I didn't mind the clothing part, but the toys, now they were important to me. I hoped Eileen would share her scooter.

Eileen was my older sister's friend, not mine. She was about seven. Eileen always called for my sister, never for me. But here she was, calling for me! Me! Perhaps she knew my sister wasn't home. I now had someone to play with!

"Mom, Eileen's calling for me! I'm going outside," I yelled, my voice echoing throughout our apartment. Without waiting for a response, I ran to the door, slammed it shut behind me, and raced down the narrow stairway, the pounding of my worn leather-soled shoes reverberating throughout the stairwell with each step, all the way down to the porch outside facing the sidewalk.

"Eileen! Is that a new scooter?" I cried out immediately, as both my feet landed on our front porch.

"Sure is!" she responded. "Wanna race on the sidewalk?"

Well, of course, I did! We raced up and down Mozart Street, Eileen on the scooter, me running beside her. Then she shared her scooter! I raced on the scooter with her running beside me. It was a hot sunny afternoon in the middle of summer, but we kept racing back and forth, trading places with her scooter. She was nearly half a foot taller than me, giving her the advantage of size in addition to age. I was a slight kid and a little shorter than average for my age. And, so most of the time, Eileen beat me. But I found I could run furiously fast. I began to outrun Eileen.

And then, somehow, for some reason, Eileen must have gotten mad at me. Perhaps I beat her in our race too many times in a row. Perhaps she got tired before I did and just didn't want to admit it. I really don't know. But she stopped running and looked at me directly in the eyes. Her blue eyes staring into my blue eyes. Her white-blonde hair wringing wet with sweat. Beads of sweat dripping down her forehead into her eyes and onto her cheeks. She wiped the salty drops away from her eyes. It was then I became aware I was hot and sweaty, too. We were both breathing heavily from running so fast and so hard in the midwestern summer heat.

"The devil lives under your gramma's porch, you know," she said between heavy breaths.

"What?" I asked. "What's the devil?"

Eileen was quite excited to tell me. She stood up straighter, her expression becoming more intense as she focused all her attention on me, locking her eyes into mine.

"The devil is a red man with shiny red eyes, horns, and a long pointy tail," she said. "He carries a huge, pointed fork so he can stick you. He lives in fire—forever and ever in hell."

This was way too much for me to take in. First, there's a devil wanting to hurt me. He lives under my gramma's steps. And he also lives in another town called hell. And somehow, he doesn't burn up even though he's in a forever fire. But then, what's forever?

I decided to take this one step at a time. Let's just find out what hell is, and where it is.

"Ah, where's hell?" I softly asked.

"Hell is where you go when you die," Eileen said, her tone dropping, sounding quite serious.

"Die? What's die?" I asked, deciding that taking one step at a time was not working as well as I'd wished.

This was big. Really big. I decided I had to get this straight. My heart was quickening. My legs were shaking. I was even having a difficult time catching my breath. I tried and tried to breathe more deeply and slowly, but I just couldn't.

"You don't know what die is?" Eileen shrieked, appearing shocked, making fun of me. "Well, die is what happens when you don't live anymore," she said, almost laughing. "You disappear. It happens when you get old. Like your gramma. She's gonna die pretty soon."

For the first time ever, I considered this thing called time. A pretty complicated issue, if you consider it. I became aware my gramma was older than Mom and Dad, and they were older than me. And I had two siblings older than me, and two younger than me. Doesn't it stay that way forever I thought? But then, what is forever? And what's this thing called die? How could someone just disappear? Where do they go? I was sure

Eileen thought I was stupid, but I figured she knew stuff I didn't, so I risked looking even more stupid and pressed her for more answers.

"What happens when we die?" I asked.

"The devil takes his pointy fork and sticks you and drags you down to burn forever in hell," Eileen said, standing even straighter and making even more intense eye contact. We were standing about two feet apart, close enough to feel each other's breath.

Clearly, Eileen was sure of her information. I wanted to look away. But she knew things no one else was telling me. Even my own mom denied things, like about the fruit peddler and that flying thing. I was convinced I had to know what Eileen knew. And she appeared quite willing to share. Much different from Mom.

"Everybody?" I faintly asked.

"Yes. Everybody," Eileen stated strongly with an air of complete assurance. "Even your mom and dad. And when the devil drags people down into hell, they never see their mom and dad again. People are alone with the devil in hell. Forever and ever in fire," she said. Then added, with an upturn of her head, "Humph," gliding swiftly away, taking herself and her beautiful red scooter home.

I stood there in silence. Completely confused. And terrified.

I clearly saw the images Eileen just described. Red man. Sharp fork. Forever and ever in fire. Die. Never see your mom or dad or gramma again. Your mom and dad burning forever in hell. Me, too. Everybody. So first, I thought, I live here, on Mozart Street, then die and burn forever in hell with the devil poking me. And he lives under my gramma's front steps, waiting to get each person when they die. No chance of getting away.

Breathing deeply, I tried to hold myself up in the midst of terror. My whole body trembled. The front porch stairs were about fifteen feet away.

I walked slowly toward them, trying to get a good look. The steps were dark grey with white crisscrossing slats on the side, the white paint flaking and dotted with the orange smudge of rusting nails. Bending over very carefully, trying to see under the stairs and in between those peeling white slats touching the ground, I saw nothing but dirt and maybe a few little stones. No red man with horns and a pointy tail. No sign of a big sharp fork. No, nothing there.

Slowly, I took a few steps backward, not wanting to turn my eyes from the stairway. Standing a safe distance away, seeing pictures in my mind of all Eileen had said, I felt terror at the thought of Mom dying and burning in hell. Terror at the thought of me dying and also burning in hell. I shook all the way down to my feet.

And then, in what was perhaps one brief moment— or perhaps many moments— I can't really say— many thoughts, feelings, images and concepts flashed into my awareness— as if a loving wise elder just stepped in. Those questions I'd so diligently asked Mom earlier and Eileen just a moment ago suddenly had answers.

The image of the blimp came first into my awareness. I sensed this loving presence showing me the blimp was from another lifetime. One lived before coming into this family. Before having this Mom.

"Oh, that was another life!" I said out loud.

"Yes," I felt the response. "One of many, many you have had."

And the old man with the horse and cart selling fruit—well Mom doesn't remember those because she wasn't there either.

I realized then Mom was confused because she knew blimps, fruit peddlers with horses, and carts were around before I was born. And she doesn't understand how I could possibly know about them now, never having seen them. Mom never considered we have all lived before.

"So, Mom's not lying," I said silently to myself, breathing a sigh of relief. "Wow! Mom's not lying!"

So, we don't ever die! We just leave this life here and go on to another! Learning from each life and moving through time. With a loving place beyond time holding us all. Witnessing everything. Each and every one of us.

There is no hell when we die and there is no devil, despite what Eileen had said. Of that, I was now sure.

What I understood was this: I am not who I think I am. And neither was Eileen or any of us who walk upon this earth. We are so much more.

I realized then the nearly five-year-old self I was, who stood right there in that very moment on Mozart Street, would be here and would perhaps grow old—and will someday leave this place. But an eternal part of me will come back again and again if I choose. Maybe not here. And maybe not with this family. But I will continue. As will we all. Because there is this piece of each of us traveling through time seeing it all and learning. Life is about learning, growing, choosing, and sharing. And an eternal part of us witnessing it all, holding everything within a huge field of love. Of this, I was now absolutely sure.

As I stood there, facing those steps, I felt as if I'd been kissed by the fragrance of a soft magenta rose and held in peace. My body stopped shaking and I felt my feet touching the ground as the warmth of the sun touched my head and shoulders.

I glanced at my feet held inside those hand-me-down worn red leather Mary Jane shoes, standing there on the concrete sidewalk. I looked up and down the street and noticed the tall elm trees living in the small muddy area between the sidewalk and the cars, their arching branches moving gently in the softness of a breeze.

All those questions I so diligently asked Mom and Eileen were answered. Just not in the way I expected.

Surely there was a purpose to our days beyond winning a race with a shiny red scooter, as fun as that truly can be.

Now you would think, wouldn't you, I would run inside and tell Mom I now know why she doesn't remember all those things I'd been so intently asking her about just this morning? Somehow, part of the experience also guided me to keep this to myself. And, so I did.

But I did run inside and tell Mom about Eileen trying to scare the daylights out of me about the devil. That's how I saw it at the time.

I ran up those grey porch stairs and then inside up the dark narrow hallway into our second-floor apartment. Finally finding Mom still scrubbing dishes in the kitchen, I yelled "Mom, Eileen told me something scary I don't believe!!!"

"What's that, Pammie?" she said with a bored sigh.

"She said the devil lives under our porch steps!"

"That's not true, Pammie," Mom said softly, barely audible, with apparent disinterest.

Yeah, I already knew the devil wasn't there. But at the time, I wanted Mom to know what Eileen said, even if she wasn't interested.

And then I went into our front room to play with Teddy.

I held the Mozart Street Experience close to me, throughout many years of darkness, telling absolutely no one. If I had told someone, like my mother, she probably would have eventually talked me out of it, and I would have forgotten it or distorted it into something else. But instead, I kept it close, told no one, and remembered it always, exactly as it happened.

In the decades leading up to getting bucked off Gabriel, throughout the many trials of my life, and there were many, I silently kept reminding myself of this experience. I am not my personality, yet I travel through this world with my personality. I kept close to my memory there is a deeper loving meaning and purpose to all experiences taking place in this very physical life here. Even during those times I didn't understand, times when I felt so separate from any sense of love, I tried to keep this close, reminding myself there is a wiser self and a deeper home than this outer world seems to show. I held that to my heart.

And now, as I sat there, this cold February morning, my neck held tightly in the brace, for the first time I let myself feel gratitude for the Mozart Street Experience. Gratitude for holding me throughout my entire life. Even though I'd spent decades feeling alone and separate from any loving Spiritual source, as I experienced the Mozart Street Experience again that morning, I became aware I had been held all along. Tears of gratitude dripped down my face.

As I was nearing my fiftieth year, I began to open my 'bandwidth of awareness' into a deeper truth of spirit in my life, and in everyone's life. I finally stopped pushing it away.

At the time of the Mozart Street experience, the big takeaway for my nearly five-year-old self was that we are here to grow, to learn, and to evolve. Now the word, evolve, was not used, but the concept was presented, and even at nearly five, I understood.

And another takeaway was we all have a soul—an eternal part of us different from our personality—our personality being the part of us that acts in this world, and lives and dies in this world. The word soul also was not actually used, but again, my child self somehow understood the concept. What I understood then was there is an eternal part of us traveling through lifetimes, learning, growing, sharing and being held within a loving timeless presence. And somehow, time itself isn't quite as we understand it.

And also, every life matters and is held within this huge field of love. No exceptions. Every. Single. Life.

Another takeaway was that our entire world is alive with love. It was a beautiful wonder to behold—yet quite unusual for the forty-eight-year-old I was as I recollected the Mozart Street Experience from the distance of decades later sitting there facing the beautiful western field after breaking my neck. But it was entirely normal for the wonder a five-year-old holds every day.

You might ask how is it a young child does hold something like this? Well, consider for a moment what the life of a five-year-old is like. Everything is a wonder. The sun rising in the morning. The opening of a flower. The flight of a bee or a bird. A snowstorm. The love of a brown teddy bear. A five-year-old lives in wonder.

Something we forget as we grow older. Because we all experience fear. And we always remember fear. And believe listening to our fear will make us safe. Shortly after the experience on Mozart Street, I did experience fear, a deep terror.

My younger sister Blythe, who was three at the time, was kidnapped. No one had any idea of how it happened.

I remember the terror of coming to grips with the possibility Blythe was completely lost and gone from us. As a baby girl.

Of course, we called the police. The entire neighborhood went on a search and rescue effort. Someone, I don't know who, heard her crying from a garbage can where she had been stuffed. Thankfully, she was alive, but how could anyone do this? I had no answer.

To my young child self, parts of the world were not safe.

CHAPTER THREE

IS THIS A DAY TO DIE?

"Death is not the greatest loss in life.
The greatest loss is what dies inside us while we live."

—Norman Cousins

To Mom, the world wasn't safe either.

Intense conversations between Mom and Dad went on for days after finding Blythe safe. Mom was fearful this could happen again. I recall the pain, the anger, the intense grief. The fear. And the relief Blythe was okay.

Mom insisted we move. She didn't want to live in a large city. Dad had grown up in Chicago, so he resisted, but eventually, he agreed.

And so, early the next spring, we moved from Grandpa's apartment in Chicago to our own small ranch house far out in the suburbs. Our house was a shell with just a roof, outside windows and walls. Many houses were built like this in the early fifty's suburbs. We had no interior walls or ceilings. We had plywood for floors. Sand for a basement floor, with no steps into the basement. No kitchen cabinets. The only walls were in the bathroom, the one place with privacy. A brown army blanket draped the bathroom doorway.

It was the only way we could afford a house.

Even though our house was small, and not finished, I didn't care. Similar to Chicago, my siblings found friends living nearby, but there was no one my age around. So, I spent a great deal of time with our dog Sheba, my only companion, exploring the woods across the street. Mom was okay with my wandering. Sheba and I made friends with every tree. They were mostly tall old oak trees. A shallow creek wound its way through the hilly woods.

Over a period of a year or two, Dad built the rest of the house with his bare hands. The exciting smell of sawdust permeated our house all those years. He poured a concrete floor in the basement. Put up walls and ceilings dividing the bedrooms. Made kitchen cabinets. Put in oak floors throughout the entire house. Put in each door, one by one. I was at his side for nearly every nail hammered and every screw drilled.

By the time I was seven, all the walls and floors were in. We had a kitchen. And doors hung on all our doorways. We also had a few pieces of furniture and a small television set in our living room. Our house looked pretty much like everyone else's in our neighborhood.

One day I was invited over to a classmate's house for her eighth birthday party. Mary Ann lived in a big ranch house near the school. Her mom made barbecued beef sandwiches and served them with potato chips, coca-cola, and cake and ice cream for dessert. I had never had some of the food she served. It was quite a big party with lots of girls—an entirely new and exciting experience.

I got sick after the party. At the time, I blamed it on the barbecue beef, something I'd never eaten before. This ended up being my first 'full-out' invitation after my Mozart Street Experience, into a deeper experience of life.

I got a terrible stomachache. After many hours of watching me and thumping my stomach, Mom decided I had appendicitis and needed surgery, immediately. By this time, it was the middle of the night.

"Pammie, I think you have something inside your tummy that needs to be taken out," she said after one last stomach thumping. "We can't wait until morning."

Before taking me to the ER, I heard Mom and Dad whispering while pacing outside my bedroom door. From the ceiling light cast in the hallway, I could see their shadows shifting back and forth as they moved around, whispering.

"Red," Mom said in a low and urgent tone, "Pammie is very sick. We need to get her to the Emergency Room. I think she has appendicitis."

"How can you be sure?" Dad responded.

Mom was very familiar with medical issues. She always wanted to be a physician and had studied a great deal of anatomy and medicine on her own. Money prevented the pursuit of her dream of medical school.

She described the thumping she did on my abdomen—noting my pain increased as she let up pressure, rather than when she put on pressure. "That's classic appendicitis, Red. I think she needs surgery. Now."

"But Fran," I heard Dad say, "we have no money. How can we do this? Are you sure?"

"If she has appendicitis and we don't get her surgery, she could die," Mom said, with the authority of knowing a fair amount about medicine.

I suddenly became aware of the urgency here. Now I understood why she'd been asking so many questions and thumping my tummy with such deep attention.

Dad didn't appear to like the option of me dying of appendicitis any more than Mom. And so they both decided I must go to the Emergency Room immediately and place this decision before doctors.

She woke our doctor in the middle of the night, and he and an associate agreed to meet us at the small unstaffed, empty hospital emergency room.

The doctors spent about an hour physically checking me out. They took blood and urine tests. Then they declared yes, indeed, I did have appendicitis and, yes, indeed, I did need surgery. Immediately. Not later. Now.

When they told us I needed surgery, Mom and the two doctors asked me to wait outside in a dark, empty hallway, sitting alone on a single brown, cold folding chair, while they discussed my surgery.

Mom emerged from the room, her shoulders slumped and wiping tears from her face. She'd been crying. The doctors followed her out. All their heads were down, facing the floor, seeming to be quite unhappy.

I tried to look at each of them, but no one would make eye contact with me.

"Let's go home, Pammie," Mom said.

I nearly passed out as my heart sank. I wouldn't be getting surgery after all. Now I was the one fighting back tears. I'd been pretty brave up to this point, but I couldn't bear the idea of this pain any longer. Did this mean I was going to die? How can they come to this decision when the doctors had been so clear I had appendicitis and needed surgery? Immediately. To save my life?

Both doctors turned to me – the youngest and littlest among the four of us standing in the dark, empty, sad, hospital corridor, for the first time looking me in the eyes. One of them touched my shoulder as he spoke.

"If anything changes with your pain Pammie, you must let your mommy know. Do you understand?" the first doctor said with a sense of urgency and firmness.

"Right away. You understand, don't you Pammie?" asked the second doctor who had his hand on my shoulder.

They both wanted me to have surgery and were unhappy with Mom's decision to take me home. All I could do through my tears was nod I understood.

I was in so much pain I could hardly walk. Hunched over, barely able to raise my right leg, I limped out with Mom pulling me by my hand down the hallway. We slowly inched our way down the long corridor out of the hospital and onto the dark empty street where our car was parked. I didn't want to leave. I wanted surgery.

As we got into our old beat-up '52 green Chevy, we said nothing. Mom lit her cigarette, then started the car. Finally, I broke the silence, "Why can't they take out my appendix?"

"Because, Pammie, it takes money we don't have," she said with just a hint of sharpness. "And we don't have insurance either."

Ok, I think to myself, now I get it. These things cost money. Hospitals and doctors don't help people who need help unless they have money to pay. Even if it's an emergency. Even if it may mean someone's life. A pretty awful awareness.

I knew we were short on money. Mom and Dad owned our house and the Chevy, but we didn't have much else.

I'd often heard talks between my parents about how paying for one thing or another was going to "drive us to the poorhouse." Mom was always worried about losing our house, just like what happened in Iowa. My dad worked hard as a painter every day, but I knew he wasn't paid much. They were doing the best they could.

"What's insurance?" I asked as we began our drive down the street bordering the hospital. That's when I learned insurance pays for medical bills, but we didn't have any. Dad's company laid him off when they were low on work. And when they laid him off, he lost our insurance, too. But even this understanding about the lack of insurance was not what made the drive home so difficult.

What was difficult was my growing awareness Mom made the decision to take me home and gamble I would make it through the night without dying of appendicitis.

Her tears in the ER with those doctors were from facing such a decision. Should she gamble my life? Or should she get surgery for me and maybe lose the house? With four other children needing a roof over their heads? Surely, she'd been told she would be expected to pay, by hook or by crook. But probably by foreclosure.

I heard myself silently plead with my mother, "Mom, please let me live. Please love me."

I pondered how little I must be worth to Mom. If I was somebody else, would she have been willing to save me? If I was one of my siblings, would her decision have been different?

There was a long silence between us as we drove home in the dark, Mom inhaling smoke from her cigarette.

I considered those doctors in the emergency room. Their children surely would have gotten this surgery. As we drove through our small town, past the large stately homes near the hospital, I looked at each of those homes and thought, "Any child living in that house, and that house, and that house, would be able to have this surgery." As we neared our own small, tiny ranch house in our neighborhood of small, tiny ranch houses, I considered yes, even here, these kids likely would have been able to have this surgery.

The tools and the ability to do the surgery to save my life were all around me, to save everyone else but for some reason, not me. It was a choice my mom and those doctors made.

I felt unbearably alone. But I was completely silent, knowing my words, my voice would make no difference.

I felt abandoned by my own mother and by my own community. In a world without safety. Or love. Several years later this feeling was reinforced when both of my younger siblings had appendicitis and both had appendectomies.

As Mom and I made our way home from the ER early that morning, I saw my dad watching for us through the kitchen window as we pulled into our driveway. He came out to pick me up, carefully cradling my head in his left shoulder. His hazel eyes met my blue eyes, and I saw his concern and grief, perhaps, I thought, at knowing I may die. He carried me into my bedroom and placed me in my bed.

Well, that night, my pain did get worse. Quite a bit. I didn't think it could. But it did. I was delirious with pain and called Mom to tell her I was worse, just like the doctors said. Like we all agreed.

Mom came to my side, touching my left shoulder, desperately pleading, "Pammie, tell me. Is your pain worse?"

I heard the desperation and fear in her voice, wishing I wasn't worse. I pictured our family living in the village dump. Just like the one on Red Skelton's television show when he played a bum. I saw the sign above our heads spelling out "Arnesen's Poorhouse". And it would be all my fault because I asked for my life to be saved.

"No, Mom," I said, "I'm not worse."

"Okay," she said, obvious relief in her voice.

I closed my eyes and turned my head away from her. Remembering the Mozart Street Experience, I consciously released myself from this life, fully expecting to die—to move on into another place, knowing there is truly no death.

I immediately fell into a long, deep, and dreamless sleep.

Waking many hours later, hearing the chaotic noises of our household, I was completely shocked and confused I was here in this life. Why am I not hearing music and seeing the beauty of heaven, I wondered? Horribly disappointed I was here in this household, in this physical world, and not in heaven with music and light and love, I asked, how is it I can be here? What happened?

I decided the love I experienced on Mozart Street rejected me. They didn't want me either. Just like Mom. Just like the doctors.

I heard the crashing of pots and pans from the kitchen, the canned laughing from a television program my siblings were watching, the screeching on the kitchen floor of a chair being dragged across the tile, and the barking of our dog, Sheba.

But my stomachache was essentially gone.

This was the day I gave up on a mother's love. And on a father's love. And on the safety and sanctity of human caring within a human community. For a mother, a father, and physicians within a hospital system to turn away from what could be a dying child was beyond my understanding.

It was not as if we lived off in a jungle somewhere and our only option was to wait it out—to see what Providence would bring. No, the tools and expertise to do surgery were right outside our own door. And I had been denied.

I decided I was on my own. My parents neither had the money nor the knowledge to navigate the world enough to protect me. And so, in many ways, I walked away from my mother and my father that day. And, also, our human community of doctors and hospitals who failed to help me in my deepest need.

But even more, I felt abandoned by the love I experienced on Mozart Street for not receiving me when I gave up my life. I felt completely unwanted and abandoned by life and by any sense of eternal love beyond this life.

I decided, then, I must be worthless. I can't stay here. And it seems I can't go there, to some eternal loving place beyond, either. Stuck in the middle, with only me. Nowhere to go. No one wants me.

I felt an inner sense of homelessness with no escape as if I'd been dropped off somewhere behind enemy lines and did not belong in this life or in any life beyond this particular time. A deep sense of alienation. I felt as if I'd been ripped away and separated from any form of human and spiritual safety and compassion.

Life was never the same.

I lost my innocence that day and sheltered it in a deep basement bunker—what we therapists term "shadow". And I began soldiering myself through life. Putting one foot in front of the other. Not knowing what else to do. Doing my best to just survive. To make it through each day.

It turned out to be a difficult year.

I noticed something changed with Mom, too. She was missing in action most of the time. She rarely groomed her hair and never wore make-up. She started wearing boy's shoes and boy's jeans, at a time when moms generally wore dresses.

She said it was because boy's clothing was cheaper and more durable. We were short on money, and we needed to spend money elsewhere. More than once I watched Mom chase the oil man down the street when he tried to bypass our house because he didn't want to deliver oil to a family who owed him so much. Sometimes he would agree to put in just a little oil so we could have just a little heat during those cold midwestern winters. And sometimes oatmeal was our breakfast and our dinner.

During those days, Dad was also missing in action. He went to work every day unless he was laid off. Which was always just before Thanksgiving and lasted until Spring. During those months, he disappeared during normal work hours. Sometimes he had extra jobs, but mostly he visited friends and relatives. People I'd never heard of.

When he was working, he took the train into the city and worked as a painter at a building called the Monadnock, in the south loop of Chicago. He always wore a suit on the train. I knew he didn't paint in a suit, yet that's what he wore to work. One day I asked him why.

"I feel safer wearing a suit," he responded. "Everybody wears one."

At the time, I remember thinking he was hiding his real work from others. Just about everybody on the train were businessmen wearing suits, and he wanted to fit in. Somehow, I saw it as him feeling shame for who he was and what he did.

And so, I felt shame for all of us.

We lived in a small but rich town, with no diversity. Most of the early settlers were white and wealthy. In those days in our town, if you were poor, you were surely not good enough. It made no difference if your dad was a World War II Navy Veteran or if your mom was beautiful, smart and artistic, you were still an outcast. So, Dad pretended on the train.

But I couldn't.

I had to go to school and interact with others. Fortunately, we lived on the poorer side of town, so I didn't have to interact with the rich kids. But we were poorer than most of the others even on our side of town.

And so, I was shy and quiet and skipped school at least thirty days each year. Often more.

I felt relief only in moments walking with our dog, Sheba, in the woods across the street from our house. Taking in the tall old oak trees, the blue jays, the cardinals, the red-winged blackbirds, and watching squirrels and butterflies, was the only way I felt connected to anything with meaning or beauty. It was my only relief and where I spent most of my time when I wasn't in school.

On this one particular summer day, I can't say for sure there was any precipitating event. I can say, however, I do not recall any.

I just got tired of 'soldiering,' tired of feeling so alienated, so completely alone and on my own. So bereft without magic, without a feeling of love, in my life.

I do remember I decided I was done. Completely. Irrevocably. Done.

I was eight years old.

I calmly walked into our only bathroom. This was the one place in our household of seven people, one dog, and three cats, where you could be alone and undisturbed—at least for a few moments. Pretty soon, however, I knew someone would be banging on the bathroom door screaming to get in. So, I knew I must be quick and get on with it.

Once inside the bathroom, I opened the closet door and looked inside for the bottle of ammonia, planning to suicide. Seeing it, I quickly grabbed the bottle and sat down on the side of the nearby bathtub.

Wasting not a second of time, I unscrewed the cap to the bottle and brought it to my mouth. I breathed in the smell. It burned my throat and mouth. I wasn't deterred. I opened my lips and began tipping the bottle toward my open mouth. I knew I had to be quick, or I wouldn't be able to drink it all. And I intended to drink it all.

"You know," a presence standing before me and a little to my right said, "you're just a little kid right now. You don't have to do this."

I paused for a moment, taking notice of this presence so suddenly in my bathroom with me, and moved the bottle slightly away from my mouth. I decided to give him my attention. And while I did not see him with my eyes, I sensed his presence and understood his words, although we did not speak in words.

He was very tall. From what I was able to discern, he seemed to be a Native American, standing before me straight and strong. I could not see his face. But that didn't matter. He was holding clear intent and an unshakeable love. A strong candle and a fragrant rose.

We spoke nonverbally. Our communication and contact were crystal clear and unmistakable. And for some reason, I wasn't shocked out of my mind. Or scared of him. This experience seemed perfectly natural. Familiar actually.

"Why not?" I said when he told me I don't have to suicide. "There is no love here."

"Well, that may be true at this moment," he responded. "But you're just a little kid right now, and the future can bring you love."

"I don't believe that," I said. "I'm done. I can't do this anymore."

"Sure you can," he responded.

He somehow showed me how I can someday drive a car and travel to other places and meet other people. He conveyed a future where I would build love.

I saw the images and felt the warmth and the truth of a future with love deep into my heart. Not a 'selfish' love, but an authentic love for myself, for my life, and for others. A future holding the magic and innocence I lost just the year before.

And I didn't have to die to find this love. This was important. I didn't have to die to find real love. It wasn't just in heaven. I could build a future here that has love. Here. On this earth among the woods and the homes and the fields and the people. But it was a future involving me walking a path making choices toward love.

And I was the only one who could make those choices for myself. These were not decisions made by any other. Not a human other. Not even a spiritual other. Only me, in this physical body I have. So, I understood that only I, this personality, has the freedom, the responsibility, the sovereignty, to choose this path toward love. Or not.

He convinced me to carry on, to continue to soldier, for the time being, while keeping an awareness of my ability to make a future of love when I'm old enough to direct my life and make choices. He gave me an invitation into a deeper life. A deeper life with an authentic love. He reminded me of an eternal, divine self, and of my soul, being held within me, and of the truth of my Mozart Street Experience, of eternal, unbounded love, known to us by many names, spanning all time, and no time, that does include me.

With this meeting, a part of me accepted I did belong, understanding, even at age eight, this is all part of a process of living, learning, loving and choosing. And somehow, I had agreed to all this before coming into this particular life. This was an important awareness. The Mozart Street Experience was the touchstone for that.

But a small unknown part of me remained hidden in silence, in the shadow of the basement bunker, refusing to accept any invitation, any sense of hope or love. Feeling abandoned. Somehow directing my life but yearning to find a way to come home.

"Ok," I said to him while holding up the bottle of ammonia and screwing on the cap, "I will put this away for now. But I will not put away the idea of coming back to all of you and leaving this life at some point in the future if I do not find love here."

I guess, even at age eight, I knew who I was talking to and knew he was one of a group of others. And I guess, even at age eight, I did understand this personality I was had the right to sovereignty—to be in charge of my own life direction—to make my own choices—and they are sacred—even in the face of what would, in retrospect, appear to be a spiritual guide.

I stood up and walked over to the closet and placed the bottle of ammonia back on the shelf where I'd gotten it just a few moments before. I closed the closet door, opened the bathroom door and walked out.

As if nothing had happened.

You might think I would run out and tell someone, anyone, a sister, brother, Mom, or Dad what just happened. Who I just met. What he had shown me. You might think I would have been shocked out of my mind.

But I didn't. And I wasn't. As with the Mozart Street Experience, I kept this to myself for decades.

That February morning after getting bucked off Gabriel, as I sat there sipping my now quickly cooling coffee, I wondered why I was not aware of further contact with the tall spirit in the bathroom when I was eight. Not even in dreams. Years have passed, decades even, since then. I wondered why. The angel hovering over me in the arena just a few days before, as Gabriel raced those wild circles around me, was a female angelic presence. A very different feeling experience from the tall spirit. Yet both had conveyed a solid knowing intent and a boundless loving force. A candle and a rose.

As I got up to fix breakfast and pour a second cup of coffee, I reminded myself again that throughout all the decades of my life leading up to breaking my neck, I was not abandoned by spirit. Spirit had been walking with me. Quietly, without my awareness. For most of my life I denied this, walking through the 'battlefields' of my life thinking I was alone. When I was not. I decided to note this new awareness, and again let myself feel gratitude, tears streaming down my face as I fixed myself a bowl of warm oatmeal.

After finishing breakfast, I returned to my living room chair again, facing the vast western field. As the sun was shining down on the fields of wild grasses, trees and a pond far off in the distance, a hawk circled above.

My mind wandered again back to the memory of the day in the bathroom, all those years before, when I decided to put the bottle of ammonia back into the closet. As I walked out of our bathroom into the hallway leading to the living room of our house that day, my youngest brother was petting our dog, Sheba, while watching Howdy Doody on television. It was a sunny summer day outside and wanting to feel the earth under my feet and the trees shading my head, I walked barefoot outside into the woods across the street and spent the rest of the afternoon walking and resting among the trees, the creek, and the small little hills.

My experience all those decades ago in the bathroom was as if I had stepped out of my eight-year-old earthly life for a moment and into a discussion with an advisor in another, more real, existence. Years later, I came to call this guide, this loving presence 'Tall Man,' because he was so tall.

And so I carried on. I soldiered. Feeling alone yet trying to keep an awareness of a larger picture. Of deeper levels to life. And deeper levels to time itself. Trying to hold hope for a future where there is love—perhaps not now, but perhaps someday, as I honored my sovereignty and learned how to make my own choices.

But a child part of me remained stuck in silence, held in a shadow place forgotten by me, grieving over not feeling loved by my mom and dad. Grieving over feeling abandoned by a human community. Grieving over feeling abandoned by a boundless eternal love. Looking for someone to care. Silent and unknown to me, yearning for a savior.

CHAPTER FOUR

THE FIRST YES AND THEN ANOTHER AND…

"These are my last words to you. Be not afraid of life."

—William James

As the years went by I forgot about my desire for love. I was still quiet and shy. Invisible, actually. Remember those kids in school who spoke only in whispers? The ones with such a soft voice you could barely hear them when they spoke? For the most part, that was me. I just wanted to be quiet, fit in, not raise a ruckus. I passively and quietly trance-walked myself through childhood and into adolescence. Even in junior high and high school, I skipped a lot of school. No one noticed. No teacher made contact. Not until Mr. Raspiller. He was my ninth-grade Biology teacher.

"Say, Pam," he said one morning after class as I picked my books up from the desk to leave. "Can I speak with you for a moment?"

I was pretty shocked. A teacher. Wanting to speak with me? I nodded a yes, then paused to hear what he had to say.

"Pam," Mr. Raspiller continued, "You could be the best student in my class if you just did your homework."

I was stunned. And speechless. He noticed my shock.

"I mean it. Really," he added. "If you just did your homework."

I nodded to him in silence, then stumbled out the door, leaving him standing there. I just couldn't say anything.

But Mr. Raspiller kept on encouraging me. Every day in class while he taught, he made eye contact with me. He called on me, encouraging me to speak, even at times when I hadn't raised my hand. I spoke so softly he sometimes had to repeat what I said. But my answer was always right. And when I got enough courage to raise my hand, he called on me every single time. Every. Single. Time.

And then one day, he made a point of complimenting me in class in front of the other students. He did it masterfully—in such a way other students would not think I was 'special,' or a 'teacher's pet'. Which I surely wasn't. With his comment, the other students began to make friendly eye contact with me and I didn't feel quite so alone.

I started doing some of my homework, and my grades began to improve, in his class and in other classes. With Mr. Raspiller's subtle encouragement every day, for the first time, I began to believe I might have the ability to go to college. By the time I graduated from high school, I was on the Honor Roll. A first for anyone in my family.

Mr. Raspiller interrupted my trance-walk and somehow, through his attention, invited me to consider better options for my life. I have always held on to his encouragement. His words guided me safely in some of the most difficult trials I dragged myself through on my path to finish college. I never told him how much he did for me. I so wish I had. Teachers, when they are engaged with their students, are worth more than their weight in gold.

"Thank you, Mr. Raspiller," I now say, "you were the first person who helped me change the direction of my life."

You see, watching my parents struggle with money, I was certain college would secure my financial future and would make it possible for me to live independent from my family, to make another kind of family. A happier, stronger one.

And so when I met a nice young man in high school who asked me to marry him sometime in the future after we both graduated from college, I accepted. Brian was a few years ahead of me and we both would be working our way through college. But like Gabriel, I did not love him. Like Gabriel, I did not know why. But I accepted his offer of marriage anyway. In retrospect, I believe I didn't want to confront my fears. If I felt authentic love for him, I would have to deal with my fears of losing him or of him not loving me back. If he left me, I wouldn't have been devastated—because he didn't mean much to me anyway. A pretty awful awareness, but Brian was a safe guy. Since he was a good person, I figured that was all I was going to ask for in my life. Safety.

But after my first year of college something happened, upending my entire prearranged life, and issued me an invitation, that if I accepted, required me to gather the courage to choose love over fear. Love over safety. It was my first huge yes, my first huge choice.

There are no coincidences. Only sacred synchronicities, with invitations.

In those days, school loans were not available, so I was working my way through college part-time as a waitress at an ice cream shop and part-time at a Jewel food store down the street from where I lived with my family. By saving nearly every penny, I was able to gather enough money to get through the first year of college. But I would be short of money the second year.

As I was agonizing over how to pay for the second year of college, my boss at Jewel offered me a full-time job at a neighboring store one town over. Perhaps, I thought to myself, I could work full time for one year and save money for two years of college. Then there would be just one year remaining to worry about paying. Brian was good with my plan. And so I accepted the offer.

Jack, the store manager, and Barbara, the front office manager, must have seen me walking across the large parking lot towards the new Jewel. They were standing at the entrance, watching me as I entered the store. I hadn't met either one of them as they completely relied upon my other manager's recommendation. But they probably knew who I was by the pink Jewel uniform and the white nurse's shoes I was wearing. Certainly a dead giveaway.

"You must be Pam," the huge man said just as I stepped out of the heat of the summer morning through the doors into the cool store. "I'm Jack, the store manager. And this is Barbara, the head cashier. You will be her assistant."

'Hoss' as everyone affectionately called Jack, towered over us at about 300 plus pounds and six feet five inches, and Barbara was tiny, at about 90 pounds and four feet nine inches. As the three of us were talking in the cashier's office and I was recovering from my long walk in the heat and the massive difference in size between my two new managers, I noticed a guy halfway down the store aisle stacking oranges in the produce department. Not wanting to be distracted by him—as I already certainly was – I turned away and faced Barbara who was behind me.

"Hey Hoss," a young man's voice said, "Who's this?"

I spun around and the guy stacking oranges was resting his very strong arms on the cashier's counter directly behind us. His smile showed his straight white teeth with his green eyes focused intently on me. It was Jim.

It was truly love at first sight. Jim said it was for him as well.

All summer and fall of '67, I couldn't get him off my mind. I kept remembering my experience as an eight-year-old with Tall Man. And kept wondering if this was part of the vision he shared with me all those many years ago. I felt certain I'd known Jim before, in other lives I thought, and wondered if all this was a sign from Spirit I should attend to. Jim told me much later he also couldn't get me off his mind and wondered if we had known each other somehow in another time as well. But all this was very early in our relationship, and I didn't share my awareness of other lives with him until getting bucked off Gabriel. And, at the time we first met, he didn't believe in past lives.

After a few weeks of getting settled working at Jewel full time, one Saturday morning in late July '67, Jim stopped by the office as I was putting cash and checks together for a deposit.

"Say, Pam," he said, "I see that big rock on your left hand. You engaged?"

"Yes, I am Jim," I said.

"When's the wedding?" he immediately asked.

"Well, I don't know. Brian and I are planning on finishing college before getting married."

"You're a sophomore, right?" he grilled further.

"Yes," I said, "I sure am."

With that, he abruptly turned and took off to finish his work stacking paper towels. With our little conversation, he determined I was in college. I was engaged. But there were no immediate plans to get married. This last piece was important to him. He told me years later he and a guy in the meat market had been discussing his crush on me. The meat market guy told him I was engaged. Jim hadn't noticed. But then the meat market guy told him to find out if a wedding date was set, and if one wasn't, I was 'open game.'

From then on, we would pass in the grocery aisles and smile at each other. Usually, Jim would make some comical crack or another. I was amazed with his sense of humor and his cheerfulness. I knew he was interested in me and I very, very mildly let him know I may be interested in him.

I didn't know anything about him except he was a hard worker and seemed to make work into a game. I so admired his work attitude and his cheerfulness. I learned, of course, this was Genuine Jim.

Years later, he told me he noticed how hard I worked, too. I was never holding back at getting a job done, and I stayed until it was accomplished. So even without speaking much to each other, we recognized each other honored the value of work. To both of us, this was important. Jim was a first-generation American farmer. And I was a first-generation American who knew the experience of hunger and frigid cold nights in the winter.

The problem for me was I was engaged to Brian. But I was completely 'thrown' by Jim. I'd never felt that way for any other guy. Ever. Certainly not Brian, my fiancé. I worried I could not marry Brian when I felt this way about Jim. I was not the kind of person who dated two guys at the same time, and it was completely out of the question for me to cheat on Brian. But I'd never broken up a relationship either. Guys always broke up with me. This swirled around in my mind all summer and fall as I worked full-time at Jewel taking evening classes at college. One of them was "Logic" and Brian was in my class in assigned seating right next to me. Logic had no answers for this dilemma.

I had neatly arranged my life to finish college, be a history teacher, and marry Brian. We were working on a future together better than both our parents were able to provide. Both of us would be the first in our family to finish college. I was desperate to get out of my family, and Brian seemed to provide the easiest and appearing to me, the most realistic route.

But Jim didn't know any of that. He just kept making jokes, working hard, smiling at me, and making sure I noticed him. Which, of course, I did.

One afternoon, early August of '67, I was upstairs in Jewel's break room sitting at the table drinking a coke when Jim walked up those stairs. I was the only one in the room, and it appeared he might have been looking particularly for me. He looked up toward the table through the open railing of the stairs, and, seeing me, proceeded into the break room. He sat down at the table across from me.

"Say, what do you think about this?" he started.

I was quite curious. We hadn't had an actual conversation before. But clearly, we were going to have one now.

"Mr. Wright, the superintendent of our school district, came into the store last week while I was stacking a load of cereal boxes and asked me if I would teach math to seventh graders this coming year. What do you think?"

I didn't know he had a college education. He told me he had a Bachelor's Degree in Physics and recently spent several years in San Francisco working at Lockheed Missiles and Space Company tracking satellites before coming home to get a Master's Degree in Physics, which he was working on as we spoke. So, he certainly was qualified. But he'd never taught before and had never considered teaching as a career move. Teaching would put his pursuit of a master's degree on hold, for the time being. He wasn't sure what he wanted to do.

I so admired teachers. Of course, Mr. Raspiller came immediately to my mind. From my experience with him, I knew how important teachers were. I told Jim about Mr. Raspiller.

"You know, Jim," I started, "I think teaching is a fantastic career. If you like it, that is." Even then, I believed it was crucial to be in a career reflecting your heart. I waited for his response.

"Well, I don't know if I'd like teaching. And it's only three weeks till the beginning of the school year. I haven't got the slightest idea of how to prepare," he said. It was obvious he felt daunted at the prospect of handling a class of seventh graders. I could certainly understand but I continued to weigh in on the side of teaching.

"If you don't like it, can you leave? I asked, aware my break time was running out but quite intent on finishing this conversation.

"Not for one school year. It would be a commitment for nine months," He responded. He had already thought of this.

I was so aware of how handsome he looked, facing me—his intense green as grass eyes and his handsome strong square jaw. Usually, he would be joking with me as we crossed paths in the grocery store aisles. But this time, we were talking seriously about his future. I felt honored. I didn't know at the time he had specifically sought me out for advice and was having this kind of conversation with only two others, his brother and a coworker at Jewel.

I told him I believed he would be able to handle the students in the class, pointing to his sense of humor and the thoroughness of his education. I told him I respected teachers but cautioned him about developing a career he truly enjoyed whether it was teaching, physics, or back at Lockheed tracking satellites.

We both got up from the break table and walked down the stairs together through the back end of the store and into those lovely grocery aisles where he always prodded me with jokes. This time it was more serious and terribly exciting for me. I did not let on, as far as I was aware, of how much I liked him.

About a week or so later, again as I was the only one upstairs in the Jewel break room, Jim came up those stairs and it was obvious he was looking for me. He saw me sitting there eating a sandwich for dinner.

"Look at my new suit, Pam," he said, as he modeled a smart brown suit. He wanted to know if I thought the pant legs were the right length.

Oh my God, he looked so handsome! And in a suit! No one I knew ever had a need to wear a suit. And here he was modeling for me!

"What a fantastic suit on you," I responded. "You look so professional!"

Jim told me he accepted the teaching position and bought three or four suits at a local clothing store to wear at his new job. In those days, teachers wore suits and ties. School would start in about a week.

"I'm going to continue working here," he said. "Just part-time, like now. I've always had a part-time job."

So, Jim would still be here, I thought, posing a dilemma for me. I knew Brian was beginning to wonder if I was interested in someone at Jewel. I tried to keep everything to myself. I did care for Brian. He was a decent person. But how could I be so interested in Jim? It was troubling to me. I just didn't know what to do. As the fall evenings got dark earlier, Brian began picking me up at Jewel, rather than me walking the four miles home. He always parked his blue Ford right outside the front windows, for all to see he was waiting. Jim noticed. I know because he made comments.

Then, one Wednesday evening in October of '67, on my day off, I was called into Jewel by one of the cashiers saying she needed help with a problem. I found out later Jim put her up to calling.

Jim came over to the office where I was counting the day's money, and while resting his arms on the counter, he said, "Hey Pam, there's a blue Ford sitting out in front."

I looked and indeed there was a blue Ford parked right outside the window, just where Brian always parked. But I knew it wasn't him. The Ford looked very much like Brian's, but it wasn't his. I drove my mom's big Oldsmobile to the Jewel because I was coming for just about an hour. My mom said it was okay for me to drive her big old car.

"I'll bet you a beer that's Brian's car," he said with a smile and his characteristic twinkle in those big, handsome green eyes.

"Oh, I don't drink beer," I responded.

"Well then, I'll bet you a drink it's Brian's car," he answered quickly.

"Well then," I shot right back, "I'll bet you a drink it's not Brian's car."

We both stood in silence as we watched a man leave the store, walk over to the blue Ford, unlock it, put his groceries in, and drive off. We looked at the empty parking space and then turned to look at each other.

"I owe you a drink," he said with a knowing smile and a twinkle in his eye.

Jim followed me home, me in my mom's big old Oldsmobile and he in his new 1967 blue Pontiac LeMans. Jim wanted to go to a bowling alley out of town. We went into the bar and sat down to have our conversation and for Jim to make good on his lost bet. He was six years older than me and quite accustomed to going into bars and drinking, having spent all his years in college and in San Francisco doing just that. He drank several beers but seemed perfectly fine to drive.

He told me more about the time he spent in the San Francisco area working at Lockheed Missiles and Space Co. under contract with the U.S. Air Force tracking satellites. This was during the Viet Nam War and he had a deferment through the Air Force since Lockheed was under contract with them. He loved his job, but when his mother died, he wanted to come home to keep his father company, with the idea of spending his time in Illinois getting a graduate degree in physics. He had grown up on a farm and was living with his dad while working and going to graduate school. He said he planned to return to San Francisco to work again for Lockheed when he finished his master's degree and felt his dad was okay. But his new teaching job put his master's degree on hold for the time being.

Jim took me home about one o'clock in the morning. In just a few hours, both of us had to be at work. We'd had no discussion about dating again or about seeing each other. He was a complete gentleman, of course, another early example of Genuine Jim. We did not kiss or have any kind of romantic exchange. Even though there was no indication this could be anything other than a friendship, I knew my neatly arranged world had been completely and forever upended, as if the pieces of my life had been thrown into the whirling gust of a windstorm. I was terrified. I was very 'taken' with Jim. What if he didn't love me back?

After work my sister Laura and I took our mom's great big Oldsmobile out to a local drive-in restaurant for a coca-cola—that's what young people did in those days—and we talked about it. I knew I couldn't go on with Brian but I was terrified of breaking up with him because I did not know if Jim and I would ever have anything beyond joking in grocery store aisles. Laura reminded me if I didn't take a chance on seeing if anything was going to happen with Jim, which wouldn't be possible if I didn't break up with Brian, I would always wonder and would always be unhappy with him. I knew she was right. I couldn't stay with Brian when I cared so much about Jim. It just was not possible. And the memory of my experience with 'Tall Man' kept coming into mind, reinforcing I needed to pursue a genuine love—which by now, I knew I didn't have with Brian.

And so, without talking to anyone else, I broke up with Brian later that evening and gave him back his ring. He seemed just a little sad about it, but not surprised.

The following weekend Jim noticed at Jewel I wasn't wearing the engagement ring and asked about it. "I broke up with Brian," was all I said, rather nonchalantly, trying, of course, not to make a big deal out of it. And then we began dating—in November 1967.

I came to discover Jim had the knack of buying just the kind of car that would in the future become a classic. '55 Chevy; '57 Chevy convertible; '60 Chevy convertible; and '70 GTO. He loved cars.

And he loved to drink beer. Budweiser specifically.

A year later, he asked me to marry him. I said yes. Even though I was terrified he would stop loving me, I said yes anyway. I was hopelessly in love with him. Like nothing I'd ever experienced before. Saying yes to him was one of the most courageous acts I have ever done in my life.

In October 1968, wearing a white wedding gown, my veil flowing all the way down onto the aisle of the church, I knew. That this was the beginning of a great adventure, I knew. That this would break my heart wide open, I also knew. Walking arm in arm with my father, seeing Jim standing at the altar waiting for me with the grandest love in his deep green eyes, I knew. With my love for Jim, I began to risk my life for the very love of life. Just as Tall Man had shown.

I said yes to the invitation into our human experience and to the dance with fear and love, head and heart, hard and soft, self and soul, death and eternity. Through this dance, I found my way through a very dark night of the soul only to find there never was any darkness. There was only the story of darkness.

Nearly thirty years later, as I sat there, sipping my coffee, gazing out our living room window at the eighty acres of wild grasses that had been Jim's family farm, I was overcome with gratitude for Jim and for my bravery in saying yes. This was one of the best and most courageous decisions of my life. Yes, choice, as Tall Man had advised, is how we grow and evolve ourselves.

But what I was about to come into in the decade after our wedding became the biggest trial of my life.

CHAPTER FIVE

ENTER THE DARK NIGHT

"Only when we are brave enough to explore the darkness will we discover the infinite power of our light."

—Brene Brown

Well, that thing about Budweiser became a problem.

One summer morning in the thirtieth year of my life, I woke to a feeling of deep emptiness. I don't mean empty of energy. Or empty of ideas. Or empty of plans. I mean empty like a glass when it is empty of water. Dry, actually. But not just a little dry, bone dry. So dry if you blow into the glass, it whistles with the deep and hollow tone of empty.

I'd had no warning. At least none I was aware of at the time.

By the time of this experience, Jim and I had been married about ten years. We had three daughters and a house in the suburbs with a white picket fence. Jim was an eighth-grade science teacher. His colleagues called him "Mr. Nice Guy," because truly he was. I was a stay-at-home mom. On the surface, it was a picture-perfect life—the American Dream. One as a child I thought I would never achieve. We'd broken out of our family heritage and fully entered the middle class.

Having the financial resources to stay at home and take care of our children, have a decent car that didn't break down, have money to pay for heat and even air-conditioning in the summer, and money to pay medical bills was beyond anything I experienced as a child or imagined I would ever have as an adult.

"How could I be unhappy?" I wondered. "We were living the American Dream."

But in truth, several years before, I had slowly, small piece by small piece and imperceptible to me at the time, given up on the courage to create an authentic relationship with Jim. Somehow the love Jim and I shared when we married seemed to have evaporated. At the time I had no idea of why. I settled for a minimal relationship with Jim, just as I had earlier with Brian, and sold myself out, giving up on the love Tall Man had shown me all those years before. And I'd given up on my dream of finishing college and on having any dreams of my own.

I consoled myself into blindness, passivity and silence, with the sense of financial security and 'safety' I believed as a child I would never experience as an adult. My inauthenticity and lifelong passivity, my 'silent domesticity,' was my payment for what I thought was security.

It's similar to the ancient agreement horses had with humans when they were domesticated.

Woman: "I will be and do what is expected of me and you will provide security."

Man: "I will provide security and you will present well and make our family respectable."

Of course, neither Jim nor I was conscious of any of this. We had bought, hook, line, and sinker, into the common social group-think of our time.

Jim drank until blacking out every single night. I thought he drank because he didn't love me and he fell into a deep unconscious sleep because he was just tired. While he was always decent, he wasn't present in our relationship. Those green eyes of his ceased making eye contact with mine. My heart, ever so slowly, shattered. I had no idea at the time how deeply and how devastating Jim's drinking, and my unknown complicity in it, was hurting us all. We were blind. Alcoholism creates blindness. All addiction creates blindness.

But on this one particular morning, my entire life shifted forever. My eyes, very painfully, began to open. It took a long time, however, for me to more fully see truth.

Just as I woke from a very sound sleep, through closed eyes I became aware of the brightness of the summer sun. I heard dishes clattering, my children talking, and Jim's footsteps walking throughout the kitchen downstairs while he was preparing breakfast. It seemed to be a typical Sunday morning.

Slowly, I opened my eyes to take in the light. And then I felt it more fully. The emptiness. With a deep and foreboding sense of nothingness. I felt as if I had no floor to stand upon, no wall to rest upon, and no belief holding meaning or significance. Something in my life had shifted and had left me adrift, unmoored and blowing about in a desert.

I opened my eyes a little further and gazed at the blue-flowered curtains covering our bedroom windows. I looked around the room. Everything was just as it had been the day before, but I was acutely aware nothing felt the same.

It was as if everything in my life before this day, who and what I was, had been a facade in a movie set and was now collapsed, leaving nothing but dried up shells of building fronts and cut up piles of the fallen scenes of my life scattered about on a desert floor, baking in the sun.

It seemed as if a large and knotted plastic rope tying together my life's now collapsed facades had somehow started a slow and ever-quickening retreat, pulling into some unknown place all the beliefs I clung to so tightly just the evening before. Each knot in the rope held a belief about myself and about life I could no longer honor.

"Your lovely house with the picket fence means you've arrived."

Really? Arrived where? Who says? It doesn't matter.

Gone. Not true. I can no longer honor that belief. No one determines another has 'arrived.' There is no destination called 'arrival.'

Is there some board of social directors somewhere deciding who matters and what is of value?

No. There is not. That knot slipped right out of my desperately clinging hands. It was no use hanging on. It was gone.

Doesn't it matter, I hopelessly asked this vast emptiness pulling the smelly, knotted plastic rope from my hands, doesn't it matter I, finally, have arrived in the middle class? I have a house. I have medical insurance. I have a working car. I can pay for gas.

"Doesn't it matter," I pleaded with whatever force was withdrawing this synthetic lifeline of all my life goals and had, in one way or another, tied my life neatly together and defined me for years. "Doesn't that make a difference?"

No, I heard. It does not. There is no board of directors who establish worth, value, or meaning to one's life.

"Jim says he loves me," I said.

Somehow, I managed to hear a response as I felt the knotted rope pull further away against my clinging grip, "No. This is not what love feels like."

I had to recognize we no longer were expressing to each other an authentic love. Had we ever, I wondered?

Faster and faster away from me, the plastic rope went far beyond my grasp. Along with it went all my beliefs about what is real and what is important in my life – a nice house, a sweet-looking car, good clothes, good position – all now a rope of knotted plastic inventions reeking of the stink of everything artificial – and quickly pulling away from my grasp. Never to be believed in again.

As I laid in bed, trying in vain to grasp the rope, as awful as it was, trying to bring it back to me, trying to believe again in all the materialistic vanities that had defined me so tightly just the evening before, I noticed the knotted plastic rope was also pulling away all other beliefs I held about the meaning and goals of all life. It felt as if our human culture was a concocted group of false beliefs and false stories we vainly tell ourselves and each other, with no grounding in anything real or authentic. A collection of 'group think,' or 'domestication,' I could no longer believe.

Beliefs such as, 'more is better,' 'life is about progress and achievement,' 'one must pull oneself up by the bootstraps,' 'competition is the name of the game,' 'survival of the fittest,' 'winning is the goal,' 'you must be one up, not one down,' but most significant was 'having money and possessions means you are held in favor by Providence, and not having money and possessions means Providence has found you undeserving and unworthy.'

Before this experience, life was a linear game of progress with sure winners and losers. And winning mattered. It established worth. And made life safe.

I saw my life and all human life at this point in time as one mechanized robot meeting another, falling in line without question for beliefs created by some vast entity to feed a largely artificial and very hungry circular belief system. Unmoored from all that is genuine. I, and humanity itself, it seemed, were dead.

But no one knew it. We were just held together by beliefs and stories (told and held by whom and for whose benefit I did not know) like synthetic knots tying our lives together in a large extended plastic rope, tying our lives to some form of materialistic and artificial safety. Traveling in circles, pretending we were progressing.

"Is anything real?" I called out to the emptiness and heard only deep silence.

"Isn't this enough?" I asked.

"No," I heard as the answer. And then, more silence.

At the time of this experience, I had not forgotten but had left behind as unimportant and insignificant my experience with Tall Man in the bathroom when I was eight. And I discounted the Mozart Street invitation as well. Those experiences were kept silently to myself, now bound tightly in a box with leather straps, tied to another rope, tossed deep into a sea, far beyond my grasp. Far beyond the desert I was now in.

It was many more years before I opened the box. Those experiences were moments of grace held in a safety deposit box for retrieval when Gabriel insisted on more.

Had I been able at the time to hold those experiences closely to my heart, I might have done better with the next few years of my life. But I was now walking deeply into mystery and darkness. With no apparent guide. Or so I thought.

Questions I had pondered (yes, I really did) when I was five, seven, and eight years old, and put aside for some future date, came thundering back.

"What is real?"

"What is love?"

"What do I trust"?

"What is truth?"

"Is anything absolute?"

"Who decides?"

Nothing was ever the same for me again. Nothing.

Generally, we all have the great good fortune of experiencing our lives day by day, moment by moment, but rarely can we look back at a defining moment in our life where we know the very earth shifted beneath our feet. On this day the earth shifted for me. I had no idea of why, what, or how. I just felt the empty – a huge expanse of empty with no boundary.

And I knew I had no escape.

A frightening freedom comes with this kind of experience. It was the beginning of deep personal sovereignty. Grace comes in many packages. Most of them are disguised and wrapped as something else. That was the case with this unmooring. It came disguised as a nightmarish experience, yet it came to save my life.

Who knew? Certainly not me.

I had no idea this was another invitation further into a deeper relationship with life, with my very soul. It was an invitation into a very dark night, nearly costing me my life, but oddly, in the end, giving me my life. I had no idea my soul was calling to me, calling me to let go of false stories, false identities, materialistic vanities, trying to get my attention, trying to give me the fragrance of a rose. Calling me home. Asking me to light my own candle. And to remember who I truly am.

At the time, I'd forgotten so much of the wonder of my five-year-old self I could smell only synthetic plastic rope. I had no context with which to place my experience of this deep loss and unmooring. This was the beginning of the deepest part of my walk into the dark night.

But when grace is locked in a safety deposit box and thrown into the sea, one must go deep to retrieve it. And so, I guess that's what I had to do.

I inched my way out of bed, placing my feet on the carpeted floor. I felt the soft carpeting under my bare feet, but I couldn't feel my life. I reminded myself I knew who I was. I was the mother of three children. My husband was a science teacher. My name was Pam. I lived here in this house. My family was downstairs. I will be going to meet them in a moment. What will I feel? Will I feel?

As I stepped into the kitchen, I saw Jim whipping eggs to scramble for breakfast. Our girls were in the family room watching television and working on puzzles. I saw a commercial on television using cartoon animals urging my children to ask their mommy to buy a sugary cereal. Plastic. Artificially created cereal, so unmoored from the grains of the earth our ancestors of just fifty years ago would find it unrecognizable.

My daughters looked up at me and smiled.

I looked around our house. Yesterday my life and house was a beautiful Hollywood movie set and today it had all collapsed. Collapsed. Nothing was saved from the collapse. Nothing.

Well, at least I thought at the time nothing had been saved. I was wrong about that part. There were more shreds of knotted plastic rope waiting to be let go. But those parts were unknown to me at the time – parts being held in the shadow of an unconscious basement bunker, awaiting further invitations to bring them into the open. To remember. And to heal from.

I hoped this emptiness would pass. I watched and waited through breakfast. It didn't. I noticed with some detached wonder I know we must eat, but even eating had no meaning, no authenticity to it. Just rote behavior.

"What is it that gives life to life?" I kept asking myself. "What is real?"

And so I went back to my old pattern of behavior from childhood. I wanted to die and thought of suicide every day. I gave up any sense of hope and began to soldier again. Like I did when I was seven after my appendicitis experience. Passively waiting for something to happen to make it better. Taking one step at a time, just putting one foot in front of the other. I had children to take care of, after all. Their lives mattered. I couldn't collapse. I had to survive. I had to buck up for them.

I had the same nightmare every night for nearly a year.

It is nighttime and the dark sky is pouring down rain—thick dense cold raindrops beating heavily upon my body and the mud beneath my feet. I am a soldier behind enemy lines, plodding through deep mud, hauling a dead soldier over my left shoulder, hoping somehow to bring him back to life. Bullets are whistling by from every direction. Off in the distance, bombs are exploding into the night sky.

Of course, as was typical of me at the time, I shared this with no one. I had no faith anyone cared to listen. I believed I was alone in this vast sea of humanity and did not belong. That I had been dropped long ago behind enemy lines when I had appendicitis. Stuck in the middle, alone, again, with just me. Silent.

My love for Jim and his love for me hadn't saved me. I thought it would. But I was wrong.

I felt no sense I could talk with Jim or he would understand me even if I did. He drank until he passed out every night. Neither one of us had any knowledge or understanding of alcoholism.

I just didn't know what to do. The emptiness provided no answers.

In the middle of this, my mother was dying of cancer. At the time, her illness seemed to bear little significance to me. I thought I left her years ago and moved on when she abandoned me with appendicitis. But I'd never considered how to take care of the little girl in me who I, myself, abandoned right along with my mother those many years ago. I expected Jim to rescue me with his love. But he hadn't. I had no knowledge a wounded part of me was trapped and held in a bunker. When we have been deeply wounded as children, that's what we do.

Who knew? Certainly not me.

Sometimes soldiering is the only thing one can do. And so I did.

As Providence would have it, another invitation would enter my life. This was the hardest and most dangerous of all. But the grace ended up being significant. I finally rescued myself. I found my voice. And I finally felt seen, accepted and safe within our human community. I developed a sense of a sovereign self, able to stand on my own on this earth, both feet planted safely and with love. But I had no idea of any of that then. It took me years of dragging myself through mud and carrying the soldier.

One morning, after a particularly long night, plodding in the dark, muddy battlefield, I woke exhausted and suicidal. I didn't think I could carry the soldier much longer. I decided I needed help. The same day, a newspaper article appeared about a new therapist, a psychologist with a master's degree, in our area. The article said he had experience with depression and alcoholism. It seemed it could be a good fit. And so, of course, when Jim got home from work, I asked him if we could pay the thirty-five dollars for both of us to go to a meeting with this new therapist. He refused and told me to go without him. And so I did.

Benjamin's office was a few towns over and upstairs above a record shop. I walked up the stairs and saw his office door open with him sitting behind his desk, waiting for me. He smiled as I entered and said, "You must be Pam."

He seemed like a decent guy. What did I know? Apparently not so much. At least not so much I was paying attention to.

I smiled back and acknowledged yes, indeed, I was Pam.

He was perhaps about six years older than me, about five feet six inches tall, and wore black horn-rimmed thick glasses. He had dark thinning hair, blue eyes, and a mustache. Slightly overweight. He was not a particularly handsome man. But he showed a nice smile.

Benjamin got up from his desk and invited me into another part of his office suite—where three couches were arranged in a U-shaped pattern in the center of the room with bookshelves lining the walls filled to the brim with books. Obviously he loved books.

I was so desperate I finally opened up to someone for the first time in my life. I told him of my 'unmooring experience.' Of my recurring dream trudging through a battlefield. Of how isolated I felt from others. Of how suicidal I was at times. Of my concern with Jim's drinking. And that my mother was dying of cancer. He listened.

I saw Benjamin regularly for quite some time. Because he took the time to listen, I figured he cared. No one had ever listened to me before. To use my voice, and then for someone else to take the time to listen, was an entirely new experience for me.

But he dismissed my concerns of Jim's drinking, my desire to finish college, and my pain of the dream with the soldier on the battlefield. He even dismissed my suicidal desires.

He knew my mother was dying of cancer and suggested cancer would be my fate if I didn't become independent from Jim.

And then one day he told me I was special.

"Special," I thought at the time. I've never been special to anyone. Certainly not my mom. Or my dad. Not my community who had abandoned me to appendicitis all those years before. Surely not to the love I experienced on Mozart Street when I asked to be taken back to heaven and was denied.

"No one is "special," I responded to him. Then he said it again. Wanting to believe this, I said, "Everyone is special."

"Well," Benjamin quickly replied, "if everyone is 'special,' then you're 'special special.'"

Being called special, particularly by someone who knew all my secrets, felt like being given a drink of water at a time when I was wandering in a desert, dying of thirst.

Can you hear the soft echoes of the voice of the little girl left alone in the shadow world, locked deeply into a basement bunker?

Benjamin also dismissed my 'unmooring experience,' terming it an existential crisis (which it was) but discounting it as having any meaning or importance (of which it did). He said my feelings of isolation were from my need to make better connections with people other than Jim. And then he suggested himself.

I was entirely passive in this therapy—being passive was my life pattern up to this point. I was waiting for Benjamin to rescue me, to fix me, completely believing I was unable and incapable of 'fixing' or helping myself.

A victim looking for a rescuer.

My sense of loss of meaning, of life, of love, got worse rather than better. I began to feel as if I was encased in a plexiglass cage separated even further from all humanity while passively trance walking myself through life.

I was concerned about the impact this could have on my children. Can they tell I am so distressed?

All the plants in my house died. I just couldn't water them. They died only for lack of water. My children must have noticed, but they said nothing. What could they do but watch and hold their breath as they saw me slip away? Jim didn't water the plants either. I didn't know why.

I guess he thought watering plants was a woman's job. Eight beautiful plants died because I just couldn't bring myself to bring them water while I, myself, was dying of thirst.

And so Benjamin began to suggest sexual contact with him might be a solution to my sense of living in this plexiglass cage.

I refused over and over, until one day I was so exhausted, I just couldn't refuse. I never said yes. Never. I just didn't continue saying no. I was too exhausted. And too scared. This is therapy, after all. I never regarded it as anything else. And from what he said, neither did he. I let my body be used to pay for what I thought at the time was my salvation.

I began to see Benjamin as my savior, as rescuing me from myself, from my desire to kill myself, from the potential of my own mother's fate with cancer and saving my life.

Of course, the plastic knotted rope tying me and the innocent child in me to false beliefs that others are responsible for rescuing me from myself, that I cannot rescue myself, and that in general men are the rescuers, was a synthetic piece of knotted rope of 'group think' awaiting a painful retreat. I was unconscious of all this.

At the time, I didn't even know I had an innocent child needing rescuing. But she knew. She was still standing outside the Emergency Room in the dark of night pleading for help. I had no idea she even existed. I remembered the experience, even though I never spoke of it, but I had no idea I abandoned a part of myself outside the Emergency Room so long ago. But apparently, Benjamin could see her. He was a therapist, after all. And therapists know these things. He must have decided he could use her for his own purposes. Without my awareness.

When we are children and we get injured, we lose pieces of our innocence, parts of ourselves. This happens to all of us, to one degree or another. We bury those parts of ourselves, unknown and unremembered, stuck in time, waiting to be rediscovered and brought home to ourselves in some distant, more loving, more forgiving future of ours. Generally, a similar trauma, if healed, will bring those parts home. And so traumas are invitations to heal.

Very gradually, Benjamin managed to convince me to question my understanding of my own feelings and beliefs, and in the process, undermine any sense I had left of who and what I was or could do. The unmooring experience and my intense suicidal desires made his effort significantly easier for him than if I had walked into his office intact.

But, of course, who among us ever walks into a psychotherapist's office intact? Probably not a one of us. Certainly not me.

Years later I understood. But not then. It took years of grief, darkness, and near suicide. And help and support from many who understood, waited, witnessed, and cared.

I kept soldiering on, continuing to meet with this therapist with his new therapeutic 'intervention.' I got much worse. I did not think it could happen. But it did.

One night in the middle of the night, I decided to suicide. I was convinced Jim would make a better father than I a mother. He would make sure he found someone who would take better care of our children than me. I was determined. I had a plan. Neither Jim nor my children would be able to find me. I got up out of bed and walked past my children's bedrooms on the way to the stairs.

"Mommy," one of my daughters called, at just the moment I walked past her door. "Mommy."

Continuing to walk past her door, I stopped at the top of the stairs, listening to her softly calling. Then I decided, oh well, surely it wouldn't hurt to go to her bed, this one last time, to comfort her. I went to her, leaned over and held her as she lay in bed.

"Mommy," she pleaded, more asleep than awake, "Don't leave me. Please, don't leave me."

I was dumbstruck. I stopped my suicide plan immediately.

While holding her softly I said, "I am not going anywhere. I am here. I love you." And I knew that was true.

Suicide plans canceled. I returned to my bed and pondered what to do next.

As I lay in bed, my eyes open and gazing at the ceiling above, light from the moon reflecting through our curtains, I knew I could not continue on like this. Perhaps I needed to consider divorce. I thought back to Jim's and my first meeting, in the grocery store. I believed loving him was the right path for me. And I knew I loved him, yet I did not feel anything. And he didn't seem to feel anything either.

At the time, I had no idea of the consequences alcoholism was having on both of us. I had no idea of the consequences of Benjamin's therapeutic 'interventions'. And I had no idea of the trauma I was holding outside the Emergency Room, held in a basement bunker.

But perhaps I did have a glimmer of awareness in the flame of a candle in the darkness that night. And with the scent of a rose in the love I felt for my children.

I decided I needed to go to school, to finish my education, regardless of what Jim did or what Benjamin said. I thought back to Mr. Raspiller and how he woke me from my passive trance-walk through high school, provoking me to hope for a better future I, myself, could direct. He seemed to be rooting for me from some distant and very real past. Even then, as I lay there in bed staring at the dark ceiling, I held on to the memory of Mr. Raspiller. Yes, our human community does matter in our healing.

We get hurt in community. And we get healed in community.

I made a commitment to myself that night I was going to go back to school. I knew it wouldn't be an easy sell to Jim. His fall into alcoholism infused him with a fear of strong women. I knew I was in for a fight.

So now we started the 'season of fighting'. My lifetime of passivity was just beginning to end. A new, unknown, part of me began to emerge.

Turns out, I could be quite a 'scrapper.'

I signed up for classes at the local Junior College. I was going part-time. This we could afford. I had one year of credits to get before transferring to a four-year college.

In his ongoing resistance to my going to school, we had many fights. One time, Jim threw my racquetball equipment on the roof of our house. Another time, I took all his clothes out of our closet and threw them onto our front porch. And another time, I yanked off the side rear view mirror of our GTO as he pulled away. In a rage, when he told me I couldn't go to school one summer, I ran a mile in seven minutes. Another time, while speeding away from our house on the way to class, I burned rubber for nearly a block down the street as I popped the clutch on our four on the floor GTO. Sometimes he didn't come home on days I was scheduled for classes. And so I found babysitters. And more I cannot recall. But I kept going.

I was still seeing that therapist. Jim was still drinking. My mother was still dying. And I was still dealing with the deep sense of loss of meaning, but my fight with Jim about going to college, my resolve around that one issue, and my memory of Mr. Raspiller, held me.

It was amazing how Jim's resistance began to bring out my voice and my action to save my own life. It was an entirely new experience for me. And oddly, it was just what I needed. Grace comes disguised in many packages. Thank you, Jim.

The therapy, however, was devastating. I tried to deny it, thinking somehow it held my way out of the plexiglass cage, as Benjamin had said. Somehow, I continued to think he could rescue me, could save my life.

And then one day, in my last semester of Junior College, I decided to sign up for a marriage and family class. It was taught by Mr. Zimmer. And now, here we go with another invitation. And I hadn't completed the other one, the one with the therapist with his terrible intervention strategy, as yet. But sometimes we get more than one at a time. Sometimes we have to deal with multiple invites. And sometimes one invite eventually provokes a response to the previous one not 'appropriately' responded to. As this one did. But it took time.

Mr. Zimmer handed out a chart outlining different dysfunctional family systems and the problems associated with each one. It identified the major behaviors generally associated with both the husband and the wife in different columns. I immediately looked to the column associated with the wife, scrolling down the list of behaviors and beliefs associated with various 'dysfunctions.' I identified myself, beyond any doubt, as codependent and married to an alcoholic. Someone who is 'codependent' is someone who relies upon another for their self-esteem and sense of worth. It is a denial of one's autonomy, accountability and sovereignty. It was what I was doing with Jim and Benjamin. To this day, forty years later, I remember the exact moment and the exact place I was sitting when I came to that awareness. It was huge.

Benjamin and I had never talked about this. If we had, of course, it would have undermined his rationale for his 'therapeutic interventions'. I didn't know there was a term "codependent". I was both shocked and not shocked alcoholism and my voiceless complicity were a large part of our problems. It all made sense.

I immediately went home after class and excitedly told Jim, who by now was nearly passed out from drinking so much beer, he was an alcoholic and I was a codependent. And he needed to stop drinking. He agreed to get counseling.

But as I already experienced with Jim so many times before, the next morning he didn't remember our discussion or his agreement to get counseling. Blackouts, after all. But I figured he was trying to avoid the issue. At the time, I didn't understand blackouts any more than I understood alcoholism. I found a counselor and made an appointment anyway.

"Okay now, so what brings you two here?" the middle-aged man asked.

"Well, Pam, you should probably say," Jim said. "We're here because you insisted."

"We're here because Jim is an alcoholic. He needs to stop drinking," I said in a very cool, detached, and matter-of-fact fashion. I proceeded to tell Julian, the counselor, of what I had learned in my marriage and family class from the chart. I may have even pulled out the chart and shown it to him. To me, this was proof of Jim's alcoholism and my codependence.

Now, I must say—as an addictions counselor—a couple coming into my office and presenting like this would be a total gift. They would be so close to recovery as to smell the scent of roses. But this counselor knew nothing about alcoholism. Since we knew nothing about alcoholism either, we did not know that not every counselor knows how to help alcoholics.

In the session, I went over why I was concerned with Jim's drinking. Jim shared he drank at least a six-pack of beer every day. I shared he passed out every night. Jim argued he fell asleep. I argued I couldn't wake him up. Julian agreed to see Jim for counseling on a schedule of once a week. Seventy-five dollars a week on a very small teacher's salary is a great deal of money. But I felt it was worth it.

I figured I would let Julian and Jim concern themselves with Jim's drinking as I turned my focus on my last semester at junior college. I did not pester Jim about drinking nor did I give it another thought. Somehow, I thought Jim's therapy with Julian would magically make him decide he didn't like drinking so much and instead wanted to spend more time with me and our kids. But that never happened. Like I said, I knew nothing about alcoholism.

My mother's cancer began to take a turn for the worse.

And I began, slowly, to wonder about Benjamin's interventions.

CHAPTER SIX

THREE MOTHERS AND A BUNCH OF GHOSTS

"If you don't get out of the box you've been raised in, you won't understand how much bigger the world is."

—Angelina Jolie

We rarely sat down face to face and we hardly ever spoke. Sad, given we were mother and daughter. So having a meal together was an unusual event. But this particular morning Mom called and asked to meet with me for brunch at a local restaurant.

When your dying mom asks you out for breakfast, you agree. And so I did.

I wasn't sure what we would talk about and felt nervous about meeting with her. But I did want to get a sense of how she was doing with her cancer. I figured we could use some of our time talking about a job I recently accepted. This might capture her interest.

Several months before this meeting, I'd answered an ad in our local newspaper for a job as a part-time reporter. In newspaper lingo, the position was called a 'stringer.' With no prior experience or educational background for such a position, I applied anyway, only because I felt the whisper deep inside telling me to do it. Usually, a bachelor's degree is required for such work and I was two years away from that. It is only in looking back over the years I see the whisper was guiding me into an opportunity to learn to use my voice. To break my silence and passivity.

I loved sorting out the issues and writing about them. This job allowed me to ask others lots of questions, and to learn how the world works. It also gave me an opportunity to observe and ask just about anything of anybody. I loved the research and the questioning, always making certain of all the facts. This was exciting, and I wanted Mom to know I was finally doing something I liked. It seemed a good conversation starter.

We met at Lum's, a breakfast place not far from where we both lived. Mom arrived early and was already sitting in the entrance area as I opened the door to walk in. Immediately seeing each other, we nodded a silent "hello."

It was late winter, so Mom was wearing her old long black coat. Even though her coat was old and dated, it was in good shape. On this day, she was wearing a blue cotton blouse with black slacks. She almost always wore black. But the addition of blue accented her striking blue eyes. And the black accented her very dark, yet greying, hair. She looked pretty good. I sighed with a measure of relief, having known her for decades to be poorly groomed and poorly dressed.

"I put our name in," Mom said, responding to the concerned look on my face as I glanced over at the mob of people already waiting for tables. "They're getting a table for us now."

Just then the cashier, a short, stocky, dark-haired woman, nearly breathless from keeping track of who needs a table, who needs to pay for breakfast, and who needs a table cleared, came to us and said, "We have a spot for you." It was just a spot. She led us to a small table for two right in the middle of the noisy breakfast crowd. Since the table was so small, we would be able to hear each other above all the noise. But I was so anxious I wasn't sure I wanted to hear what Mom had to say.

As we sat down facing each other, Mom appeared to be feeling strong, not yet showing the consequences of her quickly escalating cancer. Her medium-length dark hair was groomed, framing her oval face, emphasizing those striking blue eyes. Somehow, she was able to put forth the appearance of some measure of strength. Her skin was light and pale, as always, with hints of the beauty she had as a youth. When she was younger, and groomed, people compared her to Elizabeth Taylor. Which was true, I thought, as we sat facing each other over the breakfast table.

Mom ordered pancakes with maple syrup. She loved sweet things. I ordered scrambled eggs. We both ordered coffee. Nice warm coffee with cream.

She took a sip from her coffee. Wasting no time in superficial conversation, as she placed her cup back on the table, she said, "How's it going with your therapist?"

For the last few months, Mom always asked about Benjamin. In her experience, to be able to pay for therapy was especially wonderful—a special privilege. She was grateful I was able to. I didn't like her asking about my therapy. It agitated me. I knew something was wrong with the therapy, but oddly, in retrospect now, I was unable to identify exactly what. My life was getting worse rather than better. Jim had expressed concerns, too. And so I was quite defensive. When therapy is working, I thought, my life should be getting better, not worse. But this was my first experience with a therapist.

I held onto the hope Benjamin could rescue me.

I bristled at her question, cocking my head to one side, and even furled my eyebrows a bit, yet trying very hard to be polite to my dying mother. I managed to utter a well-mannered response.

"Oh," I said, "I'm having a hard time with it all, you know, Jim and the therapist, but I'll be okay."

I wanted to shut up Mom and stop her from asking any more questions about therapy. Trying to change the subject, I told her all about my job as a newspaper reporter.

"Mom," I finally said, "they print every word I write. Have you read any-thing I've written in our paper?"

"No, Pam," she responded softly. "I haven't. But I will."

Her response was not surprising. I figured she probably wouldn't end up reading anything, but at least I told her. She continued talking about therapy but switched it to her experiences rather than asking about mine. So part of my agenda to shut her up worked.

"I know therapy can be difficult," Mom responded. "I wish I had been able to get therapy when I was a young mother. I'm glad you can. Perhaps I would have been happier if I had. Perhaps it would have been easier for all of you kids," she said.

I flashed back to all the years watching my mom drag herself through life. Sitting for hours in one green living room chair or at the kitchen table reading late into the night, piles of dead cigarette butts in the ash tray next to her. Three days of dirty dishes filling every inch of counter space in the kitchen. Four baskets lying in the living room mixed with both clean and dirty laundry. Stacks of books piled up next to her read-ing chair—The Complete Works of Sigmund Freud; The Interpretation of Dreams by Freud; The Neurotic Personality of Our Time by Karen Horney; and Understanding Human Nature by Alfred Adler.

"Yeah, I wish things had been better for you Mom," I said, relieved the subject had switched to her and feeling the truth of my wishes for her warm my chest as the two of us for one brief moment made eye contact. Tears welled in my eyes as I considered Mom's life was going to end with so little sense of satisfaction.

"I wish I had accepted the scholarships from the Chicago Art Institute," Mom continued. "That is the biggest regret of my life."

I was surprised. I always thought her biggest regret was having children, especially having me. I felt I was a burden on her. But of course, she wouldn't say that. Mom would have had so many more options in her life if she hadn't had have five children and hadn't been so poor. Five children cost a lot of money.

"Why didn't you take those scholarships, Mom?" I carefully asked, aware this might be opening up a mine field.

"Artists don't make much money. And I didn't believe I had the talent anyway," she responded, shifting herself in her chair as she looked down at the floor.

Wow, I thought. She's never been this open with me. Perhaps having a terminal diagnosis opens one up to honesty. I softly took in a breath, feeling grateful for her frankness.

"I did believe I could be a physician," she said, looking up, her eyes flashing a brightness for just a bit of a moment, then fading. "But we didn't have money for medical school."

We both broke eye contact with her last sentence and sat in silence as we looked down at the table, then lifted our coffee cups to our lips for another sip of warm coffee.

I thought about a conversation a few years earlier with my grandmother Olga, Mom's mother, about this exact topic. Olga said she'd been enraged with Mom's desire to go to medical school. She said she was never going to let Mom do anything leading to medical school when she, herself, was working at a laundry earning only five cents an hour. Olga said Mom was arrogant in considering such a plan. "How can she think she could go to medical school when all I'm doing is ironing clothes for a nickel an hour? Who does she think she is? Someone special?"

I winced with grief for Mom as I remembered Olga's words and her unspoken but commanding rule: You may not outclass your parents by doing better than they.

"When I couldn't go to medical school," Mom continued, "I was so angry at everyone I didn't want to do art school either. So, I didn't do any of it. I wish I had. I think I would have loved art and done well if I just believed in myself and gave myself a chance."

I nodded slightly. The waitress interrupted our conversation by pouring more coffee, asking if we needed anything. The slight pause gave me a moment to remember a time when I was in grade school and Mom surprised everyone by taking up oil painting. All she painted were portraits of Black women. Each portrait was slightly different. The dark skin tone varied just a bit. Some faces had larger eyes, some a smaller nose, or a squarer face. But they all had similar dark hair, either pulled back or cut fairly close to the face and head. And they all held kind expressions, with slight smiles and soft dark eyes.

After school one day, motioning to the two new paintings she had placed on our kitchen table, I asked Mom about the surprising portraits of Black women. "Mom, why are you painting faces of Black women? I've never known a Black person. Have you?"

Mom was facing the kitchen sink washing some dishes, looking out the window as she replied. "Yes, Pammie. When I was a little girl, before I was four years old and put into an orphanage, a Black woman took care of me. She was kind."

And that's all she had said.

I stood at the kitchen table, glancing between my mom's back and her paintings, watching her take in a few quick breaths, holding back a sob. I knew, even then as a little girl, Mom was trying, in vain, to recreate the image of the one woman who had provided her with a sense of love. A sense of what a mother was.

A few tears dripped down my face as I, too, held back sobs of grief for Mom's loss. I was afraid to ask her anything else, so I quietly left the kitchen.

Decades after the day in the kitchen with Mom, and years after our conversation in the restaurant, Jim researched what happened to Mom. As an infant, she was left in the care of a group of Black women who were servants on a large farm in Tennessee, while Olga spent long stretches of time traveling up and down the Mississippi and Ohio Rivers, working at putting together city directories, and having an affair with my mother's father, who was married to another woman. Someone, we cannot be sure who, came and took Mom, along with her younger sister, to an orphanage in Chicago.

Mom never had a chance to say goodbye to the kind woman who took care of her. When she was taken at age four, she couldn't have even known what goodbye meant. And so as an adult, she yearned to finally know this woman's face. To paint her. To see her, and to feel again what she had lost but couldn't quite remember.

Even as a little girl, and years later as an adult facing my mom in the restaurant, I knew there was no going back. There is no chance for a re-do. There is no chance to find the one woman who was my mom's first mother of her heart. And there is no chance to go back and decide instead to go to the Chicago Art Institute. To honor her gifts.

Regret is a painful load to carry.

"Don't do that to your life, Pam," Mom said as we faced each other in the restaurant, dragging out the word "don't" and emphasizing the word "your."

"I won't, Mom," I said while picturing in my mind all the fights Jim and I were having about my going to school. I knew my words to her were rote. I didn't think I could honor them.

After brunch, we decided to go to my house—which was an unusual event, even though her house was only two miles away. Mom rarely visited and my children hardly knew her. She didn't know how to be a Mom or a Grandmother, not having had much of a mom and no experience of having a grandmother. In some ways, even in life, Mom had been raised by a ghost and was already a ghost to our family.

I brought her upstairs to show her how Jim and I decorated our girls' bedrooms. Being able to have a nice house with space for bedrooms and then to decorate them with wallpaper and nice furniture was an event unheard of in our family lineage at the time. Jim and I were breaking into new paths. I wanted her to know we were going to be okay, hoping it would bring her some peace.

Mom sat on one of my daughter's beds, laying down on her side, her head propped up by her hand. I took the cue and sat on the same bed facing her.

She took a deep breath and paused, giving herself time to determine whether she wanted to go into a difficult conversation. I wondered, with some anxiety, what was to come.

"On the way over here today," Mom said, pausing again to take another slow deep breath, "I passed a squirrel on the road who had just been hit by a car. She was lying there, struggling, but not able to get up. Trying to live but going to die," she said, tears welling from her eyes. "Just like me," she continued, stifling, then inhaling an emerging sob.

"I found a hard lump in my liver yesterday. Surely this means the end is near. The cancer has spread and is now terminal, just as the doctor predicted," she said.

I sat in silence, not knowing what to say. Or what to do. So this is why Mom wanted to meet—to give me a message. She is dying. And to live fully your life's gifts so you do not die with regret.

Tears fell down Mom's cheeks. I'd seen her cry only two times in her life, both of them years and years before. I was stunned and didn't know what to say.

"I'm sorry, Mom," I finally managed, feeling compassion for her human struggle, but not feeling love for her. "I wish this wasn't so. I wish I could change this."

"Oh, I know you can't Pam. Nobody can," she said. "It's just the way it is. And I have to accept it."

"I know," I said. "And I will also have to face this someday. We all will go sometime; everyone faces this passage."

I was stumbling on my words, trying, but failing, to offer a bit of shared humanity to the journey she was now entering, while also remembering the time when I let go of my own life all those many years ago when she abandoned me.

I wondered if she opened up this topic to allow me to express pain for her upcoming death. Or perhaps she hoped to hear some expression of my love for her or some regret at not having her presence continue on in my life. If that's what she wanted, that's not what she got. I just didn't have it in me at the time. I'm not proud of that. It wasn't I was angry and wanted to deny her relief. At the time, I was unaware of anger. And I surely didn't want to deny her relief. I just didn't feel anything other than great sorrow for her un-lived life. I wished she had not been abandoned as a child. I wished she had known the mother of her heart. And I wished she had fulfilled her dream of pursuing art.

As for me, I was aware of feeling nothing about losing Mom. Nothing. I already gave up on her when she failed me as a child when I needed her most. I closed my heart to her so many years ago and walked away, refusing to believe in love, locking part of myself in a basement bunker, quietly soldiering the rest of my life until I found what I thought was love in Jim. But even that was failing me now. I was in a very difficult place.

Basement bunkers are deep. And one's own ghosts are difficult to see. The therapist I was seeing at the time was the only one aware of the little one stuck in the bunker.

After Mom left that day, we all limped on. Mom slowly dying. Me, hardly breathing. Jim, continuing with his counseling but drinking into oblivion every night.

As Mom's cancer worsened, she became confined to bed. Laura, my older sister, had recently married. She and her husband offered Mom a room at their house while they paid for around-the-clock nursing care. To everyone's great relief and gratitude.

I went to see her occasionally. Not as frequently as one would think, given I knew she was dying. And just a few miles away. It seemed every time I planned on seeing her, I got sick. So I went infrequently. I wasn't aware of feeling much, just getting sick every time I thought of seeing Mom.

One afternoon, about two months after our breakfast meeting, I was able to get myself over to visit her at Laura's place. Mom was lying in her bed and I sat on a bed opposite her's. Not knowing what to say, I began talking about school. I knew Mom wanted me to go to school, so it seemed a safe topic. Maybe I'd get more of a response from her than sharing about my job as a reporter.

"I like this marriage and family class," I said. "Perhaps I will major in psychology."

Mom wasted no time interrupting me.

"Pam, you know I will be dying soon, don't you?"

She looked directly at me, our eyes meeting in one very brief moment.

I decided to accept her invitation into truth.

I moved over to her bed, sitting next to her, holding her right hand. It was an unusually intimate movement for me to make. But I didn't think or consider any other options. I just did it.

"I know Mom," I said, lightly stroking her right arm. "Please tell me, what can I do to make this easier for you?"

"Please take care of yourself, Pam," she said, whispering in labored breathing while beginning to sob.

I was struck silent while I puzzled over this request. I was concerned about Mom's comfort, not my own. Then I wondered, could it be Mom loved me and cared about my life? Mine? I asked myself, is Mom concerned about my life when she is losing hers?

Mom noticed my puzzlement.

"Pam, please take care of yourself," she repeated more forcefully, between her sobs. "So I don't worry about you."

I finally got it. Mom did care about me.

"I promise you, Mom, I will take care of myself," I said, hoping I could honor this promise to my dying mother. "I want you to have peace."

I recalled the boy's clothing she always wore when I was a child. The dirty hair she rarely groomed. The piles of spent cigarettes always around her.

The portraits of Black women she painted from images haunting her heart daily. The piles of books she read. The beauty and the talent and the intelligence she had but never used. The silent grief she held inside all of her unexpressed and un-lived life.

I finally realized Mom didn't want me to do as she had done. And so I said again, "I promise you, Mom, I will take care of myself. I promise."

Mom smiled when she heard that, then nodded and whispered "Yes, good. Thank you."

We had made a pact.

She closed her eyes, then fell asleep.

That was the day I made a commitment to Mom. And to myself. An unbreakable commitment. And perhaps, too, when I began to consider accepting her love, to be open to it for the first time in twenty-four years.

The little girl, stuck in the bunker, well, she was a little closer to being rescued by me. Me.

Later in the week, I took the watch I was wearing during this conversation to a jeweler in town for him to engrave, "To Pam, Take care of yourself, Love, Mom." There was no way I was ever going to forget.

Three weeks later, the Thursday morning before Easter Sunday, Laura called.

"Mom has taken a turn for the worse," she said. "The nurse says she will not live much longer. It looks like she is slipping in and out of a coma," Laura continued, matter of factly. Then she added with a hint of grief as she pulled in her breath, holding back a sob, "Pretty soon she will be permanently in a coma. This is the beginning of the end, Pam."

I went over there that morning, leaving Laura's house mid-afternoon, coming home to take care of my family. I went back early Friday morning, planning to stay as long as it took, knowing Mom was in a coma and dying.

One by one, within a few hours, all five of us kids arrived. Everyone planning to stay for the duration. We spent most of our time in her bedroom, surrounding her in silence, as she breathed with difficulty.

At one point, somewhere around midnight between Friday and Saturday, Mom started to struggle, fighting her own death, turning her head from side to side and saying over and over and over again, "No. No. No."

Laura and I went to her side, Laura on her right and I on her left. We each took one of mom's hands and stroked her arms. First Laura and I looked at each other, and then, nodding in silent agreement, we looked to Mom, somehow intuitively knowing what we needed to say, in unison we said, "It's okay Mom. We will be okay. You don't have to worry about us. We will be okay. You will be okay."

And with those words, Mom settled down. She seemed to have heard and to have understood. Laura and I stayed there, holding mom's hands for some time.

None of us knew the exact moment she slipped away. She left softly and quietly. Like when she sat at my bedside when I was a child having nightmares, leaving softly at just the moment I drifted off to sleep. She slipped away just like that.

I was thirty-one years old.

Of course, Mom visited me after her death. Several times, actually. As I said, it's a family tradition among us women.

Just after Mom's death, early Saturday morning between Good Friday and Easter Sunday, as I was leaving Laura's house for the first time in nearly a day, I walked alone to my car. Looking up at the dawn sky—just before sunrise—that liminal time between night and morning, I noticed millions of stars. Coming from forever and casting off into forever. Now Mom is out there. Deeply in my heart, I felt she was in the beauty and the love of it all.

Suddenly, I was gripped with Mom's first message. She shared an immense joy and sense of freedom, gratitude, and love for her life here and for her life beyond. I stopped for several minutes before entering my car, taking in Mom's sharing of love, gratitude and freedom. Mom told me not to grieve for her, she was finally at peace with how her life here proceeded.

Life and death, somehow complicated and intertwined. Love, joy and grief. Companion cousins.

"Thank you, Mom," I said out loud as I opened the door to my car for the short drive home. Jim was waiting at the door for me as I arrived. Collapsing on the floor of the entryway in unexpected tears and grief, Jim sat on the floor with me and held me in silence. It was the first time I'd felt any grief about Mom. And it had been a long time since Jim held me with such kindness and tenderness. I was grateful for his presence.

After making funeral arrangements, my two sisters and I visited Olga. The one who abandoned Mom in so many ways so many times, just yesterday, last week, and decades before.

The same Thursday Mom slipped into her final coma, Olga was hospitalized with heart failure. The thing is, she hadn't been told her daughter slipped into a coma. Olga knew very little about what was going on with Mom. Her last visit had likely been about four weeks or more before. And the one before that, a few months before. They rarely spoke. It was another family tradition. But, of course, Olga's soul knew. And responded with the grief of heart failure.

We three thought Grandma needed to know, but not by a phone call or a message delivered by some unknown person. We wanted to be caring emissaries for our Mother. A new family tradition.

We drove together to visit Grandma in the hospital. We all agreed we wanted to be kind and caring with Grandma. When Olga saw the three of us walk together into her room, she opened her mouth with a slight gasp, likely knowing why we had come. We surrounded Olga's bed, each of us giving her a hug.

"Mom died last night, Grandma," Laura began.

"She died peacefully," I added.

"With all of us surrounding her and holding her," Blythe said.

Grandma cried.

Her crying puzzled me. I couldn't recall her ever showing affection for Mom.

"It's a terrible thing for a mother to lose her child," Olga said through her falling tears.

At the time, I was thinking Grandma was trying to make this all about her. I was feeling anger towards Olga for abandoning Mom as an infant, then somehow letting her be taken hundreds of miles away and put into an orphanage. Grandma didn't begin being a mother until my Mom was nearly seven years old, and even then, she was unloving.

Perhaps Olga's tears were about her beginning to feel regret for how she abandoned my mom, I thought, with some bitterness. But here we have it again—regret—another family tradition. One I noticed more than a few times quite recently, and one I vowed to break.

While it was difficult for me to have much compassion for Grandma, since we all had children of our own, I believe we each understood the pain of losing a child was beyond any comprehension any of us ever wanted to encounter. And so, I know I let a little crack of compassion slip through for Grandma. Not much I must say, however. I did have more forgiveness to do.

We told Grandma all about the funeral plans for the coming Tuesday at 2:00. "I hope you can be there, Grandma," I said. "I hope you are okay by then."

Grandma nodded in agreement, tears dripping down her face. Smiling gently, we each gave her a hug and bid her goodbye. Although she was discharged from the hospital, Grandma didn't make it to Mom's funeral. She went on to live nearly another decade.

In the early morning, the Monday after Easter, I woke in the dawn remembering Mom just died. Then, I became aware of someone standing next to my bed. Slowly I opened my eyes.

It was Jim, holding a cup of freshly made warm coffee, his green eyes sparkling for the first time in so long I could not remember. "Here's some coffee for you, Pam," he said. "I'll be taking off for school in just a few and wanted to make sure you're ok."

Oh Gosh! How I loved it he brings me coffee in the morning! But much more, how nice it was to see his green eyes sparkle, finally meeting mine! It had been such a long time since we had eye contact, but with Mom's passing, Jim seemed to feel considerable compassion for me. I could see it in the softness of his eyes.

"Thanks, Jim," I said. "Since the funeral is already arranged, all I'll need to do is make sure everything is good to go here so there's nothing last minute for tomorrow. I'll be fine."

We kissed a gentle goodbye, as we've done every single morning for over a decade, and he set off for school. I got the kids off to their school. It was after that, when I was alone, things got tangled.

I became aware of Mom at my side, following me around. Mom appeared to be frantic and grasping for my attention.

I thought it was my imagination. So, I ignored her.

Pretty soon it felt like Mom was grabbing my shoulders, trying to shake me. Then I remembered many conversations years before when Olga talked about Guy, her nephew, visiting her after he died in the South Pacific as a POW in World War II, and telling her of things she couldn't possibly have known but which were confirmed by our government nearly one year later.

So, I decided to listen, not knowing what else to do. I sat down on a velvet, stripped chair in our living room. "Okay Mom," I said out loud. "You have my attention."

Mom conveyed information to me, not in concise words, sentences, pictures, or images, but in a combination of everything. She indicated people were touching her and moving her body around. She couldn't bear it. But even more concerning was someone was gluing her eyes shut. She was sure she wouldn't be able to see when they were finished.

"Pam, help me! Get them to stop! I won't be able to see when they glue my eyes shut!"

I gathered as much love for Mom as I could, drawing on my earlier experience of her just after her death outside Laura's house while standing by my car, believing I wouldn't be able to communicate with her unless I was able to hold her in a space of love.

"Oh, Mom," I said out loud, "you have died to this lifetime. And it's now time to pass into the Light. You have eyes to see without a body. Do you see the Light?"

I visualized a loving light—like a portal for her to walk through.

"And you have a body that can move without the body you had here. Do you know that?" I asked.

I sensed quiet from Mom. She seemed to be listening and checking out what I said.

"There is peace and love and freedom in the Light," I continued. "Do you see it?"

I sat in my velvet stripped chair for some time, holding a loving space.

And then suddenly, Mom appeared to be gone. I did not feel her angst about the funeral preparation process anymore.

But I did experience her again.

As the days went on after her death, I felt an increasing urgency to give my life meaning, yet not knowing what that meant. I was terribly frightened of proceeding with my life—of actually accomplishing college graduation. But I had made a pact with Mom.

It could be said an unspoken rule in my family was "Try, but make sure you don't succeed." Fighting was trying, you see. Going to classes was trying. But, graduating? Well, that was a 'horse of a different color,'—graduating from college would be a form of success. Something no one in our family had yet done.

My mom did try. While I was a teenager, for a short time she went to the University of Illinois, Chicago, and majored in pre-med. And did quite well. But did not graduate. My dad developed a cancer, which he survived, but which forced Mom to quit her education and go to work. When things improved, she never went back.

Seeing Mom die feeling the grief and regret of unfinished dreams was more painful to me than losing her. It provoked me to push further past the "trying" piece and to graduate with my bachelor's degree. But I had a long way to go—I had more than two years before any graduation.

One night, not long after Mom died, I woke from the same recurring dream of trudging in the muddy battlefield, hauling a soldier over my shoulder, bullets whizzing by with bombs blasting in the distance, and wanting to kill myself. Again.

I went downstairs and sat sobbing on the floor in the corner of our dining room, denying myself suicide, asking for help. I had sleeping children upstairs, after all, I couldn't bear leaving them. But how can I live with all this?

Suddenly, I felt the clear presence of Mom, shaking me, practically yelling, "Wake up, Pam! Wake up! Now! Wake up!"

Mom was frantic. And wanted me to remember the pact we had made.

Somehow, I knew Mom meant waking up was getting away from that therapist, that therapy, and finishing college. I knew then, beyond any doubt, staying in Benjamin's therapy was not taking care of myself. And I had to finish college.

The next morning, I called Benjamin and told him I was suicidal—and didn't think I could hold on long without killing myself. I told him his sexual interventions hadn't prevented me from feeling suicidal, they had actually intensified them. I told him I still felt encased in a plexiglass cage that seemed to be killing me. Benjamin called a psychiatrist he knew, and I was hospitalized for a short time.

I saw them both for a while. The psychiatrist, Dr. Kack, didn't care if I worked with both of them. Or even question why. I didn't tell the psychiatrist about Benjamin's 'interventions,' but little by little, I edged further away from Benjamin. He didn't seem to mind. I knew I somehow needed to break clear of some grasp, some hold he had on me. But I didn't understand what it was. Unconscious shadows and basement bunkers are deep.

At times when I met with Benjamin and we talked of suicide, he shared people said drowning either in a pool or in a bathtub was a very peaceful and profound way to die. That was odd "information," because, after all, Benjamin never expressed any belief in life after death. So, how could he say someone could convey thoughts to the living after death? But even more odd, I did not see this as a problem with Benjamin.

Jim was still drinking. And without understanding alcoholism, I was still complicit with it. We were both just trying to survive. But we were hardly living.

I hung on to my promise to Mom.

PART TWO

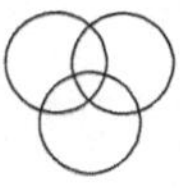

FINDING GROUND
TO STAND UPON

FROM A WHISPER TO A ROAR

*"And the day came when the risk it took to remain
tight in a bud was more painful than the
risk it took to blossom."*

—Anais Nin

Well, my promise to Mom meant I must honor my voice. And take action. The newspaper job surely gave me practice with both. For the first time in my life, I had a voice, independent of anyone else. And I was paid for my words. I began to experience myself as accepted within a community of others. It was an entirely new and profoundly healing experience for me. Turns out, it was just the beginning of feeling accepted in a community and of finding my voice.

Being a stringer for a newspaper paid something, but not much. And tuition for the four-year college I was entering, rather than the junior college I'd just finished, required more money than Jim and I had. The shit hit the fan when it came time to find the money for a four-year college. My newly emerging 'scrapper' had to fight much harder for school after Mom died. Now I had to fight with Jim about money and about going to school.

I went to the financial aid office at the four-year college I wanted to attend and spoke with a tiny, skinny, blue-eyed old man who told me I didn't qualify for any aid from the school. I begged. I pleaded. I literally cried. "Surely I qualify for financial aid. With our income and three kids there is not one more penny to pay for school," I said. And of course, this was true.

"Oh, but Pam," he replied to my tears and my pleading, "I am sure if you go home and look, you will find the money. I am sure it is there. Go home and look."

And then he dismissed me.

I drove home, crying all the way, completely unwilling to let myself be shut out of a degree because of money. I was not going to be a victim to this. I would find a way. I took this skinny, cold, steely bit of a man literally and went home and physically looked for money.

For the first time ever, I began by looking at our checkbook. Going over the entries, there was lots of money every day, every week, every month spent paying for beer. I tallied it up, and then tallied up the money spent in the past many months for useless therapy with Julian. If I had all that money, it would go a long distance toward paying tuition. I went into the basement and checked out several years of checkbooks, going through each one. Hundreds of dollars to pay for beer. Yes, the skinny, cold, minuscule man actually had it right. I got in the car and went to our bank. Our only bank account, a checking account, was in both mine and Jim's name. But I had never paid a bill, nor had I ever balanced a checkbook. I didn't have the faintest of ideas of how to manage a checking account or how to deal with banks. I figured I would learn. I was a reporter, after all. Asking questions was my job.

"I wish to close down this account please," I said to the teller.

"Ok," she said. "What would you like to do with the balance in the account right now?"

"I wish to put it in another checking account in my name only," I responded.

The teller paused for a brief moment, then gulped, likely just becoming aware I had taken my husband's name off our joint checking account without his presence or apparent consent. But she did it anyway.

I was not done.

I went home and called Julian.

"Say, Julian," I said to him when he called back, "When Jim and I came to you nearly a year ago I told you Jim was an alcoholic. And you know what? He is still an alcoholic, and he's still drinking. Your therapy hasn't fixed him."

"Oh, I know he's drinking, Pam," he responded with clear resignation.

"Well, today I took his name off the checkbook and so today is your last appointment with him. I am not writing one more check to you for therapy." Then I hung up on him.

A short time later, Jim came home from work, carrying under his arm his customary six-pack of Budweiser.

As he stood in our entryway, clinging to his beer while placing his brief-case on the floor, we made focused eye contact. He must have seen the resolve in my eyes and knew what was coming. As I looked into his green eyes and he looked into my blue eyes, neither of us flinched. We just stood there, facing each other in our entryway, our eyes fixated on each other. In silence. Somehow, he must have known he couldn't mess with me; and that it was over.

"I took your name off our checking account," I said, finally breaking the silence. "Today you will see Julian for the last time. There is no more money for him. And there is no more money for beer. It's over Jim."

You would think he would have put up a fight, but he didn't. Our unflinching eye contact held fast.

Our children were asleep when he came home after his appointment. I was sitting on the couch in our family room watching the news as he approached me, feeling firm resolve as he sat down right next to me.

"Julian referred me to an alcoholism counselor in his office," he said, "I met with him tonight."

"What?" I said. "An alcoholism counselor? What's an alcoholism counselor?"

At the time, I had no idea there were specific counselors specializing in addictions. And also, Julian had one in his office all along. One known as one of the best alcoholism counselors in the entire Chicagoland area. Right there. In his office. Julian had just wanted to keep Jim's money to himself rather than referring Jim to Bill, as he should have at the very beginning. Close to $3000 spent on useless counseling.

For the first night since I had known Jim, he did not drink. And, of course, he did not pass out. I had never, in the thirteen years I'd known him, ever experienced him not drinking himself to sleep every single night. And he threw away the six-pack of beer he'd brought home earlier in the day.

Somehow, ever so slightly, a fresh air began to sweep into our house, into our relationship, and into our family.

He started seeing Bill on a weekly basis and appeared to like him, seeming to feel a sense of hope I hadn't seen in him in years. Bill introduced Jim to Alcoholics Anonymous and The Twelve Steps. Eventually, Bill wanted to see the two of us together. Of course, I wanted to go, figuring I could tell him all about Jim's drinking. Codependent, you know.

Jim and I drove the thirty-minute journey to Bill's office, the same place where Julian, Jim and I had our very first appointment. Of course, Bill wanted to know all about my experience with Jim's drinking. And, of course, I eagerly told him.

About halfway into the session, Bill turned his attention toward how I was feeling about my own life. I shared my intense desire to complete college and my love of learning. Bill learned I was committed to our marriage and to our family. But not to be partnered with drinking. That was clear. Then he asked if I would be willing to read a book.

"Of course, I'll read a book," I responded. "I love reading and learning. What book is it?"

"It's called *Alcoholism is a Family Affair*," he said, as he handed me the book.

I took the book into my hands as I looked at the title. *Alcoholism is a Family Affair*. I was silent as I read the title several times. I turned the book over and looked at the back. I looked at the table of contents.

Suddenly, I lifted up the book and pitched it full throttle right at Bill. I stood up and yelled, "Jim brought this into our family. I didn't do this. He did!" And then I walked out.

I stood alone outside in the parking lot, unable to get in the car. Jim had the keys and he was inside with Bill. If I had had the keys, I would have left without Jim. But I couldn't.

And now, this is where the resolve to heal turns benefits and pain in both directions. As it always does when it comes from a larger love. Sometimes appearing unbidden.

After a few minutes of standing out there in the cold parking lot, I returned to the office. Bill and Jim were sitting in their same chairs, talking. "I'll read your book, Bill," I said. He handed me the book again. And again, I was silent as I read the title. Looked at the table of contents. Looked at the back of the book. Turned it around in my hands. And then

I did it again. I lifted up the book and pitched it full throttle directly at Bill. This time he put his arms up to prevent himself from getting hit in the face by the book. I walked out, again.

I stood outside in the cold unable to get in the car and drive away.

After a few moments, I walked back inside and sat down with Bill and Jim. They were both amazingly gracious with me, appearing to understand how painful this was. Bill offered me the book a third time. This time, I accepted without looking at it any further, placing the book into my purse. Our session ended.

Jim and I walked out as I blamed him for all our problems. When we got to the car, I kicked the car over and over while screaming it was him, and not me, bringing alcoholism into our family.

It was years before I realized I, myself, had grown up in an alcoholic family. By this time, I was a counselor treating alcoholics and their family members in a treatment center when I recognized the unmistakable, but very familiar odor of vodka seeping out the pores of a detoxing late-stage and likely dying alcoholic. And Bill was referring clients to me. I wondered if he ever told them of how I threw books at him.

Jim stopped drinking after starting with Bill. He had a brief relapse while on a retreat three weeks later, and then never drank again.

Within a very short time, he became the man I always knew he was. As for me, it took significantly longer to come to a sense of peace. I had to deal with college and with Benjamin.

I was finally able to go to full-time college while continuing to see Dr. Kack and occasionally Benjamin. Somehow, however, I was able to refuse sexual contact with him. He didn't push me as he had before. And without Jim's drinking, our relationship began to improve. My focus turned even more toward Benjamin—in a decidedly negative way.

Now, if I were writing fiction, you would be forgiven for thinking what I am about to share that happened on this one day and in the following week is too unrealistic to believe. But you can't make this stuff up. All of this did take place. And in the order and shortness of time in which I share. It was all a series of sacred synchronicities calling to wake me.

It was only after I sat in my living room chair that one cold February morning so many years later, reviewing all the events leading up to getting bucked off Gabriel, when I became aware of all the synchronicities. I was nearly overwhelmed when I realized, for the first time, such a profound sequence of events occurred in the short fashion in which they did. At the time this was taking place, all those years ago, I was so overwhelmed with just getting through each day intact I wasn't able to consider anything larger than what was directly in front of me. Due to my stress, seeing a bigger picture was not possible.

It began with a nightmare, another invitation sent by an angel. My eyes started to open.

My whole body was shaking as I tried to wake myself from the dream. Where am I? When is this? I asked myself. I breathed in the slight aroma of coffee and sensed light from the morning sun shining through my closed eyelids. Oh, it's morning, I thought. And this must have been a dream. A horrific dream. But, still, just a dream. I reassured myself.

While opening my eyes, I looked around the bedroom and down the hallway leading to my three daughter's rooms. Yes, this was the same house as in the dream. It felt so real.

As I took in a breath, I noticed again the aroma of coffee. Jim had placed a hot cup of coffee on the bedside table just before leaving for work, knowing I would soon be waking. The nightstand clock showed the alarm would ring in five minutes. Oh good, so I'm not late, I thought.

The girls were up and rustling around in their bedrooms, opening closet doors and drawers, getting out clothes to wear for school. Just then,

Caitlynn came into my room, jumping and running as only a six-year-old can, claiming oatmeal for breakfast.

"Sounds good to me!" I said as I got out of bed and grabbed my robe. "Let's get everyone dressed and downstairs for oatmeal."

While getting all three girls fed and off to school, I set the dream aside, deciding I would contemplate it's meaning during my nearly hour-long drive to school. But I found the dream too painful to consider while driving. Arriving earlier than expected, I pulled out my journal and while sitting in the car in the parking lot, I wrote it down.

I'm alone in the kitchen washing dishes. Jim and the girls are all at school. I hear the painful mourning and calling of a small child.

"Help. Help me, please!" calls the child.

I put down the dish and the washcloth I am holding, and listen, trying to hear the crying more clearly. "Where is this crying coming from?" I ask. I stand at the kitchen sink and look through the window at the backyard and the backyards of our neighbors. There are no children anywhere. There is no sign of a problem.

I walk in a circle throughout the house. First into the dining room, then the living room, then back into the kitchen and family room. Looking carefully everywhere. Nothing. There is no child calling for help. But I hear the pleading, over and over. "Please help! Please help me!"

The calling doesn't seem any louder in any one of the rooms. It's not coming from upstairs. Or from the basement. It seems to be coming from everywhere.

It's as if the house itself is crying.

The wailing becomes more urgent. I must find this child. Surely the child is in danger.

I walk throughout the house again, trying to determine from where the cries are coming. I open the front door, walking onto the front porch. The cries are louder and more clear. Now they seem to be coming from somewhere outside the house. I step off the porch onto the driveway and stop to listen.

The cries are coming from my neighbor's house. I'm very confused. These neighbors don't have any young children or grandchildren. But the pleading is loud and clear. "Please help me. Please help!" the child continues to cry. I must help this child. I walk over to my neighbor's house and ring the doorbell. The child's wailing cries are louder and more intense now. They are coming from inside my neighbor's house.

No one answers. I bang hard on the door while also ringing the doorbell, as if to say, "I'm not going away! You'd better answer. And answer now!"

The door cracks open just a little, and I can hear the child's howls even louder. "Please help! Please help me!" the child cries as if she knows help is on the way and wants me to know she is in there and is the one calling for help. The door opens a little more, barely enough for a man's face to peek slightly through the small opening.

I am shocked the man answering the door is not my neighbor, but instead is Benjamin, my first therapist. I notice his blue eyes framed by large black horn-rimmed glasses, his mustache, and his dark hair, balding at the crown. I say to him, "Who is crying? Certainly, that child needs help." Benjamin looks at me, then says with coldness, "That child is just fine. I'm taking good care of her. You are not needed here."

Benjamin then pushes the door shut against my resisting hands as the child inside screams even louder, as if she has lost all hope of being saved. I stand at the door, then step back, my hands pushing on the closed door, wondering what I can do to rescue this crying child.

After finishing the last sentence, I was shaking so much I had to stop. Any assessment of the dream would have to wait, I figured, for another time. I had to gather myself and get into class.

My first class was an undergraduate class in medical ethics, taught by Dr. Leonard. I really liked this teacher. But that's not why I signed up for the class. By the time I got to this four-year college, I'd given up on the idea of being a history or economics teacher and settled instead on a major in psychology. I was trying to figure out what was going on with my therapy with Benjamin. I figured majoring in psychology would be the ticket to that. I didn't have long to wait.

Medical ethics was a required course for psychology majors. Since it was the beginning of the school year, in early fall, we were just three or four weeks into the teachings.

I walked into Dr. Leonard's classroom taking a seat in the front row of a semi-circle of about twenty-five desks. I was a tad early, so I pulled out my notebook while gazing out the windows lining one wall of the class-room, noting the warm autumn sunlight shining into the room. Other students slowly and quietly drifted in, arriving before the beginning of class. Since I was fairly new to this school, I didn't know any of the other students. Just at ten, Dr. Leonard walked in, placing his few notebooks on the desk in front of the semi-circle.

"Hello," he said. "I hope you each had a good weekend. Today we are going to consider the specifics of the ethics of the patient/provider rela-tionship. We've considered the ethics of medical research, some of the various components of professional relationships, with a special focus on fiduciary responsibility, but now, today, we will consider the ethical spe-cifics and practices of the professional relationship between a physician or psychotherapist and their patient."

This was the way Dr. Leonard always spoke in front of class. He was dif-ferent in person. He had a Ph.D. in religion, philosophy, and psychology. He'd written numerous papers. And while he spoke with technical words and concepts, he spoke with an air of humble authority. That's probably why he was my favorite teacher.

I know it sounds odd, but believe me, I had no idea what was to come. I pulled out my notebook and pen to take notes. I was a prolific notetaker.

"Of particular concern today," he continued, "in the patient/provider relationship is the issue of consent."

And so he talked about consent. What it is and what it isn't, focusing almost entirely on what he termed 'informed consent,' which he said was at the heart of consent in a patient/provider relationship. I'd never heard of any of this before.

"The critical issue here is the provider always has more information than the patient," Dr. Leonard said.

I wrote the term in my notebook, even using some of his words, "informed consent means the patient grants permission after being informed by the provider of all possible consequences of treatment. The patient is informed of all possible risks and benefits." It seemed pretty clear. But then he ventured into territory arousing my grave concern.

"Consent is of particular concern in the relationship between a psychotherapist and the patient," Dr. Leonard went on. "When a patient is in therapy, if they are progressing, they are expected to regress to a more vulnerable childlike state, making informed consent quite problematic. Basically non-existent. And so in a psychotherapeutic relationship, the therapist must always understand the patient is not expected to provide a full informed consent. It is the therapist who must remain the adult in the room."

Wait! I said to myself, yelling internally. Regress? What's regress? And 'adult in the room'?! What's that mean?!

"The therapist provides the container and the safe space for the client to regress, to go back to the past, to recover the child within, so they can heal," he said.

And then Dr. Leonard added the final statement. "And so it is entirely unethical for the therapist to suggest sex as a path in therapy or to suggest a sexual relationship with the patient outside of therapy. It is the therapist who benefits and the patient who is abused. Consent does not exist here. There is no way a patient in psychotherapy can give informed consent to a sexual relationship with the therapist."

I dropped my pen onto the desk and gasped. So Benjamin, having advanced degrees, must have known sex with him was unethical and not therapeutic!!! Dr. Leonard glanced at me, appearing to note my shock with some concern. He continued talking. It didn't make any difference what he said for the rest of the class. I couldn't take any of it in. I sat there, dizzy and sick to my stomach. Thoughts and scenes from my psychotherapy with Benjamin rushed into my awareness, with Dr. Leonard's statements, "Consent does not exist in sexual contact between a psychotherapist and a patient. It is the therapist who is benefiting and the patient who is being abused."

Is this why, I wondered, I struggled so with suicide? And why Benjamin was giving me ideas of "comfortable" ways to suicide?

As I was agonizing over all this, the class was over and students were gathering their books and papers, walking out of class. Dr. Leonard looked at me and smiled as if to invite me to speak with him, but I looked away, horrified at all I'd heard. I quickly gathered my stuff and hurried out into the hallway.

A woman about my age followed me out of the classroom, calling to me, "Say, Pam, she said, as she moved to stand in front of me. "A few of us women are going out camping to Starved Rock this weekend. We've got a tent big enough for you and perhaps your kids. Want to go? My name is Andrea."

I had to gather my wits and disconnect myself from my shock with Dr. Leonard's statements. I wanted to run away, to hide somewhere. But I couldn't. She was standing directly in front of me.

I looked at her. She was a little shorter than I, had blonde hair and was quite pretty. The two of us were, at least as far as I could see, about the same age. Andrea was also a psychology major. I'd seen her before in class but knew nothing about her other than she's smart and I always appreciated her contributions in class. But we'd never spoken directly before.

After getting over my initial shock with Dr. Leonard's class, I was intrigued. I liked camping. And I wanted to get to know Andrea, and other women, better. I was flattered she asked.

"Yes, I'd love to go," I responded while wondering how Jim would feel about me going out camping with a group of women without him. But I wanted time with women and time alone in nature to process the dream and all Dr. Leonard had said. "Let me see what my husband's schedule is this weekend. And then I'll get back to you." We exchanged phone numbers, agreeing to connect in a few days.

Later that evening after getting our daughters to bed, Jim and I sat down in our family room to watch television. Since he wasn't drinking anymore, we now had time together with actual conversations. It was a relatively new experience and harkened back to those lovely days when we were dating and able to connect before alcoholism and Benjamin's therapy took over our lives.

I finally asked him, feeling some dread about his potential response, "Say, Jim, today another female student in class asked me if I, and our daughters, could go camping to Starved Rock this weekend with her and two other women and their kids. She said she has a tent big enough to hold about twelve people."

"Sounds fun," he quickly replied. "Does it sound like fun to you?"

"Well, it does. I don't know her very well, but she's about my age and is also a psychology major. I think she's a nice person."

"How about you go, Pam," he said. "I think it's a good idea."

I was stunned. Before his recovery, he would have fought me. Not wanting me to have a sense of self, a sense of independence, any sovereignty separate from him. It would have been too threatening. But here he was, saying he felt it was a good idea!

Jim was the first of what was to be Six Wise Men who showed up in my life at key moments. Jim stayed with me his entire life. They all showed up at pivotal events—another one staying his entire life, some staying for years, some for just a few months. But each showed up at just the right moment, with just the right words, with just the right help. Sacred synchronicity every step of the way.

So what is a Wise Man? A Wise Man is a man not threatened by a woman's power, by her right to say "No." He does not push past the "No," to get his own 'misappropriated needs' met. Like Benjamin had. Like a lot of men do.

But it's much more. A Wise Man does not take things personally. He respects himself and he respects others. He stands in his own authenticity, holding his power balanced by compassion and truth. He is able to see beyond the domestication, the 'group think,' the sexism, of our culture. Yes, somehow, he is holding a candle of awareness and a rose of compassion. A real man.

We need more of them.

When Jim suggested I go to Starved Rock with those other women, I thanked him.

"I'd like you to have more fun, Pam," Jim said. "I think being with a group of women and kids in a place like Starved Rock with a roaring fire at night would be good for you."

He was so right.

The next weekend, I drove with my eldest daughter, who was ten at the time, to meet this new friend Andrea and the two other women, at Starved Rock State Park. Jim was happy to take care of our two younger daughters while I camped. By the time we got there, Andrea and the others had already set up the tent.

All total, there were four of us women with six children, aged four to ten. Andrea and the other two women knew each other quite well. I was new to all of them. Andrea also invited a man to accompany the group. But he didn't camp at our site. Instead, he was down the road a bit. He came to introduce himself at dinner, but otherwise, he didn't spend any time with us.

The ten of us explored the area. We set up a campfire. Made hamburgers and corn for dinner. Listened to the birds. Watched the squirrels. And waited for the sun to set and the evening to chill a bit of the heat of the warm autumn day. As for me, I was looking forward to gazing at the stars and listening to the sound of crickets in the night.

The sun set and it finally became dark, really dark. Beautifully dark with the chirping of crickets and the crackle of the fire at the center of our campsite. All six kids went into the large tent for bed. They were so exhausted they went without one complaint.

The four of us women gathered around the campfire, which by this time, was roaring. For a few moments, we were silent, noting we saw nothing beyond the tall oak trees surrounding the campsite, the stars in the sky, the fire, and the doorway to the tent. The light of the fire shined upon all our faces. Everything else was cloaked in complete darkness. The oak trees, the sound of crickets and the stars above kept everyone company, holding witness to all.

I was the first to speak. I don't know what made me say it. But somehow, I did.

"I went into psychotherapy a few years ago and the therapist convinced me that having sex with him was the kind of therapy I needed," I said, rather casually. "It was devastating to me," I added almost as an after-thought, "I was suicidal before therapy, but I became more suicidal with that kind of therapy."

I hadn't planned on saying any of this. The words just spilled out of my mouth. Perhaps the dream propelled me to speak. Perhaps Dr. Leonard's talk opened me to speak. Perhaps talking to strangers made me more open to sharing secrets. Perhaps sitting by a campfire as women have done for thousands of years helped me open my voice. Hearing the words come out of my mouth took me by surprise. I had no idea what to expect from these three women. Strangers, all of them.

"Wow, me too," said Andrea, who was sitting to my right. "My psychotherapist also convinced me sex with him would be helpful."

"What?" cried Janice, who was sitting to the right of Andrea. "Last year, two physicians I had been to earlier in the month invited themselves over to my apartment for what I thought was a social encounter, and they both took turns raping me. I never told anyone."

"Wow," said Sue Ann, who was sitting to the right of Janice. "Right now I am having an affair with my cardiologist."

What were the chances? Four women. Five predatory males. A campfire. Crickets. And the darkness of night surrounding us all.

We were all stunned by the honesty. And speechless for several minutes while each of us attempted to take in the information.

Then I shared how Benjamin told me sex with him would help me out of my sense of alienation, opening the plexiglass cage I felt locked within. But now I felt even more isolated than before. I never wished for any sort of relationship with him other than psychotherapy. I told them I wasn't attracted to him in the least. I just wanted to be rescued. And I never said yes. It was very clear this was not a romantic relationship—just a therapeutic relationship using sex as a tool.

I mentioned Dr. Leonard's speaking about this in class the other day. Andrea responded she understood and believed what Dr. Leonard said. Then Andrea shared similar experiences.

We all talked late into the evening about how each of us came to this place with these men. This was the first time any of us shared any of this. And no one had an answer about where to go from here.

Eventually, the fire died down. The crickets and the dark coolness of night overcame everyone, and we decided to enter the tent to sleep. And to discuss more the next day.

I was awakened in the middle of the night by the cries of Sue Ann's four-year-old daughter calling for her mommy.

"Mommy! Mommy!" she called.

"Sue Ann, can you hear your daughter?" I called out louder than her little one.

No answer from Sue Ann.

Someone answered in a very sleepy low tone that Sue Ann was gone.

Her little girl cried and cried, "I'm scared. I want my mommy!"

Suddenly it occurred to me where Sue Ann was. From our earlier evening conversations, I decided Sue Ann was the only one in our group clinging to receiving reinforcement from misguided male 'admiration and rescue.' I figured Sue Ann had gone to the only man in the group—the young man camping down the road a bit.

I decided I was going to go get her. Like in my dream. A screaming child will be taken care of. I wasn't going to let Sue Ann's daughter feel abandoned. Being this assertive was a very unusual move for me to make. Actually, it was a first.

I got up, turned on my flashlight once outside the tent, and walked down the road to the site where I knew the young man put up his tent.

"Sue Ann, you in there?" I called loudly just outside his tent.

"Yes, I'm here," Sue Ann said, in a low soft tone.

"Your little girl is scared and calling for you," I said rather fiercely.

"Tell her I will be there soon. Just to wait a bit," she said while moaning and mumbling.

"Not a chance Sue Ann," I said, even more fiercely. "I am not leaving here without you. And as a matter of fact, I am counting to five and you had better be out by the count of five or I am coming in to get you. One. Two. Three. Sue Ann, I am not kidding. Four."

Sue Ann opened the tent door and came out just as I said "Five."

We walked back to the big tent in complete silence.

There was no discussion of this among the four of us the next day. Yet everyone knew what happened. It left a big impression on me.

On my drive home, I realized I abandoned my own little girl in the relationship with the therapist. And I needed to rescue her from Benjamin, as my dream guided. I became aware I needed to stand up for my own little one, to call her home, just as I did for Sue Ann's daughter. I didn't know what that meant at the time, but I was sure I would begin to figure it out by morning. I was determined.

The next morning, I called Andrea to talk about all of this.

"Andrea, what do you think about what Dr. Leonard said about informed consent and abuse?" I asked.

"I'd never thought about any of that before," Andrea said.

Then I told Andrea I never said yes. I just got so worn down by suicide desires, depression, and Benjamin, I collapsed and stopped saying no. "I never said yes, Andrea. I felt my life was at stake."

"Me, too," Andrea said.

The two of us agreed to ask Dr. Leonard to meet with us privately to see if he had any suggestions. And so, a week after Dr. Leonard's class on the issues of the medical ethics of informed consent between a psychotherapist and a patient, Andrea and I had an appointment with him. Before our scheduled meeting, we met downstairs in the small refreshment area of the school's building.

"I'm scared," I shared.

"I am, too," said Andrea.

"I think we should just be clear and quick. Let's just tell him about our experience in therapy and ask what he suggests," I said.

"I agree," Andrea said.

Our hearts beating fast, our breathing shallow, our legs shaking, we walked up the stairs and knocked on Dr. Leonard's office door.

"Come on in," Dr. Leonard said in his friendly deep voice.

We walked in and sat down in the two chairs already waiting for us in front of Dr. Leonard sitting behind his desk.

"Dr. Leonard," I began, "We are here because we both have experiences with our psychotherapist engaging in sex with us. Neither of us knew this was a breach of ethics until last week in your class."

"And neither of us could understand, until now, how devastating this has been for us," Andrea added.

"I had no idea this has likely contributed to some of my extreme suicide thoughts," I said.

Dr. Leonard gasped as his mouth dropped open.

After taking several breaths, he said, "My friend's neighbor is going through something similar with someone she knows. Her girlfriend is having a sexual relationship with her therapist, who is also my neighbor's therapist. It was on my mind and is why I went into such detail about the specifics of sexual contact between patient and psychotherapist last week."

The three of us sat in stunned silence.

Five women. Six predatory males all in professional, medical positions. All shared for the first time.

I asked Dr. Leonard for suggestions about how to go forward from this point. He told me about state licensure and professional regulations. This was all new information for me. I'd never heard any of this. And then he recommended a malpractice lawyer in the city. I took the attorney's name and phone number.

We thanked Dr. Leonard. I told him I would keep him informed of what I decided to do, and how things turned out. He pledged his support for my courage with whatever path I decided to take.

Dr. Leonard turned out to be the second of Six Wise Men to show up and support me in finding and honoring my voice. For which I am eternally grateful. Having appropriate help from some wise men is essential when you're confronting a dysfunctional male power structure. Which is what I was just about to do. I walked out of Dr. Leonard's office feeling stronger than I had in several years.

"I'm calling this lawyer today when I get home," I told Andrea.

"What will you do about Jim?" she asked, considering my relationship with Jim might be an issue. "What do you think he will do if he finds out about this? Will he think you've been cheating on him?"

"I can't think too far ahead, Andrea," I responded. I knew it was a good question and one which concerned me. "I am still fighting to save my life. I am still very suicidal. It haunts me daily. I need to do what will save my life."

I got into Jim's and my big station wagon and drove the fifty-minute drive home, all the while haunted by Andrea's last question. Telling Jim now was not an option. I was going to gather all the relevant facts and options and then proceed. I was also not going to tell my current psychiatrist. Of course, I was quite practiced at keeping things to myself. I was not an easy 'read,' and for that, I was quite grateful.

When I got home I called the lawyer.

But my thoughts of suicide went on fast forward. I was so ashamed and angry with myself for falling for such sham therapy. For letting my body be used as a tool for my own rescue. My criticism, my persecution of myself, became relentless.

That was the day I refused all sexual intimacy with Jim. Even though he was gentle, his touch felt like a knife blade scrapping across freshly burned flesh. I just couldn't bear it. Of course, saying no to him raised significant concern about whether he would stay with me. But I had to say no. My life depended upon it. I didn't know what he would end up doing.

As it turned out, he waited five years. Five years. During that time he focused on experiencing how to love beyond a personal, sexualized, possessive love. He truly became a Wise Man. He kept our family together and held the very ground under my feet.

CHAPTER EIGHT

NOW COMES THE FERAL CAT

"The truth will set you free, but first it will piss you off."

—Gloria Steinem

alling Sue Ann out of the tent, calling the lawyer, and refusing intimacy with Jim, marked the beginning of my 'feral cat' phase. I was now actively using my voice. The times of being silent and passive, waiting for rescue, were over.

Feral: in a wild state,
Especially after escape from captivity or domestication.

—New Oxford American Dictionary

A feral animal is unsocialized and unwilling, sometimes even dangerous, to be touched by humans. Frequently they've escaped captivity and know how humans seek to domesticate and control. They can read humans like humans cannot read them.

A human demonstrating feral characteristics would be someone totally unwilling to be victimized by anyone or anything. They have keen vision for lapses in another's integrity. But it goes even further. Such a person would also have a keen vision for lapses in the integrity of a social system or a culture.

The 'unmooring' experience I had earlier was preparation, and was required, for this phase of my life. With that experience, I disconnected significantly from artificial, materialistic and ego-centered cultural and social definitions of personal worth and control. It's a good start in one's journey to soul, a key part of the process. An essential first step.

But there was a big missing piece. While I disconnected from the social control of a 'group think' providing superficial vain definitions of worth, I put nothing in its place. My journey would have been less traumatic and easier for me and my family if I'd found an ethical therapist who recognized at the outset an existential crisis is a call for meaning. Deep meaning. A call from the very soul of the person.

Instead, the therapist used my vulnerability and searched for his personal satisfaction at my expense. But now I had to consciously understand fully the experience of being a victim and my complicity in it in order to get beyond victimization. It's a crucial part of the process of coming home to one's own soul. It's a great burning. A letting go of all our excuses, our rationalizations, our stories, all the ways we are complicit with our own victimization. We must dig up and heal our shadows. And bring those disowned parts of ourselves home. Yes, it is painful. We will bleed tears. But in the end, it's worth every step of the journey.

Here's the deal—our wounds are our gifts.

But I didn't know any of that then.

My spiritual experiences as a child were kept hidden, clearly remembered but discounted as irrelevant.

The feral phase of keen vision at lapses in integrity cuts both ways. Not only did I see through others' motivations and behavior, I saw through mine as well. I was brutal with myself. And I began being actively sui-cidal. My self-criticism and desire to end my life was constant.

I was my own victim and my own persecutor. And the dangerous part for me was I was completely unwilling to trust rescue from anyone. Even when it would be appropriate. Like I said, feral.

Jim understood the risk, but not why I was so desperate to suicide. He called an electrician to our house to ground all outlets so I couldn't easily electrocute myself. He removed all knives and all potentially dangerous cleaners, chemicals, medications. Fortunately, we owned no guns. I am quite sure if we had, I would not be here sharing my story with you. A gun would have been an extremely quick path for me to suicide. It would have been too quick of an option in the midst of my intense self-criticism. And I always needed time to work with myself to change my mind.

Within two weeks of meeting Dr. Leonard, I drove all the way into the city to meet John, the malpractice lawyer. He had a large fancy office on one of the upper floors of a huge office building in the middle of the financial district. I walked in to see him with my 'reporter's' mind rather than with my victim's mind. That was one of the gifts of having the experience of being a reporter. I now knew how to ask questions. Being a reporter combined with the intensity of the feral cat gave me the courage to journey far out of my life experience and comfort zone, all the way in to see the big-city lawyer.

As I walked into John's office, he was sitting behind the largest desk I've ever seen. At his back was a huge window framing the outdoor expanse of the city beyond. John was a nice-looking, tall, light-haired man, who was near my age. Mid-thirties, perhaps. Deep voice. Dressed in a suit.

He appeared quite kind, honest and straightforward. I could tell by the questions he asked he was nobody's fool. Even though I was concerned he might be a little too young for the task of a malpractice suit against a psychotherapist, a very unusual event at the time, through my questioning I found he was quite experienced. He surely wasn't naive like I was. I liked him. Even the feral cat in me, on high alert, was okay with him. To me, that was significant.

Of course, he took over two hours to make sure he understood my entire story. Then said he believed I had grounds for a lawsuit.

"Why do you want to sue Benjamin?" he asked, tilting his head a bit, implying to me he wanted an honest and thorough answer.

"I feel I need to take a stand. To say 'No, you don't get to do this to me.' Filing a lawsuit is me taking a strong stand," I said. "As long as I can also report him to the state for them to investigate pulling his license," I added.

"You realize there are no guarantees," he responded. "Losing is always a possibility, even though I am convinced you are in the right. What would you do if we lost?"

A good question, for which I didn't immediately have an answer. I already wondered that myself. John knew I'd been suicidal, but I hadn't shared with him how desperately suicidal I was.

I had a silent, and very quick, conversation with myself. It was kind of like the one a year before when I decided even though I loved Jim if he got in the way of my going to college, I would divorce him. I was committed to putting myself first. My promise to Mom and everything. In this situation, just filing a lawsuit would be healing for the little girl in me. I would not be complicit in denying what she needed. She needed me to stand up for her and to strongly and loudly say, "No." A lawsuit would do that. However it ended.

"I want to make it clear to Benjamin what he did was wrong," I responded. "I say no, he doesn't get to do that to me. Just filing a lawsuit is me saying no. Whether I win or lose, I will have finally taken a stand and said no."

After some discussion about how a lawsuit proceeds through court, assuring me he would be there with me every step of the way, and assuring me I could file a complaint against Benjamin's license with our state's regulatory agency as well, I agreed to file a lawsuit.

John was the third of the Six Wise Men to show up.

The lawsuit was filed about a month after our first meeting.

The little girl in me was terrified. The feral cat in me was ferocious. The reporter in me maintained an appropriate facade as required. And somehow, I promised myself I would do whatever I needed to do to survive this process. Whatever it took. I promised myself. And I promised the little girl in me. And my mother. And the mother in me. My children needed me to live.

I did not tell Jim.

Of course, I stopped seeing Benjamin. But continued seeing the psychiatrist. I said nothing to him about Benjamin's 'interventions' or the lawsuit. I was so ashamed of my stupidity. But eventually, as our lawsuit wound its way through the court process, John wanted me to tell my psychiatrist, so he could meet with him. And so I told Dr. Kack. He didn't seem at all surprised. Odd, I thought.

As I became more critical of myself, I also became more confrontational with Dr. Kack. It seemed he himself might have ethical problems. I refused to deny my feral cat instincts. By this time my voice was getting pretty strong.

You see, somehow when you are abused and you begin to awaken from it, your sight gets pretty keen. And you don't suffer fools. You can frighten people with your unvarnished honesty. Because at some point you don't care anymore, and social graces do not matter.

During one particularly contentious session, while glancing at a couch in his office, the feral cat in me blurted out, "Someone's been having sex on that couch!"

The look on his face said it all. He was shaken to his core, wondering to himself how I could possibly have known.

His response frightened me. While I didn't trust him much anyway, I slipped back to the place where I was alone, like after the appendicitis experience, with no one to hold me safe. Dr. Kack surely wasn't capable. After this confrontation with him, and as the lawsuit was just a few weeks from going to trial, I became very suicidal and wound up in the hospital, with Dr. Kack as my doctor.

Most of the time I was brutally honest when I was suicidal. I never used it to manipulate anyone. I wanted to be taken seriously. My life depended upon that. I wanted to live to raise my children. And so whenever I felt I would not be able to control myself, I said something.

I made no secret to staff members in the hospital I was concerned with the ethics of Dr. Kack's behavior. Although he was entirely appropriate with me, I didn't feel he was with another female patient on the unit. And my memory of the vision of his office couch kept coming into my awareness.

I accused Dr. Kack of blurring boundaries with the other patient. Implied sexual overtones. While I shared none of this with other patients on the unit, I did not make it a secret with him or with the staff.

A few years later, while working as an employee assistance counselor for a major corporation, I sat with other employee assistance counselors from other corporations discussing good treatment providers. The question of good psychiatrists came up when Dr. Kack's name was mentioned by another counselor sitting across from me. Apparently, my feral cat senses were right on target when I was in the hospital those years before. The counselor said he was basically run out of the country because of some ethical/sexual lapses with coworkers, therapists, and perhaps patients. I gulped but said nothing to the other counselors. And so I was right after all.

But I didn't know any of this "officially" when Dr. Kack had me hospitalized just a few weeks before the lawsuit was to go to court. Only the feral cat in me knew and raised a ruckus.

Perhaps it got a little too uncomfortable for him. Perhaps it was a little too close to the truth. So after a few days in the hospital, he fired me.

In our last session on a Friday evening, he said I had until 8:00 A.M. Monday to be hospitalized with another psychiatrist on another unit or he would transfer me by ambulance to another hospital, to the one where Benjamin was a manager and director of programs. Dr. Kack knew that. Pretty nasty of him. I was devastated.

"Where am I to go?" I asked, pleading with Dr. Kack to keep me. "Who do you recommend?"

"I have no recommendations for you, Pam," he stated in a cold, matter-of-fact fashion. "This session is over. Time for you to go."

I walked out of our meeting room into the day room area of the psych unit, openly crying. Which was very unusual for me.

Just as I entered the day room, the entire staff of the unit was walking out of their staffing room, all smiling as they circled around me. A few came up and hugged me. I was crying. And completely puzzled.

"Dr. Kack just fired me!" I cried. "I have until Monday morning to get another psychiatrist. I don't know anybody!"

Georgianna, one of the nurses I barely knew, came closer and hugged me. "We know, Pam," she said. "And we have a recommendation for you. We are recommending a man named Ray Robertson. He is perfect for you," she continued.

"How do you know?" I managed to say, choking on my tears. "How could you possibly know?"

"Many of us have known him for years," she explained. "He's been a psychiatrist for decades. He's good with people who have intense feelings. And you know, his wife went back to school when she was fifty and became a lawyer. His wife is a strong woman. So he is fine with strong women like you."

Of course, in retrospect, the nurse was trying to tell me Ray was not a sexist. And I was a strong woman who won't be 'put in her place' by anyone. (Thank you, feral cat.) But for some reason, this issue was not on my conscious radar at the time. Apparently, however, it was for them. It was clear from looking around at all their smiling faces they'd all come together to the same conclusion with the same recommendation. Had they known all along Dr. Kack was going to fire me? Had they planned this? Were they in on the entire process? Had they encouraged it? Or perhaps even instigated it?

Of course, they had.

The entire staff community there had my back and my best interests in their hearts. One more piece of trust in the community of humanity began to slowly re-engage with me.

Georgianna, the nurse, handed me a small card with Ray's office number. I walked over to the hallway phone and called his office, leaving a message with his answering service, and began walking into the day room to await his return call. I was hardly twenty feet from the phone when he called back. He must have been sitting right at his phone, awaiting my call.

"Hello," I said, "This is Pam."

"Hello Pam, this is Ray."

I was immediately struck with the calming, gravely deep tone of his voice, which I intuitively liked and felt an immediate sense of confidence with. But the feral cat was within me.

"Ok Ray," I said, beginning to gather my fierceness, "I need a psychiatrist who will hospitalize me by Monday morning. Is that possible?"

"Of course it is," he responded.

"Well, there is one problem," I countered, fire now building into my voice.

"What's that?" he asked, quite kindly.

"My first therapist fucked me. My second therapist fired me," continuing even more fiercely now, feral cat returning in full force, I yelled, "I go to court in three weeks in a lawsuit suing my first therapist. You got a problem with that!?"

"No, Pam, I do not," he responded, in a kind, authentic, soothing voice.

I was stopped in my tracks. Truly dumbfounded.

Of course, we made arrangements for the transfer to another hospital, and I finally got to meet Ray face to face.

I first saw him from a distance walking down the hallway. I didn't know he was Ray. But I watched him with curiosity, part of me anticipating it was him. He was tall, medium build, casually dressed, with long white hair and a white beard. I immediately felt I had known this man before, perhaps from another lifetime long, long ago, similar to how I felt when I first met Jim. While this felt hopeful, for some reason it also encouraged me to let out more of my feral cat. To be more authentic with all the chaos within. I watched as he stopped at the nurses' station to ask a question, then turn to look over into the dayroom where I was sitting observing him. The nurse motioned in my direction.

He walked over to me accompanied by another much younger man oddly dressed in a dark suit and tie while wearing big white heavy running shoes.

"You must be Pam?" Ray asked.

"Yes, I am. You must be Ray. And who is this person standing next to you?" I coolly asked.

"This is Jonathan. He's my intern. He will be with us unless you object," Ray responded.

I didn't like the idea of an 'observer', but decided if Jonathan was learning to be a shrink then he may as well learn from me to never fuck his patients.

"Hello Gym Shoes," I nodded in cold acknowledgment to Jonathan. "You can stay if you wish. But no comments and no questions. Got it?"

He nodded his agreement.

I was not going to give anybody respect unless they first showed me respect and competence worthy of my respect. And while Jonathan always behaved decently, throughout the entire time I was there I continued to call him Gym Shoes.

We sat down for a session in a small room with three chairs, a tiny table with a phone, and a window looking over an open, and very empty, courtyard. Ray got down to business rather quickly, but kindly, not seeming to mind I intended to be disrespectful, and insisted on calling his intern Gym Shoes.

Right off Ray asked me what I would do if I wanted to kill myself. And just like I told Tall Man all those years ago, I told Ray I believe I have a right to choose my own life course, regardless of where that takes me. My life, my choice.

Another awareness I considered even then but didn't voice out loud until getting bucked off Gabriel was I believed if I took a quick exit to this life by suicide, not only would I have the lessons a deeper part of me wanted to learn through the challenges I was experiencing in this particular lifetime, I would have to come back in another life and deal with the grief and regret of suicide with those I loved and left behind. Somehow, suicide would not let me off the hook for my responsibility to my children or to Jim, nor would it let me bypass a deeper plan an unknown part of me made before coming into this life. And even then, I was aware of refusing to live a fake life, one without soul, one without love and one without meaning. That would be another form of bypass. But I had no idea of what kind of life that would be. I knew I was in for the fight of my life.

I told Ray I was firm in my resolve to never involve any other person in any drama of suicide. I didn't want anyone to hurt or feel responsible in any manner for any decision of mine.

"Would you tell anybody if you felt suicidal?" he asked.

"That's what I have always done," I responded. Fully knowing this is a difficult road. So many times I experienced standing on the razor's edge of suicide, contemplating whether I would complete it. The very few times I lost my resolve, something always interrupted me, giving me another opportunity to choose life. Like when my daughter woke from her sleep and asked me to never leave her.

"I do not want to give my children the legacy of a mother who killed herself," I added.

Then I told Ray I wanted to be discharged from the hospital. On this day. Now.

He immediately asked if I was suicidal. I was testing him, and told him I wasn't, but figured I would make sure I didn't suicide after discharge. He said, "If I called your husband right now, would he be okay with me discharging you?"

I didn't think Ray would go so far as to call Jim right out of his classroom, certainly, Dr. Kack wouldn't have, so I told him Jim would be fine with whatever I wanted. I knew Jim wouldn't.

Ray picked up the phone and called Jim's school right then and there and had him pulled right out of his classroom for a telephone conference. How did Ray have all those numbers, right there, at his fingertips? I was horrified. Jim told him not to discharge me. And so, of course, Ray wouldn't.

I decided I met my match.

Gym Shoes smiled. It was a kind smile, perhaps a little amused, but it was compassionate. I was still going to call him Gym Shoes.

My trust in Ray began ever so slightly. He was kind even when I confronted him, or was rude, or refused to answer a question. Which was fairly often. Feral cat, you know. He insisted I participate in conferences with hospital staff members, something generally conducted without a patient's presence. A few days after being admitted, I attended my first staff meeting. It was held in a small room with a large table. All total, there must have been about ten people present. Nurses. Psych techs. Gym Shoes. Ray. And me.

I sat at the head of the table. Ray was to my right, and Gym Shoes was to Ray's right. Ray gave a general overview of my situation—suicidal, traumatized by an abusive therapist, lawsuit, but then added a few unexpected items. Ray told the group I was quite intelligent and aware. Then he added something alarming.

"And she eats psychiatrists for breakfast," he said, with a smile on his face as he looked around the table.

I panicked and immediately looked at everyone sitting around the table to see their response. They all smiled a gentle smile, nodding they understood. Likely a few of them had been at the receiving end of my feral cat and discussed this with others. Ray was trying to tell them I was just as hard on him as I was on them. To hang in there and not take anything personally. It helped them be kinder to me. Of course, that was his intent.

After about a week in the hospital, I got to go home. While Ray seemed okay as a therapist, my trust was very little, if at all. Like I said—feral cat.

In the few months or so after meeting Ray, I was minimally engaged in counseling. I kept my feelings locked within myself, known to me but no other. My only motivation in continuing any sort of counseling was to keep from killing myself while I navigated through the lawsuit and the eventual complaint to the state. A fairly tall order given the depth of grief and anger I was carrying. While I met with Ray weekly, I made little contact with him. For example, I didn't know the color of his eyes, and wouldn't have been able to describe him in any way, other than to say he was a tall man with long white hair, a white beard, and had a deep, gravelly voice.

The court trial on the lawsuit was put off, as was typical for quite a while, and we went through another series of delays. I was desperately outraged with myself. And then, one day I was sitting on the floor in the corner of my bathroom, planning my suicide. I was crouched on the floor, crying. Sobbing. Deep sobs as if my heart was breaking. Because it was.

It was mid-morning and Jim and our children were all at school. I was brutal with my self-criticism. I was sure Jim would find a much better person than me to mother our children. This was a very dangerous position for me to take. The most dangerous position of all.

I moved from crouching on the floor to kneeling on my hands and knees, then gently pulled myself up to standing, using the vanity in the bathroom for aid. I turned around and began slowly walking out of my bathroom and onto the carpeting of my bedroom, on my way out the door to leave to suicide.

As I took the steps from my bedroom to the door, I noticed a drawing on the floor my youngest daughter left for me to see that morning. I bent over and picked it up. She had drawn a multicolored rainbow with a red bird, its flying wings outstretched at the end of the rainbow. Offering me an opportunity to choose life rather than death.

I fell to the floor in tears. If she can believe in the goodness of life and hold hope for a loving future, so much so that she can draw this picture, I asked myself, can't I please just give this life I've been given one more chance? If a little dear like she can hope and can love, can't I?

I stood up and made a turn away from the door and instead walked to the nightstand by my bed and picked up the phone. I called Ray. I didn't expect to reach him directly, but through some sacred synchronistic good timing, he actually answered his own phone.

"Ray," I said, rather calmly without introducing myself. Completely disguising the urgency of my feelings, I asked "Given I will not suicide, how then am I to live?"

"Pam," he responded in his deep calm and gravelly voice, immediately recognizing it was me, "would you like to come in for a visit today?"

"Well, yes," I said, partly stuttering, "I think I would," totally shocked by his offer.

He accommodated my time schedule and agreed to meet me in the hour it would take me to get to his office.

When I got there, Ray was waiting. He opened his office door inviting me in, motioning for me to sit down directly opposite him, the wall at my back. As I sat down, I told him I did not know where to begin. I just wondered how was it I was going to live. How is it any of us live?

Somehow he led our discussion around to the issue of trust. How people trust each other. And why. My feral cat was there, protecting the little girl in me, very aware, yet quiet.

Then Ray went directly into what was probably his primary question. And what he needed to know in order to work with me. How was it sex with Benjamin began? Had I asked for it?

You see, there is this very real inner process that frequently occurs in the practice of psychotherapy called 'transference,' and 'counter-transference.'

It's an unconscious process that happens when the patient transfers wounded or disowned parts of their emotional self and places them onto their therapist. The patient then frequently wants to merge with the therapist, in an unconscious attempt to bring those disowned parts home. That's the desire for rescue part. Sometimes the wish for merging is experienced as sexual desire. Particularly if the patient was sexually abused as a child. However, sexual abuse as a child was not my experience growing up.

Transference is just a longing for completion. The healing of a wound. It's something which cannot be healed if the therapist in any way mistakes the attachment or the desire to merge as personally related to the therapist. It's all related to the unconscious shadow (basement bunkers) parts of a person calling to come home.

As for me, the little girl in me saw Benjamin as my savior. I wanted him to value my life. To rescue me. To tell me I had a right to exist. And so I didn't fight him much when he wanted sex from my body in exchange for saving my lost and disowned little girl.

Sexual contact between a therapist and the patient is like sexually abusing a lost child longing to come home. This is why sexual contact is so traumatic within any psychotherapeutic context. It's similar to the trauma of incest.

The education and supervision of psychotherapists focus on understanding this process. This is what Dr. Leonard was referring to when he said the therapist must be the "adult in the room," so the patient can regress.

It is also common for a psychotherapist to be sexually attracted to their patients. This is called counter-transference. It is something which is focused on in the education and mentoring of psychotherapists. Counter-transference is regarded as a sign the therapist needs to explore some of their own developmental issues with a supervisor. It's being the "adult."

All professional training teaches that any sexual contact between psychotherapist and patient is entirely unethical and abusive to the patient.

Of course, I didn't know any of this as I was seeing Benjamin. I was just beginning to understand the ethics, but not the psychology, as I began working with Ray.

But on this particular day, Ray wanted to begin to understand the origin of the abuse with Benjamin. And so he asked if I had wanted it.

"No," I said, practically whispering in answer to his question, while looking down at the floor, feeling a significant amount of shame. "I did not ask for any physical involvement with Benjamin. I just got so worn down, I stopped saying no. I was never attracted to him, and I never said yes. But I did think he could save my life. I did see him as my savior. I did want him to care for me."

"I would like you to know Pam," Ray said slowly in response, "I will never use my hands or any part of my body to invade your space. Even if you asked me. Even if you took off all your clothes," he said. "I promise you I will not invade your space. Ever."

I heard him speak those words but had a difficult time taking in their meaning. It was as if I went on overload and couldn't take in all he had said without repeating them to myself several times. And so he sat with me in silence, not rushing me, as I repeated those words inside myself. I could palpably feel his caring as we sat there, in silence, together.

I began to believe him. But it was just a beginning. Feral cat always attentive.

Then I told him about the unmooring experience and the dreams of dragging the dead soldier through a battlefield. About wanting to die before ever walking into Benjamin's office.

Ray moved his chair so he was sitting directly in front of me, so close our knees almost, but not quite, touched. He folded his hands together, placing them upon his knees.

We began to talk about his hands. Where they've been. What his hands have done. What they know to do. How old they are.

"Have you ever delivered a baby with these hands?" I asked.

Yes, I have," he answered. "It is a great privilege to hold a baby just as they enter this world."

I thought about the births of my own three babies. And of how my doctors were the very first to place their hands upon their bodies, holding them, ushering them safely into this world. And how precious that is.

He invited me to touch his hands. To turn them over and look at both sides, and to touch the wrinkles on his palms. I slowly traced the wrinkles on each of his palms, from side to side and from top to bottom. Then I noticed he had long, slender graceful fingers with well-groomed fingernails. He wore a simple gold ring on his left ring finger, symbolizing his marriage. His hands looked as if they could play the keys gracefully on a piano or would be especially artful with performing brain surgery.

We talked about the safety of his hands. And then he promised again he would never use his hands or any other part of his body to invade my body or my space.

It was my body. No one else's. My sovereignty. Mine.

As he said those words, I was holding his hands. I finally looked up directly into his eyes for the first time. He was already looking into mine. He had kind brown eyes.

"I think you have wise hands, Ray," I finally managed to whisper as we made eye contact.

And then I let myself cry. For the first time. In front of him.

The feral cat in me was 'gentled' just a bit that day.

Real therapy had begun. With authentic human compassionate contact. In the present moment. Ray knew and maintained this the entire time we worked together.

What was consistent with Ray was his ability to stay focused as a witness in present time and his amazing ability to radiate a palpable sense of a loving heart.

He kept his promise.

Ray was the fourth of the Six Wise Men to show up.

I learned decades later Ray graduated from high school at age sixteen, then graduated from Purdue University with a major in Pre-Med at age eighteen. He went on to graduate from the University of Chicago Medical School as a physician at age twenty-one. And then he went on to become a Freudian Analyst for many years. By the time I began working with him, he was sixty years old and had given up Freudian work, considering it to be too intellectual, believing real healing comes from emotional experiences occurring in the present moment. "What are you aware of right now?" was the question he asked most frequently. Ray specialized in working experientially with all his patients.

What I found rather surprising about Ray was despite his giftedness within the academic world, he never radiated one hint of arrogance. He introduced himself to me as "Ray". I never heard anyone call him Dr. Robertson or even Dr. Ray. He was not focused on image or titles. Toward the end of his life, I found out from someone who knew him, that at one point in his career as a psychiatrist he spent time volunteering at a toddler day care center, for the experience of "rolling on the floor with toddlers", to learn about life from them. His humbleness was inspiring.

Now you may wonder about the wisdom of Ray coming so physically close to me, a feral cat and victim of sexual abuse, in what we could say was a rather confrontative therapy session. It was brave of Ray. But it was wise. It was exactly what I needed to begin to re-engage in contact with another human being, to heal my feral cat. In the present moment. Experientially. Not in an intellectual discussion. And he knew that, but he made sure he had clear boundaries. Always. An entirely important function within experiential work. Within any work, for that matter, with a psychotherapist.

And so, what are boundaries? Some parts of the setting of boundaries Ray and I spoke of, and some we somehow agreed to through the action of our work together. First, it was understood I paid him for his time. And he would never derive any sexual satisfaction from me. We spoke of those two issues. He was very generous with regard to payment. But we did agree.

And something etched in granite, which we spoke about, was I was to be honest with any suicide ideation and be willing to ask for help. I agreed and he accepted my word.

It was also understood I came to a session willing to feel, in the present moment, whatever was arising within me. And it was entirely my choice as to whether I shared what I was feeling.

The most essential component of boundaries is what we do within ourselves in our interactions with each other. We must not take what another does or says personally, recognizing another's words and actions are the result of their own inner processes. Ray never took what I did or said personally. He maintained his own sovereignty over himself while respecting mine, modeling this for me in present time. Over and over, it was a profound lesson.

With that 'gentling' session with the feral cat, I began to engage in real psychotherapy for the first time. I met with Ray for one on one sessions and for group sessions. We did rage work, empty chair work, dream work, group processes. Everything centered on experiencing my feelings in the present moment and accepting them.

For example, sometimes my memories of Benjamin, my experiences with the legal process, or with the outrageousness of life itself, filled me with rage or grief, feelings I was fearful of expressing. A truth here is you cannot get anywhere in therapy unless you express what's inside. Because so often, once it is expressed, it begins to unwind and we find deeper feelings underneath, feelings we may not be aware of but feelings we can then heal and move beyond.

One of Ray's most famous sayings was, "Feel the fear and go forward anyway." And so I began to feel the fear of expressing my feelings, my fear of owning them and then giving them a voice. I began to express them anyway, despite my fear.

Whether in individual or group sessions, if I was feeling anger or fear, Ray encouraged me to use a tennis racket and beat on a stack of cushions. I found anger or fear to be the gateway into deeper truths and healing. And so of course, sessions never ended with 'racket work'. They always ended with me going ever deeper into the underlying feelings I had been holding back—often feelings I wasn't consciously aware of. Eventually, I would cry, then feel grief, then sadness, then acceptance, and then finally, gratitude. I learned I needed to feel my feelings, frequently starting with the deepest, darkest of rage. And process all of it within the moment I was feeling it. Ray witnessed it all, with caring.

Through the process of our work together, I first was able to experience Ray holding me safely within my own fear. But as time and our work progressed, I began to hold myself safely within my fear. I was learning to rely upon myself. It was a major step forward in my trust in this life.

Many psychiatrists might have immediately prescribed antidepressants, particularly given my suicidal tendencies. But Ray's assessment was I had been traumatized and needed to claim my power. He let it be known he was trusting me to be honest with him about any suicidal thoughts. And so antidepressants were not initially suggested.

But at one point, during the course of our work together, after the lawsuit was over and I was beginning a professional career, as I sat with a patient, I began to experience rage and had a desire to throw the patient out of my office. While I did not act on it in any fashion, I noted it. I was fearful those intense feelings might resurface and create problems in the pursuit of my career. So I spoke with Ray and asked him to prescribe an antidepressant. We were still working closely and intensely in therapy.

I began taking the medication on a Friday evening. In the middle of a session with another patient the following Monday afternoon, I suddenly felt a reassuring and comforting sense of my feet touching the earth. For the first time in my life. It was so profound I looked at my watch. It was 4:10 P.M.

Eventually, after routinely taking in, noting, and becoming deeply aware, in present time, of my sense of feet upon this earth, with Ray's approval, I discontinued the medication while still working with Ray. The felt sense of my feet on this earth stayed with me and is with me still.

Over a period of time, I learned two things. One, antidepressants have their place in working with depression and suicide risk. That is for sure. And so does good diet and appropriate exercise. A good psychiatrist or psychiatric nurse practitioner is helpful with these sorts of assessments.

And two, my experience with the patient that day was more about what I was picking up from the patient intuitively rather than what was going on inside of me. Those feelings came on suddenly and intensely. Over time with patients, I became aware that whether or not we are therapists, we all pick up on others' feelings and reactions intuitively. It is essential we, particularly if we are therapists, learn to discern between what is ours and what is another's—it's what maintaining boundaries is all about. I learned to continually ask myself, is this my issue or is this the issue of the one in front of me. And asking a question or two of the one we are speaking with can help clarify. Sometimes it is a 'tripwire' leading to our own unconscious bunkers needing to be healed, and sometimes it is a 'lead line' pointing to another's unconscious bunker calling to be healed. This is an important part of the boundaries between therapist and patient, and between all of us in relationships. It is foundational in learning how to not take things personally.

But, of course, all those awarenesses came several years after the 'gentling' session with Ray and my feral cat, when I first began to open my trust to Ray.

CHAPTER NINE

TRUTH TELLING

"Women have been trained to speak softly and carry a lipstick. Those days are over."

—Bella Abzug

Eventually, I had to confront one of my biggest fears. One I could avoid no longer.

I had to tell Jim.

One morning as I was clearing dishes from the breakfast table after everyone had gone to school, the phone rang. It was John.

"Hi Pam, this is John," he said. "Got a minute?"

Of course I did, I told him. And wondered with some fear what this unexpected call was about.

"We are going to be scheduling a deposition pretty soon," he said. "And I was wondering if you have told Jim about the lawsuit."

"Oh my God, no, not this," I thought. I angrily yelled silently to myself, "Well, what did you expect anyway! You know there will be a deposition! And Jim will be brought into this!"

"No, John," I said quietly. "I haven't."

"Well," he continued, "I've been thinking now is a good time for you to let him know. And really, Pam, I wonder if he might want to join you in this lawsuit. He was hurt also."

That was true. We all had been hurt. Jim. Our children.

"Do you think you could tell him before our first deposition?" John asked. He knew this was a big ask.

"First deposition?" I asked. "You mean there will be more than one?"

"Pam, there certainly will be more than one, for sure," he responded. "We need to be prepared. I'd like you to come in next week to go over some practice questions. It would be a good idea if Jim knew by then. What'da ya think?"

While I hadn't planned on all this happening this way, I figured telling Jim would be coming, somehow, someway, eventually.

I told him I would talk with Jim over the approaching weekend. When John heard I was willing to let Jim know, we settled on meeting the following Wednesday morning in his office in the city. After telling Jim, of course.

I had three days to think about how I would tell him. Would he think this was an affair? It wasn't for me, that was for sure. Men can sometimes be so possessive of women. In denial of a deeper, truer part of themselves, and others, they make something like this about their pride, their ego, seeing women as 'property', rather than becoming aware of another's pain, another's sovereignty. Well, the truth is, it's often something we all do. We all take things personally. It seems to be part of our human condition of dysfunction—this experience of being entrapped within the roles of victim, rescuer, persecutor. Our common form of domestication, our "group think". Something to move beyond. To become Wise Men and Wise Women. Easier said than done. That's for sure.

But I didn't know what Jim's response would be. His recovery was proceeding well, and he appeared to be steady. Would he continue to be the Wise Man he had begun to grow into? I just didn't know.

When he came home from work later in the evening, I kept glancing at him when he wasn't looking my way, and wondering, "What will he do? Will he be outraged? Will he be hurt? Will he be worried? Will he hate me? Will he throw me out?"

Over and over again, for the next few days and nights, those questions haunted me.

Saturday morning came and it was time. Our children were downstairs eating breakfast, watching some Saturday morning program on PBS, and the two of us were upstairs in our bedroom, putting clean clothes away in our closet.

"Jim," I began, "remember all those times when you asked me if Benjamin and I had 'something' going on beyond psychotherapy?"

He turned to look me directly in the eyes, "Yes, I do," Jim said. Then held his breath to await what was coming.

"Well," I continued, directly but kindly, knowing he'll be hurt, "you were right to be concerned. There was. But it wasn't an affair. It was supposed to be therapy." "It" of course, we both knew, was sexual contact.

He started to cry. I hated myself for hurting him. But tried my best to be kind to myself. It was easy to be kind to him. I felt so sorry for what he must be feeling. I started to cry.

"Are you still seeing him?" he asked through his tears. Perhaps wondering if this might be the beginning of me asking him for a divorce or something. Perhaps thinking this was why I refused sexual contact with him. "Do you love him?"

"No, Jim," I quickly responded. "And I haven't been in contact with Benjamin for some time now. What he did was terrible for me. It's one of the reasons I've been so suicidal, and why I haven't been able to have sex with you. Several months ago, I saw a lawyer in the city and made arrangements to sue him. I also plan to report him to our state licensing department for a breach of professional ethics, and hopefully, they will look at all the evidence and pull his license."

Jim looked away from me, then moved to sit down on our bed, over-whelmed. I went to sit next to him, placing my hand upon his knee.

"I'm so sorry, Jim," I said. We were both silent for several minutes. "What do you think about joining me in the lawsuit?" I finally said. "You were hurt too."

Several more minutes of silence.

I was angry with myself for being so naive, so stupid, and so willing to let my body be used as some form of tool for 'rescue'. Yeah, a rescue that nearly killed me. And hurt Jim and my family. How could I have done this? I raged at myself while we sat there in silence.

"Yes, I will join you in the lawsuit," he finally said. "And I would like to meet this lawyer the next time you go."

The following Monday I called John and told him Jim wanted to join me in the lawsuit and wanted to meet him.

"Can he come in with me this Wednesday?" I asked, not at all sure how a lawyer and a client prepare for a deposition.

"Yes, he can, Pam," John said. "I'd like to meet him. I'm glad he wants to join the lawsuit. But while we're going over everything in the conference room, he will need to sit in my office. It wouldn't be a good idea for him to be with us while we prepare. Perhaps tell him to bring something to read. Do you think he'd be okay with that?"

"Yes, I do," I said. And so it was settled. Jim would take a personal day from work and come with me to John's office.

On our hour-long drive into the city, we talked more about how I had come to this point. About my dream of the little girl needing rescue and held locked in a house by Benjamin. About Dr. Leonard's ethics class. About Starved Rock. And about how I found John. Jim seemed to begin to understand. He held steady.

Years later, Jim told me as a recovering alcoholic, on the day we went to meet John, he held the Serenity Prayer close to him and said it many times, "God grant me the Serenity to accept the things I cannot change. Courage to change the things I can. And the Wisdom to know the difference." He said it helped him hold steady. For him, and for me.

Jim began seeing Jason, who was in practice as a therapist with Ray. Jason was able to hold Jim throughout the painful lawsuit process and was always there as a backup for Ray. Jason was the fifth of the Six Wise Men to show up.

Between Jim, Dr. Leonard, John, Ray, and Jason, there was a fairly steady ground supporting me, for the first time in my life. Five Wise Men, all committed to honesty and integrity. Willing to support a feral cat like me.

Which was a good thing because things were about to get a little rough.

One afternoon after my last class of the day, I decided to run a 'trial balloon' so to speak, by sharing about sexual abuse as therapy with one of the younger male students. I was wondering how he would see this.

"I had a girlfriend who went into therapy with a male therapist and he convinced her sexual contact with him would be healing. She is suing him now," I started.

"Oh my God! She got away with murder!" he responded.

"What?! What do you mean?" I said, shocked by his response.

"Don't you know every woman wants to have sex with her therapist? To sue him for what she wanted is ridiculous!" he said.

No, I'd never heard any of that. Perhaps that's why Ray asked some of the questions he did, I thought to myself. At this point, I had not yet heard of the psychological process of transference, except through Dr. Leonard's brief explanation. And, I'd never heard of the very real 'group think' beliefs people often get into in 'blaming the victim'. Which is what this guy was doing.

"Well, that's not how it happened," I managed to continue in a very decent fashion, feral cat kept at bay. "The murder my friend almost got away with was the murder of the little girl inside of her. She was suicidal when she began therapy but became more suicidal with this therapist," I said.

"Don't you understand, every woman wants to have sex with her therapist?" he repeated. "Every woman wants to have sex with a powerful man. A therapist is a powerful man. She pulled off a coup. And now she's suing him?" he responded. "Who does she think she is?"

"Don't you understand even if she wanted it, which in this case she said she didn't, and I believe her, it would still be an abuse of power? And traumatic to her?"

He nodded a "no", and walked away, shaking his head, ending our conversation.

I could hear my own silent but unrelenting, brutal self-criticisms. My persecution of myself. The part of me buying into our common cultural 'group think'. And now, I heard how unaware men, and likely unaware women, might regard all I was dealing with. A group-think of massive unawareness, denial, and sexism. Shaming and blaming the victim. I knew I was alone before. But I felt even more alone with this conversation.

Having a few good men supporting me, men who were not wanting to take something from me as compensation for their support, men who understood the violation I experienced, was profoundly healing for me.

But now, after speaking with this young man, I wondered how I was going to manage my experience within this human community as all this comes out in public if everybody else feels as this young man expressed?

I held Jim, Ray, Jason, Dr. Leonard and John close.

While Freud himself, in a 1915 paper, warned others about the ethical risks and harms to patients sexually involved with their psychiatrists by writing "The patient's willingness makes no difference whatever; it merely throws the whole responsibility on (the therapist)," he continued to conform to the sexist group think victim-blaming in other situations. For example, as he did psychoanalysis with the daughters of several of his colleagues, he found some of them likely had been sexually abused by their fathers, brothers, uncles, or other close male family members. And he wrote about it. His peers confronted him, denied his assessments, claiming the women were making up wishful fantasies. Freud eventually bowed to his colleague's admonitions, went into the current 'domestication' of his time, and denied his own initial experience and understanding. He abandoned the wounding of his female clients, dismissing their autonomy and worth, calling their claims "fantasies". At the time, it was a profound, yet unconscious, form of sexism.

Years after Freud's death, and after the work of many other Freudian and Jungian psychoanalysts, claims of abusive sexual contact as 'female fantasies' were debunked as ways to diminish a relatively common, but frequently denied, traumatic female experience. Eventually, within the fields of psychotherapy, this form of male group-think has slowly begun to fade. However, these forms of unconscious sexism, victim-blaming, are quite present today in our society in both men and women. And in a sense, all of the ways we denigrate and separate ourselves from the humanity of others—sexism, racism, homophobia, and xenophobia—can be seen as a form of victim-blaming.

Of course, I didn't know any of that when I spoke with the young man. Along with Freud and many others, he was tapping into that same human dysfunctional pattern—a group-think sexist social control. Something I surely was stepping outside the lines of in filing a lawsuit, wanting to get to something more authentic. Wanting to make sure my "no" was expressed and heard.

Throughout centuries and centuries of our human existence, relationships between people and cultures have often been defined through a hierarchy, one form of power over another. This power can be social, financial, intellectual, political, or sexual. It's the 'domestication' we have all learned and passed down through our cultures and social structures, for hundreds and hundreds of years. Those having more money, social advantage, or credibility—in our culture it's generally straight white men—have power over those with less social advantage or credibility—generally women, Brown and Black people, whether male or female, and those identifying as gay or transgender.

There can be a dark side to this. Sometimes people are attracted to the power of a predator, mistaking their power for safety. Or a mistaken belief their rescue by another, more powerful person, is love. We could call this an extreme form of codependency. But it's generally all unconscious.

It's all in what can be called "the Drama Triangle." (Karpman) Victim. Persecutor. Rescuer. We humans frequently dance our social structures and our relationships with others, and with ourselves, within that triangle. Ultimately, it's what keeps the powerful in power. And, those of us dancing within the roles of the triangle are complicit with disempowering ourselves, with buying into a cultural group think of holding ourselves and others to those roles. All the while switching between the roles when one role seems to offer more reward, more safety, than the other. But it is a role. It is not authentic. Somehow, we mistake it for authenticity. And for safety. Because we are often unaware we are afraid. It's an unawareness relinquishing our authority over ourselves and offering it over to another individual or group, disempowering us.

Whenever we focus on power or safety, we are in fear. Those who work mightily to retain their power, are also in fear. They just don't know it. It is an unconscious force driving them.

When one is fearful, one usually looks for the nearest form of safety, rescue, or social power of some kind or another outside of themself. Like what I'd done with Benjamin. Worshiping another and asking for rescue is part of the triangle. Seeking rescue or 'fixing' from another is always a call to find authority from within.

The seeking of authority outside of myself was what I needed to release. And this was ultimately the gift of my experience with Benjamin. But it took a while for me to understand. Here's the deal, each one of us is the one we are looking for. I didn't know any of that then. I was just determined to move beyond victim.

But moving beyond victim meant I also somehow needed to understand persecutor and rescuer/fixer. The feral cat in me made sure I denied rescue or any fixing from another. But that can be a double-edged sword. I had to learn to discern between asking for rescue when it was my job to rescue myself and to accept help when I actually needed it. The last time I'd done that didn't end so well. I was determined not to repeat another mistake.

Ray always advised I feel the fear and go forward anyway. This wasn't about doing risky behaviors. This was about honoring a deeper part of myself which was afraid to exist. To trust in myself and others. And to love. Ray challenged me to live with courage and with love throughout the entire time we worked together. In present moment awareness.

While the lawsuit was proceeding through the courts, I graduated with my bachelor's degree with a major in psychology. On graduation day, I wore a beautiful blue dress I'd purchased just for this event. As I was getting myself ready, my self-persecutor kept demanding "What do you think you can do with a BA in psychology? It means nothing!" I could hear Benjamin's criticisms of my desire to graduate yelling in my ear. I could hear my family's mantra, "How dare you achieve more than your parents!"

While swearing outrageously at myself, I took a pair of scissors and threw them repeatedly at the image of myself in the bathroom mirror, shattering the mirror into tiny fragments. Jim came running from another part of our house and held me as I cried.

"What can I do with a bachelor's in psych?" I sobbed. "It gets me nothing!"

"Pam," he calmly said as he held me, slowly rocking me back and forth, "You will figure it out. Trust it, Pam. You will figure it out."

Can you see the evolution in Jim's growth? A dramatic change. Jim knew by this time how to hold me because he, himself, had already been held by his recovery program with AA, by Bill, and by Jason and Ray.

Jim helped me get myself together, then went downstairs to soothe our children who heard my uproar. Afterward, we all drove to the college for the ceremony. I went into the holding area for the graduates and Jim and our children went into the auditorium to await my graduation march.

We graduates formed two lines, each on opposite sides at the back of the auditorium. The lines were to merge, with students from each line pairing up, walking together two by two down the center of the auditorium. As I joined with the student from the opposite line, I noticed the person I was paired with was the young man who had earlier claimed a woman suing her therapist for being sexual with her was getting away with murder. We looked at each other with some disdain, then paired up and walked together down the aisle. We parted as we reached our seating area, with the young man and I sitting on opposite sides of the auditorium.

As I turned to walk down the row of chairs assembled to seat those in my line, I noticed the chair waiting for me had my name on it, "Pamela Verner." I was stunned. And I cried. I felt as if time stood still, right there in that moment, and the chair had been waiting for me all of my life. All of my life. Thank you, Mr. Raspiller. A chair at graduation from college had MY name on it. Mine. A place in this life, just for me.

Perhaps I did have a right to exist.

After graduation, the newspaper asked me to work as a staff reporter rather than as a stringer. I accepted. So, I had a full-time job. One I liked. So I found a Bachelor's Degree in Psychology does have something to offer.

One morning several weeks after graduation, as Jim and I were sipping our coffee, Jim pulled out pictures from graduation day. He showed me all the pictures, holding one last one in his hand.

"Look at this," he said, finally showing me the last picture. "See this chair, with your name on it, all this time waiting just for you, Pam. Just for you."

Jim knew what that meant to me. And he had gotten a picture of it. Yes, a Wise Man.

The lawsuit proceeded. Court delays, etc. Benjamin eventually admitted to the sexual contact but claimed it happened after we had terminated. And was not part of our therapy. All untrue.

Please note, even if it had taken place that way, it would have still been a breach of ethics. And traumatic for any patient.

When John told me what Benjamin was claiming, I remembered a time not long before filing the lawsuit when both he and I were driving home after a session on snow-covered roads. Benjamin was driving in front of me. I lost control of my car and spun a few circles in the middle of the road.

There were only three people on the road that night. Me. Benjamin. And a police officer.

Of course, the police officer turned on his lights and sirens and got out of his car to question me, my car already hung up on the curb, facing in the opposite direction. I was crying. Benjamin stopped and went over to speak with the officer and me, telling the officer he was my therapist and I was probably upset after our session, suggesting perhaps the officer should go easy on me. The officer spoke with both of us, likely making sure I wasn't intoxicated (which I wasn't—we never used alcohol), then helped me get my car off the curb. He did not give me a ticket. And then we all drove our separate ways.

I told John about this experience. Benjamin could not claim he was not my therapist. He'd already told an officer he was. If the officer noted it, that is.

"I'll call the police and see what they have to say about this," John said.

After calling, we learned the officer specifically remembered the incident because he had been one of Jim's students several years before.

Another sacred synchronicity.

Sexual contact previously admitted. Now, within the context of being a therapist. Verified by an officer.

And now the police were pulled into the process.

Benjamin was a respected member of our community. He had significantly more standing than I. But now I had to talk to the police. We might have to call them as witnesses to Benjamin's claim of being my therapist. It was terrifying. I spoke several times with Detective Myers, an officer from the police department. We went over all that had taken place in therapy. Detective Myers was professional, thorough, and appropriate with the questioning. But I had zero sense of how he was understanding anything I was telling him. I had no idea whether he believed me. Would he think just as the young man had? Just as Freud and his colleagues had? He was a man, after all. I could not read him. Which was very unusual, given how keen my senses were by this time.

And then, just after speaking with Detective Myers, in the span of about a week, we started getting harassing phone calls. Then vandalism at our house. Hoses and bricks and mailboxes were thrown into our yard. Our fence was broken. And then one day I went out to our car parked in the driveway to find the tires had been slit.

I reported it to the police. And called John. He also called the police. They found no evidence indicating Benjamin was in any way behind any of this. We never found out who was, but with John's and my calls to the police, and then the police questioning of others, the harassing behaviors stopped.

And then, just after one of John's calls to the police, on one sunny Thursday afternoon, in late Spring, just before the girls were due home from school, the phone rang.

I answered with the typical, "Hello," then waited a few moments for the response.

"Hello, is this Pam Verner?" It was Detective Myers. His voice was deep and strong, speaking as a man comfortable with his own authority.

"Yes, this is. Who's calling?" I asked, with quite a bit of trepidation, considering it might be exactly who it was.

"This is Detective Myers, from the Police Department," he said.

I paused to take in a deep breath. I knew John had just spoken with them about where we were in the lawsuit, but he hadn't yet shared with me how the conversation had gone. Now I was about to find out.

"I spoke with your lawyer, John," Detective Myers said. "And I wanted to call you myself."

"Well, thank you," I said, wondering whether this was going to be good news or bad news. It surely wouldn't be anything in between.

"I realize you are going through a great deal right now, Pam," he continued, never breaking his tone of strength and authority. "I understand you will be going into Chicago several times for depositions, and this can be frightening."

"Yes, it is," was all I could muster to say, ever so softly.

"I want you to know if you ever get stuck at any time in Chicago and need help or a ride home, call me," he said. "I will come and get you."

For a few moments, I was stunned speechless.

Did I hear him right? He said he would help me if I needed it. I repeated his words silently to myself.

"Thank you very much," I finally managed to say. "Thank you very much," I said again, softly, beginning to cry.

After we hung up, I shed more tears, feeling grateful this police officer could see through the abuse and not blame me. Somehow, he could see through our social group think and understand the strength and courage it was taking for me to take on this lawsuit. And offer help. Not rescue. Help.

I was already in the process of rescuing myself. But we don't do these things alone.

You see, accepting help in time of need is not the same as asking for someone to rescue you from something you must do for yourself. It's accepting help from one's community. And it's how we heal. And, it's how we help others heal. It's how we are all connected. As noted earlier, we get hurt in community and we get healed in community.

The terror and shame of the abuse from Benjamin and the grief of abandonment by our human community when I was a small child with appendicitis began to heal just a bit more with Detective Myers' offer of help. In a way, he represented the police department and our community. And he believed me. And somehow, I began to feel I could belong, and perhaps be safe, in our community.

Now there were Six Wise Men—Jim, Ray, Jason, John, Dr. Leonard and Detective Myers.

I felt like I was jumping out the window of the burning building that was my life, rescuing myself, with help from others. Deciding to be a victim no more.

What does it mean, to decide to be a victim no more? There are many ways we all are victims, in a sense, of things we cannot control. That seems to be a truth for all of our lives. We're not going to be able to avoid this. However, here is one place, of many, where the Serenity Prayer comes into focus—accepting the things we cannot change. And working to discern what we can change and what we cannot. It is a difficult walk, to be sure, but a very significant process to take. The truth is, being aware we are choosing our own attitude is what removes us from being in victim mode. That's what claiming our own sovereignty is all about. It means being aware our response, whether it is feelings or behavior to any situation, is our choice. We each have a choice in how we respond. That means an outer response to another or to our community. And that also means an inner response to how we feel about others, our situation, and ourselves. And it also means being accountable to the consequences of our choices.

Also confounding our ability to own our own attitudes is an inner process called projection. It's an unconscious process similar to transference, but it is found in all social relationships and is not particular to the therapist/patient relationship. We all project our problems onto others. What we avoid seeing in ourselves we will see in others. It's the way others are mirrors for us. It's the way we avoid and deny accountability for our own behavior. And it's generally unconscious. On the road to becoming conscious, it is essential to accept accountability for our own behavior. But we need to do it without severe self-criticism. So, it's important to notice what we see in others, and then to look within for where it may be inside of us.

And another, quite subtle issue silently confounding our ability to be aware of our own choices is this thing we therapists term 'secondary gain'. It's a problem because it's also generally unconscious. And remember now, by this time, I was committed to becoming conscious.

There is always a 'secondary gain' to the roles in this vicious circle of victim, rescuer/fixer and persecutor. Secondary gain is what fuels the vicious circle. The victim gains sympathy and perhaps help from others with things they must learn to do for themselves. The rescuer/fixer gains admiration from others when they do something for another which another needs to do for themself, bringing the 'fixer' a sense of false pride. And the persecutor gains a sense of veneration, respect, or power, from others who are fearful of them.

With the gift of the feral cat, I was determined to be my own authority. I carefully noted my self-talk and resolutely refused any scent of movement into projection and secondary gain from any of those roles. As difficult as my feral cat was for me and others, it was a gift that helped me own power over my life. The critical task for me was that I had to be aware of what I thought and felt, in the present moment. This was key.

I was determined to own my place in this world. As a person with a right to live. Not as a victim. I couldn't do it perfectly, however. In these kinds of things, there is never a perfect. But I did make a commitment to myself. It was a very rocky and sometimes muddy walk, with many falls, but always followed by getting up.

The depositions turned out to be brutal, as I expected. But I didn't have to call Detective Myers. Jim came with me for the first one. For the other two, I was able to drive myself. As I look back, I do not know how I did it. My grit, I suppose, along with my awareness of those Six Wise Men, and Jennifer, a new female lawyer hired by John, held me. Jennifer was the only woman involved during my entire legal process. All the rest were men. She was young, and new to law. But Jennifer knew her stuff, and she, as a Wise Woman in Training, always demonstrated unshakeable and insightful support. I'm very grateful for her.

For the first deposition, Jim and I arrived at John's office to find Benjamin and four other male lawyers were already there, waiting in the conference room. John greeted us and invited Jim to sit in a comfortable chair in his office, just outside the door of the conference room where I was to give my deposition. He sat down and pulled out a book, while John and Jennifer invited me into the office kitchen to get a drink of water before beginning. I do not know how Jim did it, sitting there in John's office and watching Benjamin walk in and out during our breaks. He told me later his Twelve Step Program and his work with Bill and Jason held him solid. He demonstrated a true heart of courage. And love.

"Pam," John said when he, Jennifer and I were finally alone in the kitchen, "You are going to do fine. You are in the right," he said. "Remember that, Okay?"

I nodded a yes but was terrified. John handed me a glass of water to bring into the conference room. I nearly fainted when I looked at the water through the clear glass. I held onto the cabinet, bent my head down and began to cry.

"You are going to be fine, Pam," John said again, this time gently putting his hand on my shoulder.

"I can't take this glass in there," I said, my hand shaking as I placed it on the countertop.

"Why?" in unison John and Jennifer asked.

"I can't bear to have a clear glass hold this water," I said, tears now rolling down my face. "This glass is transparent. I feel like I'm walking into the deposition with no clothes."

"Here," Jennifer said, and knowing just what I needed, she handed me a porcelain cup filled with water. "Can you take this cup of water in there?"

"Yes, I think I can," I said. A porcelain cup made the difference.

I carried the coffee cup filled with fresh water into the conference room where all the male lawyers were sitting around a large table. John motioned for me to sit between him and Jennifer. At my back was a life-sized skeleton, draped with a blanket, identical to a blanket Benjamin had in his office. Benjamin sat facing me, in a clear effort to intimidate me. The skeleton, cloaked in the blanket, was behind me, in clear effort to intimidate Benjamin.

My protection that day was John, Jennifer, and the skeleton. And, of course, I kept close to my heart my awareness of the rest of those Wise Men—with one of them, my husband Jim, sitting guard right outside the door. Benjamin's main lawyer was humiliating. I maintained my composure. Feral cat at bay but listening.

The deposition lasted three hours.

There were two more. All degrading.

At the close of the third and final deposition, just as I was approaching the doorway to leave the conference room, I was met by Benjamin's lawyer, who was also walking out. I stopped and silently motioned for him to walk out ahead of me. Being polite, you know. But he stopped and motioned for me to go instead, feigning a politeness he never displayed during all his demeaning grilling. I used my voice and told him to go first, "Your turn to walk out."

"No, you can go first," he said. Then while standing in front of me, blocking me from walking out the door, he said, "I'm sorry for being so hard on you, Pam. I had to question you the way I did. I hope you can forgive me."

"No, I won't," I replied, standing at the doorway, looking directly into his eyes, waiting for him to walk out ahead of me. "You are responsible for your behavior and for your questioning. You did not have to conduct yourself as you did. And I do not accept your apology." My feral cat being quite articulate.

And then I pivoted around and walked out ahead, dismissing him.

My forgiving of him came many years later. But he is forever accountable for his choices as to how he behaved.

About a week later, I became actively suicidal. My persecution of myself for what I thought was my stupidity was unceasing and merciless.

Somehow, again, I convinced myself Jim and our children would be better off without me. Whenever I got into that position, I was in grave danger of suicide. But those dark haunting thoughts came so quickly and with such conviction I had very little time to work at changing my mind.

Jim and our children were going to an event. I decided I would stay home, lock myself in the bedroom, and slit my arms and wrists. For some unknown reason, sacred synchronicity you know, Jim left but rather quickly returned home to retrieve something he had left behind in our bedroom. I didn't have time to complete my plan when I heard him come into the house. Jim came upstairs and, discovering our bedroom door locked, forced his way into our room. He noticed a few drops of blood I was trying to hide dripping from my closed arms. The wounds weren't deep at this point, as I had just begun. If he had been just a few minutes later, my injuries would have been more serious. I am so grateful he followed his intuition.

Jim called for help but decided not to wait for it to arrive. He picked me up, threw me over his shoulder, and hauled me down a flight of stairs and outside to our car, our shocked children standing witness on the sidewalk, and rushed me to the emergency room.

While the ER doctors assessed me, a police officer came and spoke with Jim. It was Detective Myers. A little later, when the ER doctors determined I was physically stable, at Jim's suggestion, they contacted Ray. Arrangements were made for me to be hospitalized at his hospital. After assuring Jim and the ER doctors I would not hurt myself or fight the ride to the hospital, I was released from the emergency room and, rather than travel by ambulance, Jim was allowed to take me.

By this time, I was filled with regret I began the attempt to take my life. And grateful Jim found me. We both cried on our journey to Ray's hospital. Jim told me about talking with Detective Myers, saying the officer was very supportive of me and of him. Jim seemed a little surprised and was quite grateful. It was months before I told him of how fully Detective Myers was involved in supporting us through the entire process.

I apologized to Jim for getting so far into suicide without asking for help, for violating my promise to him and to Ray, and ultimately, to myself. I knew my life was my responsibility. I did not want to leave the legacy of suicide to my children, or to anyone else in my lineage. These things have a tendency to give permission for others to follow. I did not want anyone to follow a legacy of suicide. Of that, I was absolutely sure. I just had to figure out a way to want to live. Of that, I was absolutely sure as well.

We got to Ray's hospital and were brought to the psych unit for admission. Jim and I sat next to each other as the psych tech asked me lots of questions. He knew Ray was the admitting doctor. At one point, he told me I had to remove the tiny thin silver chain necklace I was wearing. It was a necklace given to me by Jim on Valentine's Day a few years before. The chain held a gold heart of a cupid, symbolizing Jim's love for me. I did not want to remove it. I thought the request was stupid. He commented all necklaces had to be removed. Suicide precautions you know. No, I do not know. Feral cat now beginning to emerge. How can a thin tiny chain be used to strangle anyone? Ridiculous. I was outraged.

"No! I will not take off this necklace!" I yelled as I stood up, while at the same time pulling at the necklace, throwing it onto the floor.

I don't know how the man did it. But obviously, he was practiced at this sort of thing.

He picked me up, threw me over his shoulder, and hauled me into another room. As Jim picked up the necklace, I could hear him yelling objections to the man. Somehow the psych tech placed me on a mattress on the floor in a locked room. It was my only experience in a locked 'quiet' room.

The man stayed with me for hours while I screamed and wailed. He never left my side. Not even once to go to the bathroom. He stood there in the corner.

I laid on the mattress. I yelled. And yelled. And yelled. I raged about Benjamin's lawyer. I raged about Benjamin. I raged about the unfairness of life.

That unnamed man in the corner bore witness to it all. Quietly and kindly. Very occasionally he made a warm-hearted comment. And a few times he offered me a glass of water. Or a tissue to wipe my tears.

I finally gave up screaming about Benjamin and began to cry. And cry. And cry. I wept about my lost years. My lost hope. My hurt children. My hurt husband.

The unnamed man in the corner bore witness to that too. For hours. He never left my side. Until Ray came.

When Ray finally did come, I was able to get into another room, next to the nurses' station, to be near their observation. Ray told me he spoke with Jim, made sure he was okay, and made sure Jim knew I would be taken care of with respect. That was Jim's main concern. He wanted me to be taken care of with respect. And I had been. For which I was grateful.

Ray sat in silence by my side as I took in all he told me, and all that had taken place. Then I told him I was sorry for violating my promise.

"Will you make the promise again?" he asked. "And keep it?"

"Yes," I said. "I will."

It was the asking for help that was always a problem. It was hugely difficult for me to do. The last time I'd done that didn't end so well. And so, I felt fear and shame in asking for help. Shame in crying in front of another. Shame in needing another in any fashion. Fear I would be taken advantage of again. All my ways to persecute myself. False vanities, you see. I knew I must conquer this in order to honor my promise to live.

"I promise I will not take my life either accidentally or on purpose," I then said to Ray. "And if I feel I cannot keep this promise I will ask for help."

"Okay," Ray said. "I expect you will honor your promise, Pam."

And I did. From that day forward, I kept my promise as Ray kept his.

After quite some time sitting together in silence, Ray asked me about the recurring dream I'd had several years before of the soldier in a war zone, hauling a dead soldier over his shoulder.

"If we look at this dream," he gently said, "and we consider each part of the dream may be a part of you, what part of you would be the soldier walking through the mud in the battlefield?"

Ray knew I made a practice of noting my dreams, believing they are a form of guidance. And by this time, I'd experienced him working with others in dreamwork. He remembered this dream from our conversation several months before and wanted to explore it more fully.

Dreamwork was done by doing a form of "empty chair" work where the dreamer identifies the various positions, or characters, in the dream and becomes each one, speaking their concerns, wishes, admonitions, and guidance. A few caveats about dreamwork. First, no one can tell the dreamer what the dream means. Only the dreamer knows. Ray always respected my sovereignty over my dreams. And second, dreamwork of this kind is always done in the present moment, with present moment awareness. And therefore, one can get different guidance, generally much deeper, as the dream is revisited in the future. Somehow, it seems, dreams are living stories, bringing ever deeper truths and discoveries to us as our lives change and as we evolve over time.

"Well," I tried to answer, "I suppose I could say the soldier trudging through the mud is who I see myself as now."

Ray asked me to be the soldier and speak as the soldier, but I couldn't. I was too distressed. And so I just answered the war zone was my life—what life was like to me now, the soldier hauling the dead soldier was me trying to live in this battlefield that is my life, and the dead soldier was a dead part of me.

"For a moment, Pam," he responded, "see if you can get in touch with the dead soldier. Is the soldier really dead?"

And now here is another powerful aspect of dreamwork. We can come to them from a higher perspective, from a healing perspective, and see them anew.

I'd never looked that deeply. Was he dead? I didn't know. It was a new thought. I decided to check-in and see.

After some time in silence as I took on the role of the dead soldier, I discovered he was barely breathing. He was alive. Nearly dead. But surely alive.

"Ray," I said through tears, "the soldier is barely breathing, but is alive."

"Okay," was all he said.

After a few more moments of silence, he asked, "And with knowing this, what are you aware of right now?"

"That a very wounded part of me is alive," I said.

We sat in silence for several more minutes.

"And what are you aware of right now?" he asked, prodding me to go deeper.

"Some hope is alive, just barely, but still alive," I said, as I cried.

And then, we sat in silence while I cried for at least ten more minutes.

"I don't think I can go any further into this dream, Ray," I finally said.

"That's all fine," he replied. "I will come back and see you tomorrow."

I don't know how I got the courage to say this, but I did. I finally surrendered my false pride and accepted I couldn't do it all by myself and I needed to ask for help. It was a major turning point in my own healing, and a major step off of the suicidal battlefield that was my life.

"Please don't leave me now, Ray," I said. "Please don't go."

"Okay, Pam," he softly said. "I'll stay."

With that, he sat deeper into his chair and stayed, in silent witness as I cried, for quite some time. Finally, I said, "It's okay Ray. I'm all right being alone now. Thank you for staying."

"You're welcome," he replied. "I'll see you tomorrow."

I revisited the dream over the course of many years finding deeper and deeper meaning. I was released from the hospital about a week later. After surrendering my prideful resistance of asking for help when I felt suicidal, my walk on the razor's edge of suicide ceased. I had made a decision, a commitment, to live my life. However it unfolded.

I never did find out the name of the man standing witness in the corner. I wish I had. I wish I had thanked him. I now say, "Thank you, unnamed man standing witness in the corner. Thank you."

The lawsuit was nearing the end, with just one more hurdle. Benjamin's lawyers wanted a forensic psychiatrist to interview me, to determine whether I was telling the truth, whether this was some form of fantasy or some form of female grab at a man's power.

Jim and Jennifer went with me for what was expected to be the first of nine interviews. Jennifer came into the session with me while Jim sat in the waiting room as the resident Wise Man holding presence.

I was terrified. By this time, I weighed only about one hundred pounds, having lost so much weight from stress. If I wasn't careful with my make-up and clothing, I looked like a concentration camp survivor.

A receptionist brought Jennifer and me into the psychiatrist's office and introduced us. There were two chairs placed in front of the large wooden desk the doctor was sitting behind. He motioned for us to sit down. Jennifer sat to my right and placed the hugest briefcase I have ever seen, packed with legal papers, on the floor to her right. It was reassuring to finally have a woman, who was competent and aware, supporting me. Then the doctor told us he planned on recording our session.

I immediately panicked. My stoic facade beginning to crack, nearly fainting, Jennifer barely able to hear me, I managed to whisper, "I can't bear to have this recorded."

"What? Pam?" she asked.

"If this means I end this lawsuit here, right now, in refusing to be recorded, then so be it. I cannot bear to be recorded," I said again, deeply etching a line in granite, speaking slightly louder yet barely audible, enabling the doctor to also hear my shaking voice.

"Why?" the doctor asked, his hand near the record button, yet not pressing it.

"I feel as if I am being invaded," I whispered. "As if something is winding its way into my body. Invading me. I cannot bear it. I cannot," I whispered. "I say no."

"I will just keep notes, then," the doctor said while moving the recording device off of his desk.

The psychiatrist then proceeded to ask many, many questions, but was not brutal or shaming like Benjamin's lawyer. At the end of the session, he said he or someone else would get back to John and Jennifer about the possibility of scheduling another session. As Jennifer and I stood to leave, I looked into the doctor's eyes for the first time. He was crying, tears rolling down his face. Crying the tears I was holding back.

The next day, John called. "Pam," he said, "They are going to settle. It's over, Pam. It's finally over."

CHAPTER TEN

BALANCING ON BOTH SIDES OF THE DESK

"The warrior knows that her heartbreak is her map."

—Glennon Doyle

As I heard John's words on the phone, I breathed a huge sigh of relief, then saw in my mind's eye the image of the chair, at graduation, with my name on it.

I have a right to exist. In this life.

Stop for a moment and consider the immensity of this awareness to someone who has felt from a very young age she did not have a right to her own life. That she did not have a right to exist here on this planet. That she did not have a community in which to belong.

But now, I was just beginning to believe I may have the right to exist. To belong. Yes, even though it was barely a whisper, it was there.

The next week I went to the state regulatory agency and filed a claim against Benjamin's license—for them to investigate pulling his license to practice psychotherapy. Since the lawsuit was over, getting his license pulled became a priority. It was a long process, and I had to be pretty forceful in asking them to proceed. I started the process as I began graduate school and they finally pulled his license the summer I graduated with my Master's Degree.

Around the same time the lawsuit was finishing, I was doing a large research project for the newspaper on the issue of child abuse. As I sat in the newspaper office at the computer writing a series of articles on this topic, I suddenly became aware I wanted to be part of the solution to child abuse. It was just a whisper of awareness. But of course, I was paying close attention to such whispers.

I did not want to war anymore. Being a therapist, it seemed, would mean being involved in making peace. Finally, walking off the battlefield. And helping others walk off the battlefield.

Late in the summer I quit my newspaper job. It was difficult leaving there. My editors were the first to honor my voice. They'd shown such trust in me and so generously encouraged my writing for several years. And for that, to this day, I am abundantly grateful.

In the fall, I began graduate school to become a Clinical Social Worker. By the time I entered graduate school, with the lawsuit over, there was enough money to pay for school and for psychotherapy.

Through my work with Ray, the feral cat in me continued to be 'gentled'. But even with the 'gentling', the gifts of the feral cat stayed. My vision was pretty keen. But how I exercised it had to be checked in such a way I didn't raise a ruckus ultimately disempowering me, and also not inappropriately rescuing another, ultimately disempowering them. It was a balance I learned to walk.

I still sometimes thought of suicide. But just as Ray promised he would never use his hands or his body to invade my space, I promised Ray I would do everything to keep my life. By this time, I knew I could do that. We both kept our promises.

One of the great gifts of this kind of war, if, that is, we can say there are any gifts of struggling with the war of suicide as I did, is I had to be very aware, in the present moment, of everything I felt and everything I thought. If you don't see it, if you aren't aware of what you are thinking or feeling, and if you don't own it as yours, you have no control or sovereignty over your life. And I was determined to have sovereignty. Victim no more, remember? Persecutor no more. And no more begging for rescue. Ultimately, of course, in the end, I was able to own it all and to forgive it all, but it did take time.

Graduate school was provocative, as it turned out.

In graduate school for clinical social work, students are required to do two internships, each one lasting about nine months. Since I was going into clinical social work, my internships would be involved within the practice of psychotherapy. My first internship was on a psych unit. Remember now, I'd spent time as a patient on psych units. Several times. Now I was to be an intern in one of them. Fortunately, however, I would not be at one where I myself had been a patient. I made sure of that. But it was a daunting and somewhat scary prospect for me.

On this one particular day at my internship, after being there for about two months, I heard a familiar name mentioned by one of the nurses during our early morning staffing.

We were sitting around a very large wooden table in the conference room of the psych unit. There must have been about ten or twelve of us from a variety of medical and mental health disciplines. Some psychiatrists, some department heads, some nurses, some psych techs, a psychiatric social worker, and me, the social work intern. It was a typical start to a typical clinical meeting at the beginning of a typical workday on the psych unit. Only for me, it wasn't going to be typical.

"Annie Lynn Jans came in by ambulance early this morning," started Joanne, the nurse director. "After a dose of valium she's resting, in 'full leathers,' and awaiting transfer up here."

Everyone nodded in recognition of the name, Annie Lynn Jans. It was evident they'd treated her before. And by the nods of recognition, they knew she was a difficult patient.

I recognized the name from a previous hospitalization. Annie Lynn had been sitting in the day room when Dr. Kack fired me and the entire staff on the unit surrounded me and handed me Ray's contact information. She knew practically everything about my life.

She and I had similar issues. Distrust of men. Sexual abuse. And a feral cat.

My hands started to sweat. Full Leathers. She must have raised quite a commotion.

My stomach and chest filled all the way into my throat with the sense of thousands of swirling butterflies. Searing hot pins pricked and vibrated throughout my entire body, yet I felt ice cold. I was sure I was going to faint. I forced myself to breathe slowly and deeply, placing my feet directly on the floor with my hands touching the table. Somehow, despite my terror, I was able to conjure up a cool non-judgmental facial expression — a skill likely honed by the hours and hours of watching the same expression and demeanor on the face of my own therapists treating me.

"What's 'full leathers?'" I asked, even though I knew, breathing ever so easier, trying to buy some time before Annie Lynn arrived on our floor.

"She's on a flat board with her body, hands and feet buckled to the board with leather straps," responded Joanne. "She can't move."

Obviously, Annie Lynn must have raised quite a problem when she came in, I thought. Yep, that does sound like her. The feral cat, you know. I silently considered my own screaming experience on the mattress in the 'quiet room' not long ago.

"How long before she is able to get here?" I asked, doing a very good job at not sounding anxious.

"She will probably be up by the time we're done here," Joanne casually responded, then went on to discuss the next patient at hand.

Okay, I thought to myself, when this meeting is over, I just may walk out this door and come face to face with Annie Lynn strapped to a board being rolled on a gurney down the hallway. She would recognize me for sure.

I always feared this day would come. I knew it was only a matter of time before my past would catch up with me. But I hoped it would come after years of being established as a solid professional, and not in graduate school, just at the beginning, in an internship.

I decided it would look odd for me to excuse myself from this meeting. After hearing my story, which they will undoubtedly learn because of Annie Lynn, they would know I excused myself because I was afraid. It would cast a dark shadow of doubt on all I'd been working towards.

As the meeting adjourned, I started a casual conversation with a nurse. I figured it would keep the two of us in the conference room for a few moments after others left. As we walked out together, I glanced up and down the hallway. No Annie Lynn. She'd just been taken to her room, and we barely missed her. I headed over to the nurses' station to use the only phone available. A cell phone would have made this ordeal considerably easier, but it was the early 1980s and no cell phones were available at the time. All my conversations would have to take place in the open, at the nurses' station, essentially, in 'public.'

I was calling Ray.

"Hi Janice," I said to Ray's secretary with a casualness uncharacteristic of my usual calls. "I'm at my internship at the hospital today, and I'd like to speak with Ray whenever he's available." Janice knew me quite well and of course she knew this was an emergency.

"Ray is in a session, Pam, and can't return your call for at least thirty minutes. Jason is right here. How about you speak with him?" she asked. Jason knew as much about my situation as Ray. She handed the phone to him.

As luck would have it, the secretary at the nurses' station was called away for just a moment. No one else was anywhere nearby. Most of the staff members were already busy with Annie Lynn in her room. So, I had the great good fortune of being alone on the phone at the nurses' station.

"Jason," I quietly said into the phone, my demeanor of calm rapidly dissipating, "a patient I came to know when I was hospitalized with the other doctor has just been admitted onto this unit. She knows my entire life story."

I heard him gasp.

"Pam," he said, collecting himself quite nicely, "you can turn shit into roses with this one, you know?"

"I don't see any upside here," I replied, feeling my knees begin to buckle. I leaned on the nurses' station for support and braced my elbow on the counter while holding the phone to my ear.

"Pam, you are now one of the ones on the other side of the desk. You can tell her if you can do this, so can she," he responded.

"What the hell do I tell all the staff here about me?" I whispered into the phone. "She's going to tell all my secrets!"

Annie Lynn knew everything and would not keep it quiet. She would be shocked to see me on the 'other side of the desk.' And she would probably want to take me down.

Jason recommended I speak first with my supervisor, Ellie. He said both he and Ray knew her, and I should mention to Ellie I am now working with them. My body began to relax, and my legs began to feel stronger. I felt grateful for Ray's strong professional network and good reputation. My breathing began to settle. The secretary returned to her station, and I knew I could not speak with Jason any further. He bid me goodbye and good luck, with a request I call them to let them know how things went. I turned to look for Ellie.

She was just leaving Annie Lynn's room and walking down the hospital corridor. As she noticed me, she shook her head back and forth, in acknowledgment of how difficult Annie Lynn was. I asked if she had a moment to speak in private. We went into her office and closed the door.

"I know Annie Lynn from another time," I started.

She let out a gasp of what felt to me like disgust. Then nodded and while turning her head, making side-eye contact with me, softening her demeanor a bit with a gentle but suspicious-looking smile, she said, "Just tell me, Pam, when, where, what?"

While her response didn't surprise me, it did shake me. I felt the heat of fear in my chest, but somehow managed to keep my calm demeanor. I gave her a quick overview. First experience of therapy years ago. A psychologist. Sexual abuse disguised as therapy. Suicide attempts. Suicide ideation. Depression. Several therapists. Sued psychologist. Won in an out-of-court battle. In the process of pulling his license. Now with Ray and Jason. Getting my life together.

She did know Ray and Jason. And respected them. Jason was right to suggest I mention their names.

"Your first job today, Pam," she said, "is to go into Annie Lynn's room and introduce yourself as the social work intern on this unit. To be sure, she will remember you from another time. You are to tell her that is from another time. You've grown past that now," she said, and then she actually added, "You are on the other side of the desk. It is a good example for her to see."

I left Ellie's office to meet with Annie Lynn while Ellie left her office to call a meeting with the rest of the staff to tell them what I just told her. We expected fall-out from Annie Lynn. And given Annie Lynn's history, we expected it to fall out all over the unit.

I walked out of her office to the sounds of the television in the common room and some of the patients on the unit laughing. I wondered what they would be talking and laughing about after Annie Lynn was done with them.

I began my long walk past several nurses talking at the nurses' station, past the locked medical room used for shock therapy, past the empty 'quiet' room used for patients who are in restraints (full leathers that is), and past the staffing room we'd all been in earlier. I continued slowly down the long and dark hospital corridor to Annie Lynn's room.

With plenty of time to consider what to say, I reviewed my own experiences of psychotherapy and inpatient psych treatment. About half of it was a complete nightmare I barely survived, a fourth of it was pretty bad, but the last fourth of it was quite awe-inspiring and healing. With each step I took down the long corridor, I felt a sense of hope deep into my bones. A hope I wanted somehow to convey to Annie Lynn.

I did have considerable compassion for her. Annie Lynn did me a great service while we were on the same unit a few years before. It was through experiencing her closed heart I learned my own heart was closed and needed to be opened. She was like a mirror of me. Like what I would be if I chose to continue on as she. Without her knowing, she helped me to define and begin to face my own resistance.

I considered what Jason said about me being on the "other" side of the desk. I asked myself, is there really such a clear line of demarcation between the clinician and the patient? One of the problems with Benjamin was he did not keep a boundary, a line of demarcation, so to speak, between him and me. Boundaries are essential to maintain. They are a protective guardrail for transference and countertransference. But was a boundary an issue of 'therapists' on one side of the desk and 'patients' on another? Did this give me, as a beginning therapist, the opportunity to separate us, Annie Lynn and me, since now I supposedly "know more" and am at a "different place" and do not "appear" to be "lost"?

I am sure some therapists do, unfortunately. Likely out of fear, some create a form of hierarchy, emotionally separating themselves, creating a distance from their patients. But Ray and Jason, while they surely knew how to maintain boundaries and did not form personal relationships with patients, they did not in any way demonstrate a hierarchy, a sense of separation from various sections of humanity, a sense of separation between them and any of their patients. They did not "other" anybody. Authentic empathy and compassion, without separation, without "othering", was a key component in their work with me, and in my observation of their work with others.

Primary to their work was they did not take what their patients did or said personally. They always recognized their patient's sovereignty, their patient's right to choose. Perhaps that was the required separation, I thought. Perhaps it's the balance needed; the boundary required—to not take things personally.

I did not want to re-injure Annie Lynn. I expected she would be shocked to see me in this position. I could not predict her response, given the acting out I had seen her do in the past. Even though I knew my own feral cat, I knew I couldn't predict hers.

As I came near to her doorway at the end of the corridor, I slowed my steps. I took a few deep in-breaths and long exhales to calm myself before entering. I turned the corner and walked into her room to find Annie

Lynn sitting cross-legged in her chair, her foot bouncing up and down as if she was nervous and impatient—which she probably was.

She looked pretty much the same as when I last saw her on the other psych unit. She was tall and very, very slender with short bleached-blonde hair. Despite the neatness she generally projected, her appearance this day was disheveled. Wrinkled clothes. No make-up. All probably the result of her evening before and her contact with those 'full leathers.'

As I stood before her waiting to be noticed, I considered my own voyage through hell, and my own struggle to believe and have faith in the goodness of people in the face of betrayal. There were times when it very easily could have been me strapped onto a wooden board.

Annie Lynn looked up, expecting another familiar face from the psych unit. She narrowed her brown eyes, showing her confusion. I gave her time to take in my face and the difference in appearance between me now and the last time we saw each other. The last time we were together, I was wearing worn-out jeans, sandals and a big t-shirt. I had long straight brown hair brushing against my shoulders and my demeanor was quiet and shy. Now, I was wearing a dark wool skirt, heels, and a light blue sweater. More weight on me. My hair was shorter, groomed, and curly. I looked pretty well put together. Certainly different from our last encounter.

After a few moments, she recognized me. Her eyes opened wide as she took in a breath. I stood there, smiling gently, my head nodding slightly to the side in acknowledgment of her, inviting her to speak first.

"Pam, what the fuck are you doing here?!" she finally shouted out while uncrossing her legs and leaning toward me, "You're all dressed up! What the hell is going on?"

"Hi Annie Lynn," I said, smiling back a huge smile, then sitting on her bed to face her. "I'm in graduate school now, working toward a Master's Degree in Social Work. I'm an intern here on this unit."

"What?!" she yelled. She shook her head, laughed a few laughs, then shook her entire body – as if she wanted to cast off this new piece of information.

"The last I saw you," she cried, sounding partly angry, partly shocked, and partly joyous, "you were fired by a crappy fuck of a doc who threatened to send you to a state mental hospital! How did you get from that to this?! And what happened with the lawsuit?"

My first panic. She remembered the piece about me being fired by Dr. Kack. I didn't want anyone to know this piece. But I resolved to stay with this process and reminded myself of my deep commitment to healing—knowing somehow to keep that commitment is to honor my own journey and my own heart, because we are all essentially one.

"Well, Annie Lynn," I started, "I think I finally found myself a good therapist. One that doesn't want to screw me over. One that cares about my growth."

"Whoaaaa!" she said. "They're out there?"

"Yeah, they are," I said while adjusting my seating so I could face her more directly, all the while wishing I could give her Ray's contact information. "But I am working really hard in therapy. I'm finding it takes a lot of grit. And taking a lot of responsibility for my own feelings and reactions to things. I gotta say, things are getting better for me. It's not easy, but I can see light at the end of the tunnel."

"How did you wind up here, at this place?" she asked, puzzled at seeing me in this new context.

I told her the lawsuit was resolved without going to court. And while working for the newspaper, I suddenly decided to go to graduate school for a Master's Degree in Social Work. I'd been on this unit as an intern for several months. Then I asked her how she ended up coming into the emergency room the evening before.

"What's up with that, Annie Lynn?" I asked. "What brings you in here?

She went through a litany of problems; the same ones she had the last time I saw her. She'd changed nothing. Her mom was angry with how she was running her life. Annie Lynn continued to want to starve herself and throw up if she ate something 'wrong', Her dad was mean. Her boyfriend just kicked her out, and she may lose her job. She was occupied with blaming everyone for her problems and not owning responsibility for those things she could do to help herself.

These things are like double-edged swords. People do hurt us. Benjamin hurt me. And my family. But through it all, we still must take responsibility for our own response to the hurt. And take action to remove ourselves from staying a victim. That's what I was working on. That's being accountable. That's not falling for secondary gain.

But Annie Lynn was in victim mode, falling for secondary gain. She didn't know how to do anything else. And our social group think often reinforces such a stance. It's something many of us do, to one degree or another. She was claiming victim, fear, and shame as her identity. Her action was to ask others to rescue her and then to provoke others by alternating between victim and persecutor. She needed to learn to make different choices. So much easier said than done, however. Especially when we have a cultural system frequently supporting this kind of war. And it is a war. An internal war we often invite others into.

She paused. She looked at me. I looked at her.

I believe we both saw how quickly life can change and yet stay the same. And somehow I believe we both saw how choice can make the difference between a life well lived and a life of chaos. And yet, our choices are our sacred right and privilege. To screw up or not to screw up. And everything in between. It all boils down to choice. For me, I chose one of many paths. And for her, well, with each new morning, she has the opportunity to make a new choice. As do each of us.

We smiled at each other. She congratulated me for the good resolution of the lawsuit and for getting on with my life. I wished her well with this hospitalization and with getting on with her life outside the hospital.

While my heart felt great caring for Annie Lynn and for my own journey, it was years later when I realized my experience with her was the beginning of a deeper kind of personal healing and the setting of a 'template' where I could open my heart as a therapist and further heal myself as a person. It was the beginning of unbuckling myself from my own self-imposed 'full leathers.' In those days, it was easier for me to experience compassion for another and more difficult to extend that same compassion to myself. However, throughout the many years of my practice as a therapist, I found when I stretched my compassion for my patients, it helped me to grow in extending compassion for myself. In so many ways, others are a reflection of ourselves and are invitations into our own deeper healing. Annie Lynn surely was for me.

But it was Gabriel's insistence that initiated the deepest invitation many years later. Life is a process of growing and evolving. It takes time. And experiences. And awareness. Grace and grit in a dance together.

As I was walking down the corridor after our conversation, feeling gratitude for Jason's encouragement to be open with Ellie, I found Ellie standing at the nurses' station waiting for me. By the quick nod of her head as she saw me, the soft expression in her eyes and the smile on her face, I could see her talk with the staff had gone well.

"Let's talk," Ellie said, motioning me into her office.

Because Ellie was most concerned with how my conversation proceeded with Annie Lynn, I went over our discussion in detail. Ellie seemed pleased and surprised. "I predict Annie Lynn will be here a very short time and won't raise problems," she said, "because she will see you and see things she could do with her own life. I don't see her choosing to change her behavior. But she won't be able to play the games she has always played with us while you're here, seeing you as an example of where she could go with her life."

While I hoped Annie Lynn would choose a route different from Ellie's prognosis, she appeared to do as Ellie predicted. Since I'd had a prior relationship with her, I did not have any sessions with her as I generally did with the rest of the patients. We exchanged smiles and hellos. Occasionally I gave her encouragement when appropriate. But she stayed only one week, a short time for her, and left quietly and suddenly, without saying goodbye. I can only hope she found a therapist worthy of her trust. I can only hope she was able to find someone as wise as Ray. I can only hope she took the challenge to gather her grit, face her demons, and come to experience some of the grace in her life. Because it surely was there.

I can only hope she worked at becoming aware of her projections and of any secondary gains, vital steps in real healing.

As for me, Ellie never did tell me exactly what she said to the rest of the staff. I will say, however, they treated me quite well. It was no different from how they treated me before Annie Lynn showed up on our unit.

The second year of graduate school I accepted my professors' nearly insistent recommendations to enter into the field of addictions treatment. It was a choice I didn't initially want to make. But it ended up bringing me right up to the doorway of the home I'd been searching for all my life. Who knew? Certainly not me until the day I reviewed my life as I sat facing the vast western field of our front yard after getting bucked off Gabriel.

I was offered, and accepted, an internship as an Employee Assistance Counselor at a major corporation in Chicago. It was a 'plum' position for anyone wanting to go into addictions. A real honor. I just happened to be in the right place at the right time. I was accepted through an interview process with the two Employee Assistance Counselors who worked there and who would be my direct supervisors.

I had to dress in suits and take the train into the city. It was an entirely new kind of environment for me. I could now see why my dad always wanted to wear a suit on the train. Everybody did. But I wasn't pretending. My internship required I wear a suit.

Through this second internship, I began to bring home part of my little girl imprisoned in the basement bunker from so many years before. With entering the addictions field, I began to stand at the threshold of the doorway I had been seeking all my life.

Now began the season of suits.

CHAPTER ELEVEN

THE LITTLE GIRL DANCES WITH A SUIT

"A bird does not sing because it has an answer, it sings because it has a song."

—Maya Angelou

In all my thirty-some years, I'd never worn a suit. By this time, it was the mid '80s, and even Jim, as a teacher, wasn't required to wear one to school anymore—just dress pants, with a nice shirt and tie. But for this internship, at a large corporation, they told me I had to wear a suit.

My main experience with people in suits was as a child when Mom and we kids occasionally went to get Dad from the train station. While we all sat in our beat-up green '52 Chevy, I watched the parade of suited men get off the train and into their fancy cars. The little girl in me, still stuck in the bunker, thought suits were for rich people with important jobs. And she 'knew' we weren't one of them. My little one was holding on to victim and needed me, now a grown woman, to make new choices, to have new experiences, to believe in our worth separate from any cultural 'group think', and to bring her home. This phase of my life was puzzling and exciting. As all things can be when we begin a walk into new and unknown places.

I went to a store a few towns over and tried on a bunch of suits. They looked pretty nice. I got a grey herringbone one, a brown one, and a dark grey one. And heels to match. I looked the part of a businesswoman. Jim said so too when I came home and tried each suit on for him.

In addition to the fact the train station was the same one my dad used on his journey to work decades earlier, it was just one block south of the hospital I'd gone to so many years before on the night I was denied an appendectomy. And it was also in the wealthiest part of town, in an area where I always felt unwelcome. The little girl in me, the part stuck in the basement bunker, softly whispered all those memories into my ears, as I began my journey to the train station.

The task for me was to find a way to navigate the train commute into Chicago. Since I'd always gotten rides to the station, I didn't know how to pay for parking. I must say, that part felt pretty scary. Odd, I know. Especially, given that as a reporter, I'd grown accustomed to navigating around a variety of unusual situations. But this felt different.

I had to go there. I was beginning a new life. But this time, I was wearing a suit and figured I could somehow find a way to pretend I belonged.

I went early, parked my car in a parking space, and walked into the station. Just standing there, in the middle of the depot, dressed in a dark grey suit, among a mass of suited people, mostly men with just a few women, asking in my confident reporter's voice, of anyone within distance to hear, in a clear and self-assured way, "Can anyone tell me how I am to pay for parking?" Immediately about five suited people surrounded me, each telling me what I had to do, sharing with me how easy the process was.

This might seem like a small event for someone who didn't have a history of feeling alienated from a community, who didn't have a feral cat to heal, or a wounded child stuck somewhere, but for me, it was huge. The big takeaway, in the moment, was these suited people were kind, helpful and treated me as if I belonged. That was big.

The little one in the bunker whispered to me those on the rich side of town would dismiss me and look down upon me. And they were 'uppity' and pretentious, and unworthy of my respect anyway. Part of me looked down on them as I thought they were looking down on me, creating a separation between us. I was othering them, projecting my issues onto them, as I assumed they were 'othering' me. It was part of the 'false pride' I was determined to release.

The lesson for me through all the deep work I'd already done was I knew what we do to others, we do to ourselves. And what we do to ourselves, we do to others. I noted the little girl in me was doing victim and persecutor, both at the same time. What we damn, damns us back. Remember now, I was committed to overcoming those roles.

If I had been a homeless person, or dressed as a beggar, or been a poorly dressed Black or Brown person, my experience that day with those people probably would have been different. Racism was real and present then, as it, unfortunately, continues to be now. And this community, especially then, was not diverse. In those days, they likely would have subtly 'othered' me. While not excusing it, I was aware of this, even then. But I had the unearned privilege of being born a White person. And now I was a White woman dressed in a suit, and so they treated me as an equal. Because I looked the part. This experience, however, gave me the opportunity to step beyond my own 'othering' of them. That's what I focused upon. And that was the healing part. They became more human to me. Helping me to become more human to myself.

I noticed this incident at the train station and took it in, the moment it happened. With a sense of feeling gratitude. Which is a good thing. This is how we grow and change ourselves. It was part of my commitment to live my life, to be a victim no more.

When the train arrived, I followed the mass of suited people and boarded. While on the train, I took several times to recall, and hold in present awareness for a few minutes, my feeling experience of gratitude with those suited people.

What I didn't know then, but what recent research using functional MRIs has shown, is we humans can change our brains to become more receptive and aware of positive experiences, enabling us to become more aware of positive experiences as they arise, and most importantly, to feel more joy and compassion with our lives and others, in general. It's termed neuroplasticity of the brain.

In other words, to hold positive feelings, particularly gratitude, grows and changes our brains in healing ways. It helps us become more conscious. Research has shown all it takes is holding such a feeling experience—and it must be a feeling experience and not an intellectual thinking—for just twenty seconds, helps to grow our brains in positive, nurturing ways. Rick Hanson, PhD has written and taught extensively about this process. His book *Neurodharma* is all about this.

Our human brains are programmed to look for trouble and danger because that is what enhanced our survival on the savannah thousands of years ago. Our focus naturally defaults to danger, or anything 'different,' rather than to gratitude, kindness, and goodness. That is likely one of the unconscious things fueling racism, xenophobia, homophobia, sexism, and our human tendency to "other" people—to fuel the vicious circle in our human consciousness of the victim, fixer, persecutor. A history of trauma, loss, or neglect further magnifies this mindset in our very human brains. It was something I was committed to moving beyond. Recent research has shown we can move beyond this.

Medicine and psychiatry didn't know any of this when I boarded the train. But because of my struggle with suicide, I'd made my life's work of being aware of my thinking and feelings, in the present moment. And working with Ray, whose most famous question was, "What are you aware of right now?" reinforced all this as well.

Once in the city, I walked with the procession of suited people through the streets of Chicago. My office was near the train station, about eighteen floors above ground.

After a few days of brief orientation with both supervisors, Ron, my primary supervisor, wanted to learn more about me. "Say, Pam," he said one morning early after I arrived at the office, "Come meet with me in the conference room. Let's talk."

Now, Ron I already liked. He was a tall, slender man, with a mustache, perhaps about ten years older than me. My senses were quite keen by this time, considering all I had been through. My reading of him was he was a good guy. But I knew nothing about him.

We went into the large conference room in the corner of the building. The room was lined on two sides from floor to ceiling with large picture windows overlooking an expansive view of the city of Chicago. The two of us sat across from each other at the massive wooden table in the center.

Ron began by telling me about himself, how he had come from New York to Chicago as an Employee Assistance Counselor with this company. He began his career as a lawyer but his own alcoholism brought him into the Twelve Step recovery program of Alcoholics Anonymous.

"While I worked at the law firm, my drinking made me eventually hit bottom. A lawyer I practiced with noticed I was in trouble and took me to an Alcoholics Anonymous meeting. He kept on inviting me to those meetings. Somehow, as I experienced more and more problems with my drinking, I decided to get sober. My AA group was crucial to my recovery. It still is. In time, I became more interested in helping people recover from alcoholism than in practicing law," he added. "That's how I got into the Employee Assistance Program, first in New York and now here." And then he asked, "What brought you into considering addictions?"

"Well, my professors practically insisted I take this route," I responded. "They said I have a sixth sense about alcoholism and addictions. I followed their advice, considering they likely know more than I about these things."

Ron laughed. A huge gut laugh. He loved hearing this.

"Is anyone in your family alcoholic?" he asked.

"Well, yes," I carefully said, "my husband is a recovering alcoholic for about two years now."

"Does he go to AA?" Ron quickly asked, getting quite focused.

"Yes, he sure does," I replied. "He began his recovery with help from a counselor in our area named Bill."

Ron knew Bill and was impressed. He quickly learned I didn't know much about the disease process of alcoholism or the thought processes of codependency and alcoholism specifically, but somehow, I intuitively understood. Victim/persecutor/rescuer, vicious circle, you know. As my professors had already noticed. We talked a bit more about how Jim got into recovery and the part I played.

"Do you like to drink?" he asked.

"Well, for me," I said, "I can drink about one glass of wine and then I just don't like it anymore. It doesn't taste good. For Jim, he would drink until he passed out."

"That's one of the differences between someone who develops alcoholism and one who doesn't," Ron said. "Not everyone who drinks will become an alcoholic. The person who becomes alcoholic seems to have a body that processes alcohol differently from one that will not develop alcoholism. They often start out with a higher tolerance."

"So it's just a physical thing?" I asked.

"Well, not quite," Ron replied. "A person's thinking and beliefs do have a lot to do with it, but it seems the body initially makes a decision about this without the mind's consent."

"Is this why alcoholism seems to travel in families?" I asked.

"Yes, I believe it is," he responded. "While research on the genetics of alcoholism is currently underway, long-term studies have indicated a strong genetic component. We have to wait for better research to know for sure. But for me, I believe the tendency to develop alcoholism is genetic. We find it travels down family lines in much the same way as blue eyes, black hair, or long legs seem to travel in families."

Since the mid-1980s when this conversation with Ron took place, more research has been done on the genetics of alcoholism. It appears now that while there is no one specific identified gene for alcoholism or drug addiction, there is a strong genetic component, with many genes coordinating together and playing a part. New genes and variants for this are currently being actively researched.

"I thought I was a weak person," Ron said, "because I couldn't put my booze down. And I silently criticized myself and anybody else I could target. The criticism kept me in a vicious cycle of 'stinking thinking' and drinking. But I wasn't weak. And no one else was trying to be mean to me. The lawyer helped me realize I mattered. And helped me get recovery. The most important thing about helping alcoholics or addicts is they need to get recovery early enough before they get so far into it they can't recover— either because of deep denial or because of alcohol or drug-induced dementia. That's one of the things employee assistance programs are all about. It's helpful for the company because it makes for more competent employees. But what I love," Ron said, "is it helps people live better lives."

Ron asked me if I knew anything about the Twelve Steps. I had to admit I didn't. When we began talking about a Higher Power I began to feel whispers of a sense of coming home. Home, of course, being a deeper connection to an eternal part of me, connected to an eternal loving source. I desperately wanted to find a way to come home without dying. Could I find a sense of home here, in this life? I wondered if that was even possible. What would it be like to come home? What was home? I didn't realize it, but I was just beginning to stand on the welcome mat at the doorway of the home I'd been searching for most of my life. All this reference to a Higher Power was directly in line with my own deeper yet hidden spiritual experiences. My heart opened as I listened to Ron. And I could feel authentic joy and love in his heart as he spoke.

"The first three steps of the Twelve Step program involve surrendering your sense of power and will over to a Higher Power," Ron said. "But the Higher Power can be anything larger, more loving, and outside of our smaller selves. Like it can be the wisdom of a recovery group. The presence of a forest. Or a caring community. It could be the God of one's religion. Any religion. Or it could be Jesus. The Higher Power is anything more loving, more forgiving, and beyond our own small self-centered selves."

He was talking about surrendering to guidance from a sense of a loving God. About making a differentiation between the part of our personality self-focused on personal, self-enhancing vain agendas, and a larger, loving self, connected to a Higher Power. But known by many names. My Mozart Street Experience from so many years before shared a similar knowing— there is more to life than winning a race against another chasing a beautiful new red scooter down a street. As fun as that can truly be.

Ron went on sharing and explaining the rest of the steps. Coming to terms with what one had done wrong, admitting it and apologizing, then taking action, if possible, to remedy the situation. Because we are all connected, and what we do to ourselves, to others, and to our community matters. It's about being accountable. Accountability and forgiveness go hand in hand, one reinforcing the other. It is all part of living an authentic life—a life where intent matches action.

"So often," Ron said, "We all feel ashamed of our mistakes and are unwilling to ask for forgiveness. But for an alcoholic or addict, that can be life-threatening."

As Ron said that, I thought about my own persecuting unforgiving suicidal battle within myself and how I finally surrendered one day while Ray sat with me in the hospital after my final near suicide attempt. The day I surrendered my false pride and asked Ray to stay.

"A saying I once heard was," I responded, "if it weren't for second chances, or third chances, we would all be alone. Every one of us."

"Yes, true," Ron said as he laughed another huge, deep laugh.

Surely, he agreed. I thought about all Jim and I had been through and about how forgiveness has been crucial. Forgiving each other. Forgiving ourselves.

"What recovery is all about," Ron went on to say, "is transformation. It's about changing the intellectual circular 'stinking thinking' into an experiential awareness of one's self and connection to a Higher Power— known by many names."

"But what seems to be important, Pam," Ron said, "is the person working The Twelve Step Program experiences the steps, rather than just intellectualizes them. And this takes humility. Just intellectualizing the steps keeps us in a vicious circle and doesn't get to the heart of the matter," he added while laughing, "pardon the pun."

Ron loved to joke, but I got it. If we feel it in our hearts, we are actually feeling it. Experiencing it. Not thinking it. And that's what matters. I thought about all my work with Ray, and how the focus was always on my inner experiences, in the present moment, rather than on superficial thinking focused on the past or into the future. I knew then, that while sitting in a classroom and mentally hearing about these things is important, it does not accomplish healing. But having healing experiences does. And being aware of them, in present time. Like my experience with those suited people on the train just a few days before. And like the experience of my feral cat touching Ray's hands.

"But, of course," Ron said. "Recovery is also about sharing caring with others. It's not about fixing anyone else. It's about being the recovering person in authenticity, not vanity, and caring for others. Like what the lawyer did for me."

"Here," he said, as he handed me a printout of the Twelve Steps along with a short explanation of each, "you can read this on your train ride home tonight—if you wish, that is."

Well, of course, I wished.

On my walk to the train station, I thought about my education as an undergraduate psychology major and my education as a current student in the master's program in Social Work. Even with discussions about Carl Jung and Jung's archetypes, there had been no mention of a Higher Power or of any spiritual presence or consciousness contributing to recovery.

This was in the mid-eighties, and the line separating science and spirituality was etched pretty deeply into our cultural mental framework. Since then, however, with documentation of near-death studies, research documenting past lives, expanding research in quantum physics, and everything in between, our awareness of all this at this time in our human history is expanding. For that, I am immensely grateful.

But in the eighties, and many decades before, a Higher Power or some form of spiritual presence was regarded as a central part of the process within the Twelve Step addictions recovery system. I loved that. As I continued my walk to the train station after my conversation with Ron, my sense of hope for life itself, and for my life in the here and now, expanded with this new awareness. Like I said, I was just beginning to stand on the threshold.

As I boarded the train I decided to sit in the upper deck, to be alone and go over Ron's material on the Steps. Each one. One by one. After slowly reading each of those Twelve Steps, I looked around at all the people sitting with me on the train. Everyone in suits and looking professional. Like they couldn't possibly have any problems. Or could they?

All of us gently rocking back and forth, jostling with the movement and the sound of the train traveling along the rails. Some reading. Some talking. Some sitting in silence. Some perhaps alcoholic. Some perhaps addicted. Some perhaps codependent. Some 'perfectly' fine. Some not. Some aware. Some not. But all equal and all loved and all held within an eternal loving presence. On a journey home, in one way or another.

My education and training in alcoholism, addictions, and codependency went on the fast track, with Ron at my side for the next two years. After the first year, when I graduated with my master's degree, the company hired me to work as an Employee Assistance Counselor. Ron was always appropriate with me. Always a gentleman, treating me as an equal, with respect. Obviously, a Wise Man.

As an employee working alongside Ron, I was required to become certified in addictions. I had to take addiction classes at a Junior College and do another internship. He recommended an inpatient hospital-based treatment center not far from where I lived. So, I worked in Chicago with Ron and coordinated everything while working as an intern in an inpatient alcoholism treatment center.

Just as I was finishing the internship, the hospital treatment center offered me a job. They knew I was working at the corporation in the city but asked anyway. I considered my options and decided I found working directly with patients and their family members even more rewarding than working in a corporate environment, essentially managing treatment, and helping those patients within the business world.

It was hard saying goodbye to Ron. On my last day in Chicago, he handed me a gift.

"This was given to me by someone in the program when I'd been sober and with the program for six months," he said with tears in his eyes. "I've carried it with me for years and now I'm giving it to you."

He handed me a brass tag for a key chain. Engraved on it was The Serenity Prayer "God grant me the Serenity to accept the things I cannot change. Courage to change the things I can. And Wisdom to know the difference." Now I had tears in my eyes. Aside from all he taught me, he couldn't have given me anything more significant.

To this very day, I carry this on my key chain everywhere I go, well over thirty years later. And when I am ready to pass it on to another, I will.

Working with employees within a corporate setting was significantly different from working with patients and their families in a treatment center. Even though I'd done an internship at the treatment center, I did not realize the sea of difference between the two environments until I began working there. It was like going from a slightly warm frying pan and jumping into a wildly raging fire.

But this was in the eighties. Things have gotten significantly worse since then. Now, we have a perfect storm, or shall I say a raging wildfire engulfing our entire culture, sacrificing the lives of many of the warriors on the front lines in this battle our culture has with chemical addiction. The marijuana available now is exponentially more potent than the marijuana of several decades ago. We now have a massive opioid epidemic, with tens of thousands of people dying each year. Between April 2020 and April 2021, more than 100,000 Americans died from a drug overdose. (Centers for Disease Control and Prevention) Think of that—thousands and thousands of people dying from drug overdoses. We have an 'elephant' in our country many refuse to see, or they 'other' it by believing the individuals who develop this problem are weak. All untrue. Now, I do love elephants, but not when the elephant is an elephant of denial.

We've had pharmaceutical companies hiding their own research indicating their drugs are addictive, then turning around and marketing those same addictive drugs to physicians as non-addictive. All for profits. Tobacco companies did the same thing decades earlier and ended up paying out large sums of money in lawsuits. Now we have some states succeeding in lawsuits against those pharmaceutical companies, using the money gained to fund state-sponsored addiction treatment programs. And we have always had some physicians prescribing addictive drugs with little or no knowledge of what addiction is or the role they, themselves, play in fostering addiction.

In some ways, it was more simple and less pervasive when I began at the treatment center, however, it was just as dangerous to those individuals who found themselves in the web of chemical addiction. Back then, drug dealers were primarily on street corners. But now, it appears they have also been some pharmaceutical companies.

At the treatment center, we provided both inpatient and outpatient counseling for alcoholics, addicts and their family members. I conducted the evaluation and referral process, worked on an ongoing basis with those who were codependent, and facilitated all the Family Intervention Counseling. I loved my job. Our patients were husbands, wives, grown children, doctors, lawyers, bricklayers, pharmacists, nurses, salesmen and saleswomen, corporate executives, retired people, gang members, and drug dealers. And everything in between. A full mix of humanity. All with the same issue—just showing itself in different clothes, in different venues, in different words, from different worlds. Yet all the same. We were dealing with people on the front lines of addiction fighting in a battle for their lives or for the lives of those they loved. They all ended up sharing a circle of recovery with each other.

I worked with a parent who had to leave his daughter, homeless and wandering around a train station looking for handouts and drugs because the week before she refused any form of help. And I worked with a young man admitted for an overdose and detox only for his insurance company to deny him treatment, and for him to then go home and die of an overdose. I worked with parents who knew their two-year-old grandson was wandering around a drug house in the middle of the night abandoned by their drug-addicted daughter who refused help just the day before. I worked with an alcoholic who lost his own father when his veins exploded from being weakened by decades of drinking. He dedicated his own recovery to honoring his love for his father and for himself. I witnessed a whole family surround their alcoholic mother, inviting her into treatment. She said "Yes." A few months later, I witnessed the same mother, now in recovery, confront her own brother, asking him to accept help. He said "Yes."

It was gut-wrenchingly agonizing at times, but beautifully inspiring at others. Yes, the sadness was painful, but more often than not, we saw recovery nearly beyond belief. Over and over again. The undaunted courage of family members and their beloved alcoholics and addicts' acceptance of recovery continued to amaze me and give me hope. Every. Single. Day. And every day challenged me to grow, to understand more about addiction, codependency, and my own life.

And somehow, while no one I ever worked with knew of my past experience with sexual abuse, the lawsuit, suicide ideation and hospitalizations, I felt a form of shared comradeship with them all. All of us working with and believing in a Higher Power or some form of Spiritual guidance we were allowing into our lives. All working at walking off the battlefield in a common war.

We had a phrase at the treatment center I loved from the moment I heard it. "E-G-O is Easing God Out." Now, this wasn't about diminishing or denigrating our ego selves, our personality selves, because surely we do need a personality self to function in this world. Let's all be grateful for that. It was about surrendering a false pride, a false sense of who we are, to a Higher Self. This phrase was about getting beyond our very human tendency to cling to our vanities, our false feelings of pride, our drugs, our material possessions, our inflated identities, our anger and fears, our sense of victim, fixer, and persecutor, and to recognize and surrender to the deeper Truth of who we are. What I'd been searching for most of my life.

There is always more to learn. One particular day at the treatment center, another forgotten part of me was about to return. Part of my job was to go over to the hospital and visit people the doctors thought had problems with alcohol or drugs. Perhaps encourage them to get help. Either through AA or treatment or both.

The young man I went to see came into the emergency room by ambulance the night before. He'd been hemorrhaging. While they were able to stop the bleeding, the doctor saw the bleeding as a consequence of alcohol-induced hardening of his liver and the weakening of his veins and arteries. The very real risk was if this man continued drinking, he would eventually bleed to death. Much sooner rather than later.

I walked into his hospital room to see him lying in his bed, hooked up to various IVs, with his wife sitting beside him. They were a relatively young couple, likely in their mid-thirties. But what startled me was the smell of turpentine. It hit me so strongly in the face I stuttered as I introduced myself. I excused myself, saying I needed to check on something at the nurses' station, and I'd be back in a few moments.

I walked out of his room completely confused by the smell. My dad smelled just like that. As a child, I asked Mom one day what the odd smell was. She told me it was turpentine, and Dad smelled like that because he was a painter and worked with turpentine. Well, I knew that to be true. He did work with turpentine.

And so I walked around the hospital floor, circling throughout the entire corridor, looking for evidence of painting or of turpentine. I looked everywhere. No. Nothing there. I went back into the room and looked there as well. No. There was no paint. And there were no cans of turpentine.

I put aside my confusion and focused instead on the young man and his wife. After working with them for about an hour, they refused help. I accepted their decision, knowing I could not 'fix' them, knowing they each have a sacred right to their own choice, and to the consequences of those choices. As do we all. The sovereignty of self, and accountability to that, is sacred.

I left the hospital and walked back to our treatment center. As I entered the building, Dave, my supervisor, and manager of the entire treatment facility, immediately came over to me.

"Hey Pam," he said, sounding quite interested and engaged, "How'd it go with the young guy at the hospital?"

I didn't know he knew I'd gone over there, so his questioning took me by surprise. His concern and advocacy for recovery were unshakeable and quite honorable. I respected him greatly for his commitment to healing, and his attention to mentoring those he supervised. But I hadn't expected his mentoring to go as deep as it did in our encounter on this day. Dave began by describing the history of the man's condition, saying he'd been in treatment at our facility shortly before I hired on.

"Oh, I know all about that, Dave," I said rather urgently, interrupting him in mid-sentence. Almost breathless, I continued, "The most unusual thing about this interview was the smell in the room. It smelled like turpentine."

And with that, Dave paused, likely knowing before I did what was coming. He took in a gentle breath, looked me straight in the eyes, and softly said, "This guy's drug of choice is vodka and that is what it smells like when someone is late-stage and detoxing from vodka."

He maintained eye contact and became silent, waiting for my education and training to catch up with my words.

I stood there in silence for several moments, then said rather softly, "My dad smelled like that."

"Yes," he said, gently adding, "and your dad must have drunk vodka."

"And was an alcoholic," I finally said.

With that, we both nodded to each other in silent recognition.

Another elephant 'outed.'

Someone came up to us, requiring Dave to attend to another issue. I went into my office and closed the door, trying to process all this. I recalled my father's and my conversation when I was a teenager when he called alcohol 'firewater,' and said he tried not to join with others who were drinking. When someone handed him a drink, he shared he would go into the bathroom, pour the alcohol out, and pour fresh water into his glass, pretending he was drinking with others, but drinking water all the while. I recalled a forgotten conversation with his younger brother in California when he told me of several times finding my father lying on his front lawn in the morning, passed out from drinking the night before. I realized then my dad was a binge drinker, with long stretches of time in abstinence, with vodka as his chosen binge drug. I thought about all the behaviors and justifications for drinking and poor behavior in my extended family. I thought about all my father's mother's relatives who were always totally smashed at family events. How had I forgotten all this? Or not seen? Suddenly it all fit. I so wished my dad, and all of us had known about the Twelve Steps.

This is when I realized alcoholism was in my own lineage. Both the thinking process and the physiology were in my family line. No wonder my professors encouraged me. No wonder I had an intuitive sense about addiction, alcoholism, and codependency. It had been part of the air I breathed as I grew into adulthood. It wasn't just Jim. It was me too.

I realized then I came from a long lineage of alcoholism and the mental thought processes supporting it. And no one in my biological family had ever confronted it. Ever. I confronted it with Jim only because I was trying to save my own life. I had no idea it was in my lineage as well.

I became aware, for the first time, my gut-wrenching walk with suicide was just as dangerous for me as if I was taking in a drug. No wonder, I thought in tears and amazement, I loved working with alcoholics and addicts and their families. And no wonder my professors had been so insistent on my entry into addictions treatment. They could see a healing I couldn't see at the time.

Several days after my conversation with Dave, as I sat in my office logging notes in patient charts, there was a knock on my door. It was Kathy, our receptionist. "Pam," she said, "there is a man at the reception desk asking for you. He says he's your dad."

To say I was shocked is an understatement. I didn't know my dad knew where I worked. He did know I worked at an addiction treatment center at this hospital, and of course, he did know how to ask questions, but why would he want to find me? I hadn't seen or talked with him in many months. Many. He'd never made any attempt to talk with me before. And he lived quite a distance away. Why would he just show up?

I walked out to see him standing there, tall and well dressed, at the reception desk, waiting to see me. He always made sure he presented well. Suits on a train, you know.

He cast a warm and genuine smile the moment he saw me. I smiled back. He could see my puzzlement and immediately responded by saying, "Pam, I had to come to this hospital for a few tests, and since I know you work here, I wanted to drop off a picture I thought you might want to have."

And then he handed me a picture of the house I had been born in, in Iowa. My first home. The one we left when I was three. How could he have known the dim memory of that house haunted me? Sort of like, but not nearly as painful or extensive as how the dim memory of the face of my mom's Black caretaker haunted her years after being taken and placed into an orphanage.

Of course, I stumbled on my words. Trying to put together a sentence expressing gratitude. I did manage to thank him. But then our exchange was ended. He handed me the picture and left. I glanced over at the waiting area and noticed my next appointment was there, so there was no opportunity to process the experience. It was several years before I could give time to check out that home in Iowa. But I did frame the picture and place it on my office desk.

Eventually, through all my work with alcoholics, addicts, and their family members, I began to see addiction can be present without the aid of ingesting a chemical. That's termed 'process addictions.' Some examples are compulsive gambling, compulsive sex, exercising, religiosity, overeating, undereating, overspending, and hoarding. And even a compulsive addiction to AA, believe it or not, is possible. And a new addiction in these times is the addiction to computer gaming, technology, social media and cults. Cults, particularly, use projection and the roles of victim, persecutor, rescuer to foster their influence and engage participants in the circular thinking of addiction. These process addictions are just as dangerous to life as chemical addictions. It's our common cultural problem.

It is present any time we use a process to medicate an underlying fear and anger we are trying to avoid, deny, or fight. And often the fear itself is unconscious. Anger, fueled by the belief one is entitled to some form of relief from another, is often the doorway. The unconscious piece is making the choice for us without our conscious consent. Hijacking our thinking.

The ultimate battle of addiction is seeking 'relief' from a chemical, drug, thought process, or behavior, to gain a mental or physical 'high'. The mental 'high' can be about possessing money, material goods, or some socially defined group-think idea of beauty, power, or righteousness. The righteousness can be religious, social, or political. But it always boils down to wanting freedom from the fear of some form of perceived lack, or freedom from some perceived fear of vulnerability. And so the sense of being a victim is generally the foundation.

But the truth is, we are all victims, of one thing or another. Sometimes many. The question is, do we choose to identify ourselves as a victim as our life path? As for me, I certainly did not.

In short, addictions keep us stuck. And unconscious. Ultimately, it's about letting the part of ourselves that is entrenched within those roles, with victim being the foundational identity, make decisions about our lives without our conscious consent.

CHAPTER TWELVE

YOU CAN GET THERE FROM HERE

"The greatest tragedy of the family is the unlived lives of the parents."

—C. G. Jung

After working at the treatment center for several years, I decided to go into private practice. It was more difficult to leave there than it was to leave Ron in the corporate environment. I loved working at the treatment center, and I am so grateful my fellow counselors allowed me to work with them. But I needed more free time than this position allowed. I must say, to this day, I have some regret for leaving. Working on a team at the treatment center engaging with such profound healing was healing for me as well. Even though in private practice I continued to see amazing recovery and felt I was contributing to the betterment of humanity, I missed working on such a wonderful team. It gives me hope today to know such treatment centers and teams are still out there, fostering recovery.

But it was what I needed to do. I needed to have more personal time for family, reflection, and dreams. My work with Ray was significantly reduced. He became more of a mentor, and I saw him less frequently. The people I worked with in private practice were alcoholics/addicts and codependents, already in longer-term recovery working with deeper issues than initial first stage recovery. And I continued with my beloved practice of Family Intervention Counseling.

And then, one day, Jim asked a question. "Pam," he said, with the characteristic twinkle in his green eyes, forecasting something beautiful coming, "How about we go to Iowa and see the house where you were born? You know, the house in the picture your dad gave you?"

"Oh Jim," I quickly responded. "That's too far away."

But he was insistent. Jim wouldn't buy into my response. Finally, one day he said, "We have a three-day weekend. Since you're in private practice, you don't need to work Fridays or Saturdays. How about we go to Iowa?"

He would not accept my entirely unrealistic statement it was too far. Nothing I said could dissuade him from this journey. During our five-hour drive, I must have said at least five times, "But Jim, it's too far. We can't get there from here."

But the truth is, you can.

Each time he responded with the same statement. "We can do this, Pam. We've driven to San Francisco. To Florida. To New York. All those places are much farther than Iowa."

During the long drive, at his invitation, we talked about my childhood. At the time, I said nothing about Mozart Street, my appendicitis experience, or my experience with Tall Man. All that came out later after getting bucked off Gabriel. But we did talk about how I felt unloved throughout my childhood.

"Pam," he slowly asked, "Did your mom or dad ever tell you they loved you?"

"No," I finally responded. "I do not recall either one of them ever saying they loved me."

Jim became silent as he focused on driving, contemplating how it must have felt, never being told as a child you are loved.

"Pam," he eventually responded, "my mom and dad certainly weren't perfect, but I always knew I was loved. Always. I'm sorry that was your experience."

Jim's enthusiasm and curiosity about my childhood in Iowa was unrelenting. And he was a great researcher. He was friendly and outgoing to everyone we met in Iowa. When it came time to knock on the door of my first home, I refused, requesting he not attempt to reach out to the owners. He would hear nothing of it. I sat in the car, watching him, as he walked confidently up those steps and knocked on the front door of that house in the picture. I could see him talking with the person answering the door and within a minute, he waved to me, motioning for me to meet the two of them at the door. The owner of the house invited us in to tour their home.

We toured the house. I had some vague memories but one was very clear. It was my first memory in this lifetime. I was sitting in a crib, happily looking out a double window at a tree with a bird in a nest. I must have been just under two years old. As I stood in the room with the double window, I considered what it was like to be looking out that window as a baby decades earlier. Yes, this very window. In this very room. I felt a part of my child-self return. Tears fell down my face.

Jim knew exactly what he was doing. He wanted to provide me with a clear tracking of my life from birth to my life as an adult. He could easily do this with his own life, and he wanted me to be able to do the same with mine.

Since Jim had done so much research in his own private anticipation of this trip, he knew where my mom had lived with her parents when she was a child. He knew where my grandmother's sister lived just down the street from my mother as a child. He knew where Mom rented a place while Dad was in the Navy in World War II. And he knew we had lived in three houses in Iowa, not just the one I remembered. When my parents couldn't afford to pay for the house I remembered, we rented two others for a short time before moving to Mozart Street in Chicago. We walked around all the neighborhoods I lived in as a baby and my mom and grandmother had lived in as well. We walked around downtown, exploring everything.

We visited the hospital where I had been born. It was still there, as an old beautiful, large red brick hospital building, surrounded by a huge field of tall old oak trees. While Jim walked around the forested field, I sat under one of the many oaks and imagined my mom and dad coming out the doors of the hospital, taking me home to the grey house on Clay Street just a few blocks away.

On our way back to Illinois, we talked about all the losses in my family. And of the many before I had even been born. Jim was shaken by all the losses and abandonment. Then he suggested something odd. Well, it was odd given it came from him and not from my own training and experience as a psychotherapist.

"How about you put all this on a genogram, Pam?" he suggested. He was quite accustomed to putting together genograms, maps of family trees, in his own research on his and my family lineage. Now, the thing is, for years I had already been recommending and helping my clients put together their own genograms. But, not following my own advice, I hadn't put together my own. Jim's research already had names, dates, and locations put onto a genogram. But what Jim was suggesting, and what I was already doing with my clients, was to identify alcoholism, addiction, mental health problems, poverty, education, trauma, illnesses, and any losses and successes occurring in my family lineage as far back as I knew. As he suggested this, I thought to myself with a silent inner smile, yes, he certainly was a therapist's husband.

And so I did.

Loss. After loss. After loss showed up. Many things fell together.

I put together information we'd already gotten from a trip to my grandma's house a few years earlier when Jim and I drove to northern Wisconsin for one last visit with Olga, my mother's mother, as she lay dying. We both knew this would be our last time seeing my grandmother, and our last opportunity to learn about her life. Jim had already done significant research by this time and knew the truth to the many falsehoods my grandmother told about her earlier life. Falsehoods she told only because she was ashamed. And falsehoods we carefully stepped around as we got information and pictures to piece together more of the truth.

As she laid there, three weeks before dying, petting her tiny gold kitty, we talked all day, going through a big box of pictures she somehow had saved for decades. I started our conversation by asking her what she remembered about her own mother. "She had soft hands," she said, tears welling in her eyes. She said her mother died suddenly and she didn't know how. At the time, Olga was only nine years old and was the youngest of thirteen in Denmark. At the time of her mother's death, most of her siblings were scattered all over the world, to places in Europe, America, and Australia. It was clear her relationship with her mother had been tender and painful to lose. With no substitute. She came to this country, alone, at age fifteen and crisscrossed the country going from sibling to sibling.

I went through her huge box of pictures. Pulling them out and asking her about many of them. It was a day of tender exchange between grandma and me, for the first time. I believe it was healing for both of us.

I got a photograph of my mother's biological father. I knew his name but had never seen his face. She had one picture. And she allowed me to have it. And I got a picture of my mother's cousin, Guy, the World War II veteran my grandmother spoke about when I was a child. The one who died before I had been born. The one who visited my grandmother's bedside after he died. And I got a picture of my mother standing alone, at age four, looking forlorn, at the orphanage where she was taken. I got another picture of my mother, at about two years of age, standing with a Black woman dressed all in white, her hand at the baby's back, making sure the baby didn't fall and hurt herself. Finally, the face of the woman my mother yearned to see again, but couldn't, all those years ago. Right there, in that picture. In a box my grandmother had all along.

This day was the beginning of seeing my grandmother more clearly. I saw how she struggled with loss all of her life. And how she unknowingly and unwillingly passed loss down to my own mother. I began a deep forgiveness of her that day. I could see her loss, her yearning for love, and her innocence. And this helped me see my own mother more clearly as well. Yearning all her life to feel a mother's love. How could she give me what she had never experienced?

I knew then they had all done the best they could. Yet I also knew at the end of their lives, they wished they had been able to do more. This was clear the day I spoke with grandma, and it was also clear the day I spoke with my own mother years before, three weeks before she died.

And so, I began to put all this into the genogram.

Shortly after coming home from the trip to Iowa, someone claiming to be a distant relative of my dad's knocked on his door and handed him hundreds of pages of genealogy research, providing information about my dad's family he never knew. And then my dad shared it with me. Which was kind of unusual, given we rarely spoke. And so now, I could piece together my father's family.

Turns out, my dad's father was born on an island off the coast of Norway, near the Arctic Circle. But his mother refused to marry his father, calling him a "drunk." The story goes she was tied to stakes in the village center for refusing to marry the man who got her pregnant. But my grandpa always knew who his father was because his father married another, and they all lived near each other on the same small island. My grandfather was always ashamed of his birth, never being able to claim his father. He never spoke of this. But when he came to this country, alone, rather than taking the name he had been given in Norway, he took his father's name, as was Norwegian custom, and gave himself the last name of Arnesen. Research showed his father did have a problem with alcohol. And I found out many years after leaving my job at the treatment center my grandfather also had a problem with alcohol.

But the most stunning part of this story for me was my father's lineage was part Sami. My great-grandfather, the one called a "drunk," was a Sami. The Sami are the Indigenous people from far northern Norway and Europe and were often called the Reindeer People. Sometimes they were also called Laplanders. But this was seen as a pejorative term.

The Sami have an interesting story, one similar to all the Indigenous People of our world. And please, let's keep in mind all of us who walk upon this earth originated from Indigenous Peoples. Every single one of us.

In ancient times the Sami were well known for their shamans and for their ability to dream and predict the future. But their spiritual beliefs, their shamanism, their language, their entire culture, was denigrated and nearly destroyed as Norway began to form its' national identity. It was a loss my grandfather, his father, and most of his ancestors carried to their graves.

All this history, from both my mother and father, was crucial in helping me understand what my ancestors handed down to me through our family lineage. It wasn't all painful, negative things. Intuition, contact with the departed, and dreams providing guidance were also legacies passed down through both sides of my family lineage. This is true for all of us.

I came to realize all of us who walk on this earth share a lineage of unexpressed grief and loss, as well as guidance from healed ancestors.

The losses leave a more persistent mark through out generations. And they cover up the gifts.

Our ancestors' losses are passed down through our lineage like ghosts, waiting for retrieval and healing. Waiting for us, in this generation, to free ourselves of past patterns, past losses. As we do this, as we heal ourselves from our losses and our grief, we free our ancestors as well. And then we are more bridged to our healed ancestors. Because we are all connected. But I didn't know any of this then. It was years later in a series of encounters in meditation when I was shown this.

After our trip to Iowa and after learning of my ancestral connection to the Sami, Jim found a way to provoke me. Again.

Being the Wise Man he was, as the two of us sat on our front porch one morning, facing the vast western field spanned above by open blue skies, Jim suggested getting our youngest daughter a horse.

"Since we now live on this little farm," he said, "we can get a horse for Sarah."

Having a horse had been her enduring childhood dream. Every Christmas list since age five included the wish to Santa, "If you bring me a horse for Christmas, I will never ask for anything again."

I told him then, I, too, had always wanted a horse, but was silent when Sarah mentioned it every Christmas because I felt the wish could never be realized. I told him of my mother's experience as a child when Olga promised her a horse if she produced a ten-dollar bill. When my mother finally produced a ten dollar bill, Olga angrily refused and shamed her for ever wanting a horse. My mother grieved silently but never forgot. Passing it down, somehow.

"Well, then," Jim said, with a smile and his famous twinkle in his green eyes, "we can get a horse for you too."

It was quite some time before we bought a horse for our daughter, and then one for me, but after our conversation, we did get involved with horses. Sarah and I took lots of lessons. We leased horses. Our daughter was involved mostly in a practice termed "eventing," which combined the practice of dressage and cross country jumping. She was a natural rider. Me, not so much. But I loved being with horses.

Of course, I was continuing with full-time private practice as a psychotherapist, specializing in later-term addiction recovery, codependency, trauma recovery, and Family Intervention Counseling.

Eventually, we did buy a horse for me. Gabriel. And as we all know, he insisted on presenting me with an invitation into a deeper phase of my journey to soul. What I didn't see at the time before getting bucked off Gabriel, because, you know, hindsight is often twenty-twenty, I was completing one phase of my life and beginning entry into another. I was beginning to step off the threshold and enter into the doorway of my soul. I only saw this years later after sorting out all that took place before and after getting bucked off that lovely huge golden chestnut gelding.

For me, my entire life up to this point was about developing a sense of self, my own autonomy. This meant I had to own my voice, my right to exist as separate from anyone else, to own my sovereignty. I couldn't buy into a common group think discounting my personal experience in a misguided attempt for group conformity. I had to know how to function in this world as an adult, without looking into others' agendas and taking things personally. And with all the work I was doing within the addictions field, I began to trust our human community, finally believing I did have a place to exist.

So why is this so important you may ask.

First, it's vitally important to agree to life and our human process of growth and change. And to feel a sense of belonging. For me, it couldn't be a false belonging where I abdicated my inner sense of discernment and knowing. Experiencing the community of recovery within my profession gave me the space to stand as me.

If we do not own our own self, we are not giving consent to our lives. All addiction, and all unconscious denial taking place in the race around any mental vicious circle, in one way or another, deprives us of our own consent. As in my conversation with Tall Man all those years before, consent is sacred. It's how we grow our sense of self, and how we become accountable. And how our caring for ourselves and others becomes authentic.

But most important, owning our consent is how we prepare our self to know and to say yes to embracing our soul. Which, I believe, is our primary human life task. We are born into this life to come home to our soul. And our 'personality self' is not our 'soul,' yet our personality self's job is to recognize our soul and to surrender to our soul. I was just beginning to realize my entire life search was for soul. Trying to come home without killing myself to get there.

My soul had been calling me my entire life. Calling to be known by the self that also was me, the personality part of me.

And so, enter Gabriel. With his insistence, and with that painful invitation.

PART THREE

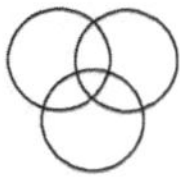

COMING HOME

CHAPTER THIRTEEN

WHAT DO DOGS KNOW? HOW TO FIND A DEAD SOLDIER

"Intuition will tell the thinking mind where to go next."

—Jonas Salk

Every night after getting home from the hospital after fracturing my neck, I went to sleep asking for a dream or some form of guidance about what I needed to learn from getting bucked off Gabriel. And then, one morning, a few days after the discussion Jim and I had after my first shower, I had an experience which began to provide an answer.

Laying there, completely motionless, caught in a liminal land between sleeping and waking, through closed eyes, I noticed the sun was shining and it was now morning. My head was throbbing in pain as I felt the brace tightly wrapped around my neck. I'd slept deeply and still all night, lying on my back, moving not one inch for at least nine hours. And then suddenly, while in a half-dream state, I felt my childhood dog, Sheba, jump on me as I lay there. I felt her love and delight in life as she licked my face.

I hadn't thought about Sheba in decades. Not once. But I began to cry as I felt my love for her and experienced her joyful, innocent presence.

My sleep had been deep and dreamless. And yet now, coming to me just as I barely wakened, was Sheba, reminding me of the wonder and of the love I lived within as a child before appendicitis.

Sheba came into our family as a puppy when I was four years old and we lived on Mozart Street in Chicago. She was a mix of a regular collie and a border collie. Of course, she was beautiful. And fun. And up for any game any of us kids could play. I loved her so. It was clear the love was mutual.

We took Sheba with us when I was five and moved into the small house in the suburbs across the street from the woods. In the mid-fifties, it was common to let your dogs roam freely during the day. And so Sheba roamed those woods. Very often with me. I was an Indian and she was my wolf companion living in the forest, wandering among the oaks in wonder. Those were the good days.

But they didn't last.

My appendicitis experience changed everything. My sense of connection and trust in any kind of Universal Love and in my family and community, and even my love for Sheba, died. It seemed as if our whole family died as well. Sheba got ignored. And often pushed aside by all of us. Even by me. And even abused. Not by me, but I said nothing to put an end to it.

We eventually sold the house Dad built with his bare hands and became renters in another part of town. We had no money for a home of our own. Sheba moved with us to our rented apartment. By the time I was a teenager and working at Jewel, Sheba was old and frail. As a family we sat and watched television while Sheba took rounds standing in front of each of us, nudging us to pet her. As we each pushed her aside, she moved on to the next person. It was a ritual we went through every evening with Sheba.

Eventually, my dad had enough of it. Holding the courage of the cancer survivor and the World War II Navy veteran he was, he told us Sheba had to be put to sleep. He said he would do it and invited any of us to go to the veterinarian with him. Not one of us said yes. When the appointment time came, he invited us to say goodbye to Sheba. I can't be sure, but I don't think any of us did. I do know, I did not.

When he returned from the vet without Sheba, I was in the living room. From where I was sitting, I looked at him and asked how it had gone. "Did you stay with her as she died?" I asked. "How was she?" Those questions arose unbidden from some unknown place deep within me. A place holding love for Sheba.

He spoke softly, his eyes filling with tears, and said, "Yes, I held her as she died. I didn't want her to be alone."

That was all he said. And then he walked away.

I was grateful for his courage.

And so I went on with my life, my heart closed until meeting Jim several years later. I didn't think of Sheba again until this particular morning, decades later, when she came running to me in my half-dreaming state.

As I pondered this, tears for Sheba's life welling in my eyes, Jim walked into our bedroom carrying for me his customary cup of hot coffee. Yes, after all these years, he still brought me coffee in the morning.

"Good morning, Pam," he said while placing the coffee on the nightstand. "How'd you sleep?" Then, noticing my tears, he sweetly asked, "What are the tears about?"

"Oh, Jim," I responded, "just a memory of a dog I loved when I was growing up." I knew I needed to explore and understand more, but didn't want to say anything else in this moment we were in.

"Well, I'm going to get off to school now," Jim said, understanding I didn't want to talk about my tears. "Are you going to be okay getting yourself out of bed and downstairs?" he asked, wanting to make sure I was all right walking around with this injury, this neck brace, and these tears. After telling him yes, I'll be okay getting out of bed by myself, we kissed a quick goodbye, as we always did every morning, and he left for school.

My head and neck throbbing in pain, crying for Sheba, I carefully made my way out of bed and downstairs, carrying my hot cup of coffee. I sat down in a chair in our living room and gazed out at the expansive western field. While shedding tears, I went over in my mind the Mozart Street Experience, the appendicitis experience, and the experience with Tall Man. Two memories kept flashing into my mind interrupting my thoughts at various points. Sheba and Gabriel. I wondered, are they related somehow? I'd asked for guidance last night and I'd gotten Sheba this morning. This couldn't be just a coincidence. There are no coincidences. Just sacred synchronicities. They must be related. But how?

Again and again, I kept returning to the angel hovering over me in the arena when Gabriel bucked me off. The angel surely saved my life by telling me to remain completely still, even though others, and I too, wanted to get up and run to rein in that wild horse. But what could Sheba have to do with this?

I put my coffee cup down, closed my eyes and sat in stillness, meditating on the experience with Sheba. I let myself feel her exuberance, her love, her joy in life as I dreamed of her just this morning jumping on me. We had so much fun together on Mozart Street and in those woods so long ago.

And then I recalled I lost all that with the appendicitis experience. All of it. It was as if the part of me who played with and loved Sheba had died. Yet a part of me had decided to go on, to find a way to live in this very human life we all have.

Those many years ago, when I turned myself over to die, I felt stuck between heaven and earth. Unable to get to either. Not wanting earth, unable to get to heaven. Feeling desperate and stuck in the middle with only me. No other place wanting me. Or so I thought.

But somehow, eventually, I managed to rescue a part of me trapped in the bunker, the part Benjamin had seen, but I hadn't known about until the abuse with him. And then, I managed to build a good life here. Thank you, to Mr. Raspiller, to Jim, to my children, to Ray and the rest of the Wise Men, to the nurses and psych techs who surrounded me and guided me one day years before, to newspaper editors, professors and teachers who mentored me, and to Ron and Dave who hired me and gave me a chance. Pretty amazing, really.

I ended up building a beautiful life after all. As Tall Man had shown me so many years before. But something was missing—and it seemed Gabriel and Sheba were trying to show the way.

I became aware of the innocent little girl who loved and played with Sheba, the innocent little one who knew of the truth of the Mozart Street Experience. The part that knows none of us, even me, are ever excluded from a loving source or from God. Could I have put that part of me into a shadow basement bunker, telling her we didn't belong, we had been rejected by God? That I didn't want to hear any truth she could tell? Could she be held there? Still?

I decided I needed to rethink everything. To look at everything anew.

The dead soldier, the one I hauled over my shoulder through the dark and muddy battlefield in the dream so many years before, came to mind. And then I remembered, the soldier was barely dead, not quite dead.

Had Sheba come to bring to me my little girl, the one I thought had died with the appendicitis? Was she that barely living soldier I was hauling over my shoulder in the dream from decades ago? She, barely alive, holding onto the truth of the universal love of God? Barely living, yet holding truth for a time when I could know it again? Was Sheba trying to bring that part of me home?

And then I thought about the angel hovering over me as I lay motionless on the floor of the arena, with Gabriel racing and stomping circles around me. I had been protected then and had been given clear guidance. I had not been abandoned.

If I had not been abandoned then, I decided, surely I had not been abandoned decades before when I had appendicitis. Sheba had come to remind me of the truth I had denied.

And so I spent the rest of the day slowly going over in my mind many life experiences, considering this time, I had not been abandoned. Perhaps throughout my life I had been guided. This was the beginning of a deeper dive into letting go of a sense of feeling a victim. Could it be, I wondered, I wasn't separate from a Universal Love, or God, after all? I had no problem believing others were guided, but somehow I felt I'd been left out. Believing myself unworthy. Denying what I already called sacred synchronicities, but somehow refusing to take in as fully real. I began to see all the invitations, surely sent by Spirit.

I'd never told anyone about any of the spiritual experiences. Even Jim. As I sat there pondering why I hadn't, I heard the garage door open. I'd been sitting in the chair, reviewing the events of my life all day, and Jim was now coming home from school. With no idea of what he would think, I decided to tell him. He'd been raised within a traditional Christian religion and knew I had zero religious upbringing. We'd never discussed any spiritual or religious beliefs except for the belief in a Higher Power within the Twelve Step Program. There is considerable room, however, within those steps for any particular beliefs, any particular religion. As long as no one is left out and as long as forgiveness and accountability are foundational. I decided it was now time to share all this with Jim.

"How has today been for you, Pam?" Jim asked with his gentle smile as he walked into our living room, putting down his briefcase and sitting in the chair opposite me.

"Today, I've gone over my entire life, up until now, trying to sense why I got bucked off Gabriel and came within a fraction of an inch of dying," I said. "Why did all this happen?"

"What do you mean?" he asked. "Does there have to be a reason?"

"Well," I said, "Why was I saved? Why are we born? Why do we exist here? What is the purpose behind our lives? What is the purpose behind my life? Is there a purpose in any of this?"

"Our purpose is to be a family," he quickly responded. "To take care of each other."

Oh, that's just like Jim, I thought. His love and dedication to family held him as he held the ground under my feet as I went through my desperate walk out of suicide and into living my life. I knew he was right on many levels.

"Okay," I said, "to be a family. I get it. And I agree. But how about our purpose as individuals within the entire human family?"

"And why did I get a warning I would be bucked off Gabriel?" I continued asking. "And then why did I get bucked off Gabriel? And why did an angel present herself and save my life? Am I missing something? I need to go deeper."

"What's deeper?" he asked. "How would you do that?"

"Jim, do you remember me telling you I believe we all have lived before? We've all had past lives?"

"I recall you mentioning it a few times," he said. "But we've never spoken much about it. Just you believed it. You never said any more or told me why. Why do you believe that?"

I began by telling him, for the first time, in full detail, about my Mozart Street Experience, my appendicitis experience, and about Tall Man.

"The significant thing about all this, Jim," I said, "is this personality, this me talking with you right now, is not all there is to this self that is me. I exist on many different levels. And I believe, in many different times. Many, I believe, I don't know. And I believe you do too. As do we all. There is more going on than we know or can even know. And I believe it is all connected to and held within an ever-abiding deep Love, or God."

He furrowed his brows a bit while slightly squinting his green eyes, holding a faraway expression, obviously going over his own experiences with himself and with me. I waited in silence, giving him time to ponder this all.

"Do you think that's why you've had dreams accurately predicting the future?" he asked. "And had experiences with those who've died—like your mom coming to you one time?"

"I think so, Jim," I said, remembering several times when Mom came and I didn't tell him. "I believe those experiences come from a spiritual place. Up until now, I've denied this, thinking I was excluded. I thought I was rejected when I had appendicitis, when I asked to go Heaven and remained here instead. I thought God, Love, Higher Power, or whatever name you want to call it, had rejected me, finding me unworthy of Heaven, unworthy of Spirit. It was for everybody else, but for some reason, it wasn't for me. But now I can't wash this belief as I consider all the spiritual experiences I've had and what just happened with Gabriel."

"You weren't excluded after all, were you?" Jim responded.

"No," I said. "I was not."

Jim smiled a warm, grateful smile, then said "Your mom and your grandma have talked about these things in the past. Your grandma talked about how Guy came to her after he died," he said. "Remember?"

"Yes, Jim," I said. "And do you remember he gave her information she couldn't possibly have known but our government confirmed nearly one year later? Remember?"

"Yes," he responded. "I do. But I wonder how any of us knows whether these kinds of things are true or not. The government confirmed your grandma's experience of Guy, but we don't generally have a way to confirm such things. How is it we know?"

Keep in mind, Jim was a science teacher. Majored in physics. And I loved science, particularly physics. That was one way the two of us had connected. But these questions are deeper than what a traditional science, a materialistic science, can answer. The science of quantum physics, discussed in the book *The Holographic Universe* Mike had given me a few weeks before, went deeper and made profound connections. But I didn't want to bring this up with Jim just yet.

He asked a good question. And one I pondered and worked with all of my life, up to this point. How is it any of us decides something is true? I'd often asked this myself.

My discerning practice began as a little girl. When you have experiences like Mozart Street, Tall Man, and predictive dreams and intuitions coming true, you spend time noting which signals you had that were true and which were not. I noticed the not true ones came from a sense of fear, and seemed to pull me down a rabbit hole of shame and blame, victim and persecutor. Not that the dreams and intuitions didn't produce fear at times. They surely did. But they didn't originate from a feeling of fear. They always originated from a feeling of 'knowing'. Generally, an instant 'knowing'. And the 'knowing' was always a felt sense—a full-body felt sense. It is difficult to define, but it is a visceral sense. And times when I followed the felt sense, it was always true. Times when I didn't, it ended up a problem.

"Jim," I said, "It's difficult for me to describe, but I feel a sense of knowing. It's visceral."

"I don't think I've ever had that," Jim said.

"Oh, I think you have," I responded immediately, having noticed many times over the years when it appeared to me Jim had quite a fine sense of intuition but perhaps didn't realize it. "I believe everybody has, at various times, in various degrees of intensity. Most of the time we either deny it or we just don't make note of it. For example, have you ever felt an instant like or dislike for someone, but had no particular facts to back you up one way or the other? But found out later your instincts were right?"

"Well, of course," Jim said. "The moment we met, I loved you at the outset. And somehow felt we were meant to be together. That's why I pursued you so strongly."

"And you were right, weren't you?" I said.

"Yep, sure was," he responded quickly, with a smile and that twinkle in his green eyes.

"That's an example. And if you look at other events," I said, "I am sure you will find you've had more."

"So, you're saying we all have an inner wisdom?" he said.

"Yes," I said, speaking slowly and choosing my words carefully. "What if, through our intuition, our dreams, and inner knowing, we are able to tap into a larger pool of information? And what if the larger pool of information is connected to us through a loving universal force, a Higher Power, or God, or whatever you want to name it? Carl Jung wrote about this sort of thing and called it the Collective Unconscious. And the book Mike gave me a couple of weeks ago, *The Holographic Universe*, is also about this."

"I always considered you were kind of special. That you had some special gift," Jim said.

It was surprising to hear this from him. Particularly because I had spent several years disconnecting myself from a yearning to be considered special—this being the particular hook I let Benjamin use to engage and hold me prisoner in the drama triangle.

"No one is special," I said emphatically. "No one. We each are different, with unique skills to bring to our lives and to others, but no one is more important, or more special, than any other. We are all included in this. Everyone. Everyone is equally precious. No one is left out. There is no one, absolutely no one excluded, or less than or greater than, anyone else."

Of this, by this time, I was absolutely sure. If I wasn't devalued or excluded, I was convinced, surely no one else was either.

"I think I've gotten complacent over the years," I said. "I think we've both gotten complacent. I mean, Jim, look at us. We live in this beautiful house on the edge of an expansive wetland nature preserve. Both of us love our jobs. Our children are doing well. We have everything materially we could possibly want. What else is there? I think I've settled for satisfaction with material life but have forgotten to delve deeper into the why of it all—into the spiritual part of life. Into a sense of a Universal Love, or God, and my relationship to that."

We humans cannot fill a spiritual yearning with a material object. Ultimately, that's addiction. Had we gotten complacent? Were we on the edge of a soft material addiction? Were we at risk of getting lost? Or had we already gotten lost? Even though we were in service to others with our careers, it seemed we needed to go deeper. To what I wasn't quite sure. But I knew it was about my Mozart Street Experience. And I knew it was about feeling a sense of home, a place I had been yearning for all my life.

"Pam," Jim asked, "What are you suggesting we do? Shall we start going to a church?"

"I don't think doing just that will bring us the answers," I said. "I think each of us needs to search within."

"I have something I'd like to explore," I said. "I want to do a past life hypnotic regression. Since I've had all these memories from other times, perhaps I should see if there is anything speaking to what I need to know about this life now. I mean, why do I remember what I remember? Why did I have that experience on Mozart Street?"

This was a huge new move for me. As a psychotherapist, while I had never experienced it, I was well aware of the benefits of hypnosis. And I had read of people experiencing past-life hypnotic regression. But before getting bucked off Gabriel, it was an arena I emphatically had not wanted to enter. My concern at the time was if I opened up to a past life, I would be pulled down a rabbit hole into doing extensive psychotherapy on another lifetime. I wrongly figured I would have to reengage in psychotherapy with a past life. Those were the days when I had a rather linear view of time, before understanding more about soul retrieval, my lineage, quantum physics, and how all this fits together. I didn't understand past lives arise to bring a deeper healing on a soul level. To bring deeper parts of our soul, parts we left behind in other lives, home to us in this life, home to the larger soul we are.

"But I have a request for you, Jim," I added, fully knowing he didn't believe in past lives but wanting to ask him anyway. "I do not want to walk into any hypnotherapist's office without protection. I don't know if the hypnotherapist will attempt to influence me, or if I will lose consciousness during hypnosis and be vulnerable to an unethical hypnotherapist. I just can't go in there alone. I want you to come with me and be a witness. Will you do this for me?"

"Yes," he said, immediately, casting a warm smile, pleased I'd asked him for support. Even though he did not believe in past lives, he wanted to support me in delving deeper into whatever might be behind those memories. But more than anything, he wanted to show up and make sure there was no abuse. Wishing he had done so with Benjamin.

We paused our discussion and gazed at the winter's sunset just outside our window. The entire western sky was lit up in various shades of orange and red, creating a stunning dance of colors across the horizon. I thought of what my dad used to say, being the Navy sailor he was, "Red sky at night, sailor's delight." Yes, perhaps a harbinger of smooth seas ahead. Of answers and of wisdom to come.

After doing a fair amount of research, I found a past-life regression hypnotherapist with good credentials and made an appointment. By this time, I was significantly recovered from the C1 fracture and was seeing clients again. As he promised, Jim came to the appointment with me and was there for the entire session.

But it didn't go as expected.

CHAPTER FOURTEEN

EVERY. SINGLE. SOUL.

"She remembered who she was and the game changed."

—Lalah Deliah

Jim stood as a silent witness in the corner as the hypnotherapy session proceeded for three full hours. I had a difficult time entering the past life but once there, a difficult time leaving. I'm grateful the hypnotherapist did not have another appointment scheduled after me and was willing to be patient and gently work through this with me.

I wasn't able to rise above the intense emotions, even though I was deeply under hypnosis. I recalled everything, in full-bodied detail and experiential awareness. It was like being in two places at the same time and watching it all while feeling it all—in the office where the session was proceeding, and in the other life. Ultimately, it took me several years to process the experience and to understand how it fit in with my life. But it was nothing like psychotherapy. It was soul retrieval. Soul healing. Bringing a lost part of my soul home to me.

I was a nun in Nazi-occupied Europe during WWII and part of the underground, rescuing Jewish families, aiding them in their escape. The moment I realized I was a nun, I was immediately overwhelmed with chills and with the feeling of needles and pins racing up and down my entire body, for at least five minutes. I could not have been more shocked, yet more sure of the reality of the experience. The nun, asking to be called 'Sister,' died in a concentration camp, while trying to forgive the Nazi soldier who shot her and who was begging for forgiveness.

The Sister, who had been lost in time, began her journey back home to the larger, eternal loving soul we were both a part of. One I was now just barely beginning to become aware of and to embody. With the regression, I witnessed her, with love, and invited her back home.

Thank you, Sheba, for forgiving me and for loving me. And for showing me the way to the little girl in me who knew truth, and how to find home.

Jim and I held onto each other, both shaken after the session, as we walked out to our car. "I didn't expect any of that, Jim," I softly said. "I'm shocked. And I have no idea what this means."

"Yes, I get that," he responded. "I didn't expect this either. But I felt the truth of the experience, Pam. It was so powerful and so real. Now, I believe we all have past lives. I have no doubt. I just don't understand how the time issue puts all this together," he added, struggling with a more materialistic interpretation of physics and sense of time.

For the next few years, I had painful flashbacks about Sister during the Holocaust. I saw it all as parts of my soul coming home. And so I welcomed those parts with love and gratitude. Eventually, I did a ceremony where I called all parts of Sister's life home. And then I began to feel more at peace.

The next morning after the hypnotic regression, hoping for guidance, I decided to take my meditation practice deeper. Instead of meditating twenty minutes each day, I decided to extend my practice to an hour each day. Most of the time, my experiences in meditation were full of mental vicious circles. Sometimes, I was successful at stilling my mind enough to experience a deep peace. And, sometimes, I experienced myself being taken on unexpected and unbidden profound journeys.

Several months after my first regression, still shaken by the experience with Sister, I decided to do a walking meditation under the stars. It was the height of summer, and late and deep in the darkness of a moonless night. I walked out onto our five-acre field. Even though I'd spent my life discerning what is true, these new experiences were so profound, so compelling, and felt so real, yet I did not personally know of anyone else experiencing anything similar. I recently read about others having experiences such as these, but I wondered how could this be happening to me? I'm just a regular person, after all.

As I walked, I heard the familiar echoing of two owls calling to each other and the chirping of frogs far off in the wetland. I noticed a few fireflies and remembered chasing massive fields of fireflies as a child. Where have all the fireflies gone, I wondered. I looked up at the dark, black, moonless sky, filled with stars, and asked out loud, "How do I know what is true, what is real?"

Suddenly Tall Man was right there, beside me. "You will know what is true from within your heart," he said. "Your deep heart has eyes to see and wisdom to know. Let that be your guide."

This was the first time I'd experienced Tall Man since decades before when I bid him goodbye and put the bottle of ammonia back in the closet as a child. And here he was. After all these years. A welcome friend. And guide.

I wondered for a moment, had he been with me all along? All these years? Yes, I felt him respond.

I knew then we are never alone. Never. We are all held and deeply loved. In every moment. Even when we think we are not.

I felt the truth of his statement. He surely was carrying a candle, lighting my way, so I could learn to see and to know. Guiding me to trust myself and make my own choices, as he had advised me all those decades ago to follow the wisdom and love held deeply within my own beating heart. Guiding me to honor what is true for me, to light my own candle, rather than to relinquish my authority to any other. And guiding me to welcome into myself the scent of the rose, to listen to the tender murmurs of my very own heart.

While there are times I feel him easier and stronger than others, from that moment on, I've been aware of Tall Man as part of the guidance in my life.

A few weeks later I told a trusted friend what I'd heard from Tall Man about the wisdom of seeing with the heart. She told me of HeartMath, an organization which has done extensive research on the electromagnetic emanations of our very human heart. (Heart Math Institute) It turns out, our hearts have a strong and measurable electromagnetic field. And, it turns out, our hearts have about forty thousand neurons—neurons being the part of our biology allowing us to understand and to have memory. Yes, just as Tall Man had shared.

Apparently, the beating hearts of all animals have an electromagnetic field as well. Horses have a particularly large heart field. And there can be a co-resonance between these fields. What she said made me think about what I read in Michael Talbot's book, *The Holographic Universe,* and the understanding of the vibrations of energetic fields making up our entire world. Our entire universe.

Recent research has validated and enlarged our understanding of many of these concepts. We are now in an area where the science of quantum physics is reaching out and touching the spiritual experiences spoken of by prophets, mystics, sages, and shamans. Of course, most scientists would not speak in those terms, but some are beginning to voice of the bridge between these two worlds.

Quantum physics is showing all is held within a huge electromagnetic field, with many frequency variations held within the field. And the strength and the frequency of the field appears to be fueled by the energy of love. A marriage of quantum physics and spirituality. A marriage of intent and love. A marriage of Spirit and Soul. A marriage of the light of a candle and the scent of a rose.

After many months of regular one-hour meditation practice, I had a profound experience. The moment I entered meditation, I experienced myself riding a horse. It was as if I was being carried into another reality, another dimension—but one far more real than the flowered chair in my living room. While I knew I was sitting in my chair, I was also aware of being taken on a journey. I silently witnessed and felt everything unfold before me.

I am in a huge vast area of red rock and desert. The sky above is clear and blue with the horizon stretching far beyond to massive red rock formations. There are absolutely no shadows. Light is everywhere. I feel comfortable and at peace.

I am riding a huge golden chestnut horse, with a thick blond mane. The horse knows its' destination and walks in a slow rhythmic cadence, rocking me with each step. I surrender myself to this golden horse and let my body move within the rhythm of the steps.

And then, I become aware I am the golden horse, walking, rocking back and forth, to the rhythm of my own beating heart. I feel the love the horse feels for all existence. The ground. The red rocks. The blue sky.

Then I am aware I am the blood of the horse, circulating and pulsating with the rhythm of my heart, throughout the body of the horse I am. As the blood, I feel an enduring love and timeless wisdom for the horse, and for all of life, within and beyond the blood I am.

And then, I become the bones of the horse, strong and solid, loving and wise. Walking with the rhythm of the beating of my heart, connected to all existence.

Then, I am aware I am the red rocks and the earth I am walking upon. And I feel a boundless love, in all realms of time, from all and for all. The horse. The blood. The bones. The red rocks. The earth. The sky.

And then, suddenly I am out in a huge endless expanse of a wet black universe, full of infinite potential, feeling a boundless, and eternal love for all that could possibly exist, in the past and endlessly on into the future. Back and forth in time. In an eternal now. An expansive love, beyond time, where even a fly is loved and is sacred beyond measure.

I stay there and feel the truth of this for some unknown time.

And then softly, I heard the chiming giving me notice my hour meditation was over.

Slowly I opened my eyes and sat in wonder. Had the soul of Gabriel come to give me the experience of feeling the timeless and infinite love of all? Everything connected within a Universal Field of Love? As One? All we see and are, including me, earth, rocks, plants, animals and all of humanity, are of God? With no separation. God is within all. Even me. Here. Present. Now.

Thank you, Gabriel, for coming to me, and for insisting on more from me than I insisted on from myself.

I sat in silence for some time, feeling held within the love of the wet, infinite black universe. And the love of earth. And of rocks. And love for all beings. Even flies.

It was clear to me then, God is within all. People. Animals. Plants. Rocks. Soil. No exceptions. And love is the deepest truth of all. Not a romantic, personal, jealous love, but an expansive, eternal, uncompromising, all-forgiving love. In an eternal, fertile, present now.

I wish I could say I was able to maintain this feeling experience at all moments of my daily life. But I wasn't. While I am able to feel it from time to time during meditation and during loving encounters with others and with nature, the feeling of love was so expansive it wasn't possible for me to experience it all the time while walking around in this world. But I fully remember the experience, the complete truth of it, and carry it with me. Always.

And then, on Wednesday, April 21, 1999, the day after the Columbine shootings, I went into my typical hour-long morning meditation. I invoked my guides, Tall Man, and my higher self, turned on my sixty-minute alarm, closed my eyes, and then was immediately shifted into a large hallway, facing an area of open double glass doors, a large meeting room with many tables and chairs scattered about beyond the doors. I was aware I was in two places at the same time and was being brought on a journey. I was in my living room. And also, in this large hallway. Two guides were standing next to me, one on each side.

"Why are we here?" I asked the guides, totally confused. I'd never experienced anything quite like this before. Then I heard myself ask them, "And why are those bodies lying there?"

The last question confused me even more. I was not aware of seeing any bodies, anywhere in this hallway or the large meeting room beyond those doors. But a part of me must have seen bodies and shielded my eyes from the vision.

"These people have died to this life," the guides said. "And some of them need help accepting the Light. They can't see us. We need a bridge between us and them, to help them get to the Light. Will you help us? Will you be a bridge?"

I paused for a few moments. Stunned with trying to understand all this. Me, be a bridge? From earth to heaven? I'm just a regular person after all.

"There are many others here helping as well," they said, seeming to notice my confusion. "Do you consent?"

"Yes," I said, with clear conviction.

And with that, I went completely blank, as if I had been put under anesthesia. I do not recall a thing. I was out for exactly fifty-nine minutes.

About thirty seconds before the chime rang, announcing the end of my hour-long meditation, I began to slowly wake, weeping out loud. Weeping with love for the shooters. I recalled only that the shooters were shocked to learn there was a God, and the love of God included them. That they could be forgiven. They were rejecting the Light, feeling they didn't qualify, because they were angry and had taken their anger out on others and on themselves. Holding themselves accountable, they didn't feel they deserved God or forgiveness. But eventually, they surrendered and accepted forgiveness. Because many loving souls, from here and from beyond, came to help.

Of course, the shooting was the Columbine High School shooting. I cried most of the day for the lost lives, the lost hope, the devastation of it all. But I cried more for the beauty of all the love coming together, from here and from beyond, to forgive and to bring everyone, every single soul, back home.

Every. Single. Soul. No one left out.

This was the beginning of a deeper search and awareness of the nature of forgiveness, and of the nature of violence, both to the self and to others. I pondered the nature of war. Of killing others. And of my long walk through my own suicidal battlefield.

By this time, I did know as truth that whatever we hate, whatever we war with, pulls us into a web of war, where we are hurt just as those we wish to hurt are hurt. We are back to that triangle. If we are one part of it, we are part of it all.

Now you may wonder how one can be forgiven for hauling out a gun and shooting dead a roomful of innocent children. I agonized over that question. I didn't have an answer. But it was clear to me this depth of forgiveness was not any form of a bypass for any individual's accountability. Accountability for destructive behavior was not denied. But the souls were forgiven.

My amazement came from experiencing the depth of the wrong and the depth of the forgiveness. The beauty of all the love coming together to bring the souls of those shooters home was undeniable.

Having someone shoot your child is a travesty beyond belief. And having someone you love pull out a gun and kill another is a tragedy beyond belief. And being the one pulling out a gun and killing another is also a tragedy beyond belief. And killing oneself is a tragedy beyond belief as well. But these things do happen. All the time. One occurrence like this is one too many.

This is the war we have with others. And the war we have within ourselves. It is the same triangle, victim, persecutor, rescuer, or if you prefer these words, shame, blame, and special. All fueled by fear. Under the cover of anger. Or 'righteous indignation.' Or retribution. Or shame.

All this was why I so badly wanted to leave as a child when I had appendicitis. I did not want to accept the terms of living here on this earth where an authentic love seemed so difficult to manifest. It takes enormous courage for each one of us to be here, to walk this earth, our feet upon the ground. I knew this even as a child when I had appendicitis and later when talking as a child with Tall Man in my bathroom. And that's why we fight so directly with our own fears, using the vicious circle of the roles in the triangle of thinking and seeking as a by-pass. It's our human drama story. One we need to move beyond.

Later in the evening, I told Jim about this experience. He immediately went to the story of Jesus on the cross. "Pam, do you recall what Jesus is supposed to have said when he was crucified?"

"No, Jim, I do not," I said, having little knowledge of Biblical passages, I ignorantly asked, "Did he say something about forgiving?"

"Father, forgive them, for they know not what they do," he replied.

I started crying all over again, recalling the boundless, forgiving love I experienced being given to the shooters when I came out of the morning's deep, mysterious meditation.

Yes, forgive them, for they know not what they do.

Forgive us all, for we know not what we do.

We must wake up.

It is time.

CHAPTER FIFTEEN

AN INVITATION INTO THE GARDEN OF GRACE

"Grace is when your own deeper self comes to rescue you."

—Tim Freke

And so, what is waking up, I wondered. Is it the home I've been searching for all my life? How would I know?

I was still under the assumption that waking up, finding home, finding my soul, was a specific destination, a specific goal and endpoint. And somehow, my arrival would be as clear to me as if I had received a note, perhaps left on my kitchen table or under my front door, telling me I finally arrived. Kind of silly I know. Spoiler alert, it doesn't happen that way. You probably knew this already. But I didn't, even then.

In the midst of all this work, I was, of course, continuing to work full time in my own private practice. But with all I was experiencing, I decided to add a new phrase to my business cards, "Integration of Body, Mind, and Spirit." It seemed appropriate. But only Jim and a few friends knew of my experiences and of my deep search. Still keeping silent. I continued to see Ray occasionally, as a mentor.

I kept exploring in meditation the relationship between these experiences, my life, and my yearning to find home, to find my soul. Doing my best at discerning. Using Tall Man's guidance about heart. And meditating an hour each day. What mattered to me was not what I was thinking, but what I deeply experienced through an open heart, in the present moment. And of course, by this time, thank you Ray, and thank you Tall Man, I had guidance and practice and knew the difference.

Within a short time, I spontaneously experienced two more very different past lives. Each came unbidden, one while practicing bodywork as a form of therapy with two friends and another while at a horse workshop I organized. It wasn't until I put the experiences of all three past lives together, combined with another experience, I finally accepted my understanding.

Two of my friends went to a bodywork presentation and learned a technique they called "unwinding." I volunteered to be the 'guinea pig' for them to practice upon. After calling on our spiritual guides, the three of us stood in one of the women's family rooms while I followed their directions to move slowly and spontaneously, "unwinding," as they had directed. I proceeded with this process for about ten minutes when I fell to the floor and, as in the hypnotic regression, I was suddenly in two worlds at the same time. I was in my friend's family room. And I was somewhere in Northwestern Europe or England hundreds of years ago where I was a woman being burned at the stake. As in the hypnotic regression, it was visceral, emotional, and detailed. I was in both places, vividly, at the same time. I felt the presence of what I can only describe as an ancient grandmother, holding me in my grief at being burned at the stake. It felt as if this sacred presence came from beyond a veil, from Divinity itself. It was impossible to deny.

I was aware of feeling enormous grief and enormous love for the ones witnessing my death, one of them being my young daughter, and the rest being the people responsible for my burning. It was similar to the expansive love I felt while gazing out at the vast black universe. And similar to the love and forgiveness I experienced with the Columbine meditation. From this time forward, whenever I felt that same depth of expansive infinite love, I felt the presence of what I decided to call the 'Ancient Grandmother.'

I smelled cherrywood smoke in my nostrils for weeks. I became aware someone who loved me wetted cherrywood so when the woodpile was lit, I would die of smoke inhalation rather than from the pain of being burned alive in a fire. I found out years later this is what some people did in those times when someone they loved was being burned at the stake.

And I had flashbacks as well. In one recurring flashback, I raged at God, "How dare you let this happen when I have done everything just as you asked? I swear to you I will never create again!" An angry, painful vow, now remembered in this life so a lost part of my wounded soul could be reunited with the larger soul we both are.

At the time of this experience, I was also working on a new kind of relationship with horses. I loved horses but now had a deeper appreciation for what they are here to bring to us human beings. I did ride again. It took courage to get on a horse after being bucked off and nearly killed. But I wasn't interested in controlling a horse, or in 'domesticating' them into any form of a riding program. I was interested in learning from them. Learning what they could teach me. I was becoming more human.

What engaged me about horses was their presence. I kept returning to the meditation experience of the huge golden chestnut horse, whose very body held the infinite love of blood, bones, earth, rocks, even flies, and of the infinite love and creative potential of the wet black universe.

Horses never vanquish their enemy. I found it interesting, and compelling to note, they do not war. We humans have brought them into our wars, but it is not natural for them. As long as they are not threatened, they seem to have a deep abiding sense of peace. And they have a specific talent. Because they have the evolution of thousands and thousands of years as prey animals, honing the skills of reading signs of danger, they can read humans much better than humans can read them. And also, much better than humans can read other humans. Horse sense, you know. It's likely because of the huge electromagnetic field of a horse's heart, as documented by HeartMath.

When horses read a human is coming in peace, they are in peace. If, however, the human presents with a peaceful shield but has an unconscious deep shadow of unrest hidden beneath, horses read this as well, and mirror back unrest. As Gabriel had done with me, highlighting my need to explore myself deeply, to bring lost parts of my soul home. Because of this, they are great companions in the practice of deep psychotherapy, providing very effective and immediate feedback to a client wanting to do such work. And so, rather than riding horses, I decided I wanted to work with them on the ground as partners in my clinical practice with clients.

That's how I ended up pulling together a horse workshop in our area with Linda Kohanov, the author of *The Tao of Equus* and *Riding Between the Worlds,* books addressing these issues. But for me, the workshop didn't go as planned. Linda and all the participants had a fulfilling event, but somehow, someway, I was unexpectedly cast into another lifetime. It was similar to the other two past-life experiences where I was very aware of being in two places at the same time. Again, it was visceral, vivid, detailed, and emotional. Like being in a backwards lucid dream, watching horrific events unfold right before my eyes, knowing in advance how they are going to proceed, being entirely unable to prevent tragedy, while at the same time working with participants within the horse workshop on a sunny Saturday morning. Fortunately, a friend helped both me and Linda with this event.

In this past life, I was the commander of an army of Knights, fighting the Cathars in the south of France, hundreds of years ago. It was a political and religious war. My son, who in this lifetime was Sarah, my daughter now, and who had brought her horse, Xavier, to the workshop, was a Knight in our battle. While we won the war, my son's horse fell on him, killing him. In a rage, I then brutally killed his horse. I felt and saw it all, in vivid detail. The thick, cold pounding rain. The smell of rain seeping into deep mud. The steam from the heat of blood flowing from the bodies of horses and of men. The screams of my son dying. The rage and horror of killing his horse.

At the end of the weekend, without sharing my experience, I asked my daughter how the workshop had gone for her. We'd had no contact during the entire time because Xavier was extremely agitated whenever I came within thirty feet of him, an entirely unusual behavior. Sarah immediately told me of vividly experiencing a past life where she was a Knight with Xavier in the South of France during the Crusades. And I, as her father, was the commander of her group. While it was a vivid and visceral experience for her, and she had many specific details all of which matched mine, she said there had been a problem with Xavier in the past life, but she didn't know what it was. And Xavier, she added, was very difficult and upset during the entire workshop, because, she thought, of the past life they experienced centuries before.

I was pretty shocked.

After the workshop, Xavier went back to his relatively calm peaceful horse self, even when I was near him. Sarah and I did a ceremony with Xavier where we apologized to him, and to all horses, for bringing them into acts of war.

As I told Jim about all this, we decided to invite horses onto our property. This meant building a barn, fencing, and pasture. Jim was preparing to retire, and I was preparing to change my psychotherapy practice to include working with clients with the consciousness of horses. He, having been raised on a dairy farm, loved the idea of retiring to a horse farm on his own property. We had just built a huge labyrinth in our front yard and planned on including labyrinth walking and horse work into sacred ceremonies along with our own personal, spiritual growth.

It was Jim's idea to build the labyrinth on our property—and to use it for sacred ceremonies. He'd come a long way in his own spiritual awareness, his own spiritual experiences, since the evening I'd been bucked off Gabriel.

And then something happened to interrupt all our plans and shake everything up. As it so often does.

The very day the workers came down our driveway to begin building the barn, Jim was diagnosed with the cancer that was to take his life.

You might ask, given I have predictive dreams and I focus on listening to my intuition, did I know ahead of time?

Yes. I did.

But not soon enough to save his life. And not soon enough to have changed those plans to build the barn. We would have needed several years' notice to save Jim's life. He lived only two years and four months after his initial diagnosis. It was a journey I would not trade for anything, except to have him back.

Jim getting cancer was not on my radar, nor on his. His father lived to be ninety-three. Jim was robust, lively, full of energy, and good health all of his life. We both thought I would die before him. My family members didn't have the long life span as those in his family. But for some reason, I guess it was meant for him to die just as he turned sixty-three. I was fifty-seven.

About eight weeks before his diagnosis, I had what was the first of several distressing experiences I knew was predictive of something big and painful approaching. But what it was, I had no idea.

My first experience was on a train ride into the city. At just the moment my body hit the seat on the train, I experienced a severe anxiety attack. The only one I've ever had. It felt as if my skin had been scrapped off my body. I could barely breathe. All I could do was sit and endure the anxiety for the entire hour. As I looked around the car, everything and everyone was peaceful, except for what I was experiencing within myself.

While desperately struggling to breathe, suddenly, Tall Man was there, offering a small piece of information, or perhaps guidance. "You have used Jim as a cloak to give you a false sense of protection. This is what you will feel without him unless you find a true sense of sanctuary within yourself. You need not look to anyone or anything outside of yourself for this. It is within."

The image of Jim being my cloak was profound. It rang true. I made a commitment in that moment to become aware and to change this within myself. To know my own sanctuary.

Within a few weeks I had another experience. I'd been having a recurring dream where the car I was driving was pitched off a cliff into a deep gorge. I kept waking myself up at just the moment I was going over the cliff. And then one night, when the dream began again and I was about to be pitched off the cliff, somehow, I reminded myself this dream is offering me a message I need to hear. One I'd been refusing to hear several times before. And so, I made the decision to remain in the dream, and witness what I was being shown. It became a form of a lucid dream, where I was aware, yet witnessing.

I went over the cliff and could see and feel myself falling into the rocky red gulch hundreds of feet below. As I fell, I realized I needed to let go of being a therapist. I needed to let go of the beautiful five acres of land we lived on. I needed to let go of being a wife. And I needed to let go of Jim. In the dream, I consciously let go of each. And then suddenly, I became aware my oldest daughter Melanie, was just about to have a baby, her third. And our family needed a grandmother.

Perhaps, I thought, if I open my eyes, I can wake from this and my family can have a grandmother. This would be a new pattern in my family. My own children didn't have a grandmother and I myself had almost non-existent contact with Olga. As I opened my eyes, I asked the dream, "What is a grandmother?"

"A grandmother is the teller of the family stories and keeper of the family lineage," I heard as I woke.

I knew this dream foretold something big coming. But didn't know what. And I refused to go into meditation to ask. I was too scared.

And then, six weeks before the diagnosis, I woke in the middle of the night screaming from a dream I could not remember. Over and over again I screamed, "Jim, someone in our family is going to die!!! Someone in our family is going to die!!!"

Jim rolled over and embraced me, saying "Oh, Pam, it will all be okay. Know it will all be okay." And then he held me as I shook off the terror and the grief.

I'm sure he must have remembered that the day we got the diagnosis. I know I did.

We were sitting together in the family room, awaiting the doctor's call. "Mr. and Mrs. Verner," the doctor said to both of us quite matter-of-factly, "the pathology tests came back confirming cancer."

I don't know why some doctors use such formal language, "Mr. and Mrs." when they are sharing such earth-shattering, intimate information. He knew our first names. He then went on to very quickly share his recommendations for a surgeon.

The thing is, the doctor had already shared with me he was sure it was cancer when he briefed me after Jim's colonoscopy a few days before. I told him then to find the best surgeon he knew and we would go wherever we needed and do whatever we needed. I kept the information to myself, taking charge, rather than waiting for Jim to make all the decisions. Rather than using Jim as my cloak to protect me, as Tall Man had guided. I told the doctor, very directly, "Do your research and have it in your hands as you call us."

And so he did.

But as Jim and I sat in our family room after getting off the phone with the doctor, I faltered in my resolve to not use Jim as my cloak.

"Jim, how are we going to do this?" I sobbed, begging for some form of relief from this terror. Wanting him to hold me and tell me everything would be okay.

"I can't protect you from this, Pam," he said through his own tears. "And I can't bear to see you cry."

I knew then I needed to be the one holding hope in the midst of terror, rather than asking Jim to do that for me. And I needed to take the lead in this, something I generally relied on Jim to do. It was now my turn to hold the very ground under his feet, as he had already done for me so many times.

This came into sharp focus six days after his surgery, on Jim's first day of full consciousness. The oncologist walked into the hospital room to discuss plans for chemotherapy.

The doctor was about fifty years old, with short thick brown perfectly parted hair and dark circles under his brown lifeless eyes. He wore a white coat hemmed exactly to his knees, making him appear perhaps squarer that he actually was. His stethoscope hung around his neck, evenly balanced. But his steps were uneven, as if he was a man in conflict with himself. As he told us who he was, I stood up and gave him my comfortable soft chair and pulled up a folding chair for me to sit in. Of course, he sat down in the comfortable chair, without even the courtesy of a thank you. I should have known what was coming.

"Jim, you have stage three colon cancer," he said, wasting no time. "This means we believe all of the cancer has not been removed."

Without pause, without checking our response, in a lifeless slow monotone, as if reading script from a computer and referring to Jim as "the body," he continued to speak. "As long as the body is able to handle the chemo, we will continue with it. Eventually, however, the cancer cells will become resistant to any chemo we can use. And we will run out of treatment options."

I tried to interrupt him, but he would have nothing of it. He refused to even look at me.

"Eventually the cancer will become resistant to anything we can do," he said, finally looking at me for the first time.

Realizing I could seize the floor, I said, "I know of several people who have had this diagnosis and have had radiation, chemo, or both, and it's been fifteen years since any need for medical intervention."

He wouldn't listen. "That won't happen here," he said with an air of certainty and detachment. "Eventually the body will not be able to tolerate the chemo and we will need to stop treatment."

Jim was looking to me for help in renegotiating this doctor's prognosis. "Now wait a minute," I said beginning to feel my own confidence and certainty, "You cannot predict every scenario. Surely you know of the bell curve?" I said, referring to statistical probabilities.

"Well," the doctor replied, turning his lifeless gaze to me, "Jim could be one of the lucky ones, but I doubt it."

Jim looked at me with complete terror in his eyes. While it might have been easy to gaze away from his horror, so intense was his pain, I locked my eyes with his, and refusing to hold on to terror, I reflected back to him my love. I called up inside of me the truths I experienced in meditations. The love in the golden horse meditation. The love of the Ancient Grandmother. Tall Man. And others. I held this. Solid. Not using Jim as a cloak, but now finding truth within myself. Knowing eternal love is the final and the real truth of all.

It was as if part of me was in the present moment of the battlefield in the hospital room and another part of me was in the present moment of sacred timelessness and grace. Sort of like sitting in a movie theater watching a horror film where Jim and I are being terrorized and chased by this doctor, cancer and death. While watching and feeling the terror, in the corner of my awareness I simultaneously felt something more real, more present and sacred. Jim and I are in a space of timelessness and love, a space more true and real than the horror story we only appear to be in on the screen. Death is not real. Only love is real.

I remembered our walk down the aisle in the church thirty-five years earlier, but just a breath of a moment away. About holding his hand while we were sharing our wedding vows. About the first time our eyes met. About how much I have always loved him. About how our love is eternal, true, and real. Without words, I reflected all that back to him.

I vowed to do everything I could to hold this for Jim.

Even though he did quite well, every time we saw the doctors, they were relentless in their dire prognosis. They refused to look at Jim. They looked and spoke only to me. Always reminding us this was his death sentence.

I have always wondered if they treated us so badly because they wanted us to leave their facility so Jim's death would not be entered into their research statistics. If so, their battle was the battle for pride in their research rather than for having compassion for their patients. Regardless of why they behaved so badly, with their behavior, they ended up aligning with cancer and death. And deserting us.

Fortunately, I was eventually able to convince Jim to go to another facility for treatment. The first thing his new doctor said to us was, "Hey Jim, you are doing quite well. Have you guys ever heard of the Bell Curve?" These new doctors partnered with us rather than with the cancer and joined us on our journey. And Jim did quite well under their care.

About six months before he died, noticing he might be fading just a bit, I quietly slimmed down my practice to make more time for Jim. One morning, while in the barn mucking out the horses' stalls, a job I dearly loved, the barn phone rang. As I held the rake and watched Xavier calmly chew his grain, I picked up the phone. It was Nora, the nurse from our medical insurance company. Our insurance provided regular nurse contact to families experiencing serious medical issues. I'd gotten to know Nora fairly well through all the conversations we'd had over the past many months of Jim's treatment. She had access to all his medical records and provided kind support. Nora joined in empathy with our journey, never projecting death ahead of time. But I figured she would know when Jim was about to enter final stages and would tell me, in a kind way.

"Nora," I carefully said, with some trepidation, "Jim and I have some money saved for a rainy day. He's always wanted to go to Sweden to visit all the farms his ancestors lived on. He has ancestral records stretching all the way back to the early 1600s. We always figured we would make sure we went. I don't know about the timing here, with Jim's illness and how long he will be strong enough to go. Tell me, Nora, is this a rainy day?"

"Yes Pam," Nora responded, "This is a rainy day."

And with that, I knew we needed to go to Sweden. Nora agreed. We quickly finished our conversation and I rushed into our living room to find Jim sitting on the couch, reading the paper.

"Say, Jim," I said, "Let's go to Sweden and visit all those farms your ancestors have lived on. What do you say?"

"I'd love to go," he said immediately, tears welling in his eyes.

I made all the plans and within a few weeks, we were in Sweden. All of Jim's ancestors lived within about three hundred miles of each other, making our journey fairly easy. We visited the farm where his father was born. We were even able to visit with some distant relatives of his who lived in Sweden. We were able to walk on all the land his ancestors tilled all the way back to 1610.

On the way to our hotel one evening, Jim raised, for the first time, his thought he would not survive this illness. We always held out hope, yet knowing we all do die. One way or another. We will all cross this bridge.

"Pam," he started softly, "I don't think I will make it through this cancer. And I don't think I have much longer to live."

"Well Jim," I softly responded, holding my promise to myself and to Jim not to cry in front of him, "if you believe this, then you need to make sure you take the time to say goodbye to our children."

He nodded his head in agreement. We both held back deep sobs. We drove to the hotel. And went to bed.

The next morning, Jim and I gathered our clothing and luggage to bring to the car, to continue on to the next hotel and the next farm. As he pulled the luggage from our room, I felt a strong urging, seeming from some unknown, yet familiar place, directing me literally to "put pen to paper."

I didn't understand, but as I've shared earlier, I pay close attention to such urgings. And this one was particularly clear and direct. "Put pen to paper." And so I did. I told Jim I would join him in the car in a moment, then sat on the bed, pulling out the pen and placing it onto my open journal. The words came so fast I couldn't read them while I was writing. This is what came:

> *The soul is the God Spark married to Humanity and All of Matter—the plants and animals of earth.*

The spirit is the God Spark married to the Transcendent.

The goal of life on earth is to marry the soul and the spirit to join the All of Matter with the All of the Transcendent.

When someone gets cancer, they have been given a sacred invitation by the God Spark of Matter and the God Spark of the Transcendent to marry soul and spirit.

The illness itself is all the illusions of the material world that form the veil of separation between the two worlds.

It makes no difference to the God Spark of Matter or the God Spark of the Transcendent if the person lives or dies—because in truth all life is eternal. It is only an illusion that it is not.

What is important is that the marriage takes place.

It can take place at any moment of earthly life— All it takes is a moment of recognition and remembrance—This is Grace.

Cancer is an invitation into the Garden of Grace.

I put my pen down and read the words. And then I wrote more—the words seeming to come from Tall Man sitting right next to me, understanding my pain.

"Our task with all of life's challenges, not just with cancer, is to hold hope and be present with what is going on right now in the present moment. A passing—when one passes from one dimension into another—can be a huge doorway for a person and a family to heal. It is the same with birth. The cost is letting go of the personal, prideful self, healing the belief we humans are separate from an eternal love, from divinity itself. This healing cannot be bought at any other price."

So, I had to surrender to the present moment. And know there truly is no separation between my human self and an eternal love. Divinity itself.

To do this, I had to surrender to the larger soul I am. That we all are. And let my larger soul hold me in this process of loss and grief to bring a healing that cannot be bought at any other price. To use nothing as a cloak. To breathe into the light while in the presence of our earthly trials.

We are Divine beings traveling in bodies throughout time, learning and evolving. As my Mozart Street Experience conveyed all those years ago. Remembering who we truly are, to marry ourselves in Divine remembrance, is the goal of earthly life. To marry the sacred with what seems to be the profane. But truly isn't.

I placed my journal into my purse and gathered my luggage, hauling it out to our car where Jim was waiting. I wasn't sure what I wanted to say.

"I have something I want to read to you, Jim," I finally said as I sat down in the driver's seat of our car. "When I put my pen to paper just a moment ago, this is what came."

And then I slowly read to him what I later came to call The Invitation into the Garden of Grace. He said nothing, sitting in silence, as I started the car to begin our day's drive through the wide, open farm fields of central Sweden.

"Jim," I said after about ten minutes of silence, "If I could trade places with you, I would gladly do so. I wish I could. I know this journey is painful and frightening. But it is safe."

"Oh Pam," he finally said, "You've always wanted to die."

"Yes, Jim," I responded, "because I know this life is not all there is. There is a more real existence beyond what we experience here. Of that, I am sure."

"Perhaps that's why you've always wanted to die, because you know there's more to life than what is here. But this time, Pam," he continued, "it is my turn to go. And it is your turn to stay."

"And it's both of our turns to do this with our eyes and hearts wide open, so we can marry our lives with the truth of who and what we are, in this life now," I said.

So, Jim found dying painful and frightening, and I found living frightening and painful. And we had to proceed into our fears. I thought of one of Ray's most famous phrases, "Feel your fear and go forward anyway." And so, of course, I knew we must. Somehow this was part of our life plan.

Jim's health began to deteriorate in the last week of our three-week trip. As he rested in our hotel room, I went to the hotel lobby and contacted the airlines to see if we could fly home earlier, asking them, please, please, please, since we paid for a slight upgrade to our economy flight, could they see it in their hearts to fly us home first class, since Jim was so weak and near the end of his days. When we got to the airport check in, the attendant, pausing for several moments after reading our name, took a deep breath and said with tears in his eyes, likely knowing our situation, "You two have been upgraded to first class. Let me take your luggage and go relax in this area to await boarding."

We both shed tears of gratitude. Jim insisted on taking the man's picture. He wanted to remember the caring shown by him and by the airlines. I can still see the man, standing there behind the counter, helping others. Yes, other people, even strangers, aid in our own healing. We are all connected. Our caring for others matters.

And then we began our slow walk into Jim's death. He did come up with a plan to say goodbye to our children. He asked each of them to write a letter of regrets and gratitudes and to come to him one by one to read and share the letters. He was prepared for each child with his own list of regrets and gratitudes.

Every evening during the last three weeks he lived, Jim and I, with our daughters and their husbands, gathered around the warm fireplace in our family room, listening to soft gentle music and to Sarah reading love letters Jim's parents had sent to each other over seventy-five years before. Letters opened for the first time since written by his parents all those decades ago.

At one point, as we were gathered around Jim, he began to sob. Deep sobs. We all rushed to his side. "No, No," he said. "I'm okay. Do you hear the music?" We all acknowledged the beautiful music surrounding us all in the family room. "Hear it," he said. "Listen to the beauty of it. It's beautiful beyond words."

I knew then he was experiencing all of us beyond the veil and feeling the safety of his passing. Drifting in and out of a coma, in and out of conscious awareness of the eternal Divine love that we all truly are.

About two weeks before he died, he wanted the two of us to share our regrets and gratitudes over the course of our thirty-seven-year marriage. Being the teacher he always was, Jim requested I write things out and be prepared ahead of time. As he had done with our children. But being in end-stage cancer, he did not have the ability to write anything down or to engage in long conversations. Even though by this time he occasionally drifted in and out of a coma, his memory was amazing. He articulated very clearly, yet briefly, with considerable love, meaning, and sense of truth. He knew he had a short time left to live and didn't want to waste one moment of our precious time together in circular small talk. He was incredibly focused and clear.

We spoke on a sunny fall afternoon. I sat at one end of our living room couch massaging Jim's feet with lavender scented lotion as he laid there, resting.

It was surprising to find we both shared similar regrets. We expressed sorrow for not sharing the depth of love we felt for each other more often throughout our lives together. I suppose it's a common regret all of us could pay attention to. We both wished we had.

And then we both expressed remorse at not exploring our spiritual connections and truths earlier in our lives and in our marriage together. We both felt our lives would have been fuller and more gratifying if we had.

And then we forgave each other and ourselves that day for all we had missed, because, you know, "Father, forgive them, for they know not what they do."

But it was Jim's gratitudes I found most amazing.

"How about you share your gratitudes first, Pam," he began.

"Jim," I started, "Your steadiness, your commitment to loving our daughters and to loving me, held me during the darkest time of my life. You held the very ground under my feet," I said, then paused for a few moments as I wept. "I don't think I would have survived without your love and your support. But here I am. And here we are. Thank you."

"You are welcome, Pam," he softly said. "I'm grateful I could be there for you and for all of us." And then wasting no time with getting to his agenda. "I have three specific gratitudes I want to make sure you know."

"First," taking in a deep breath, speaking slowly, he said, "I am grateful I learned from you of the sovereignty of women. I had no idea when we met, I held women second to men or had discounted them in any way. Or used sex as a measure to validate my own worth," pausing to gather his breath, he then continued. "But through all the stress and the chaos of our relationship and all we went through, I realized I had. I learned to fully respect you, and all women, not just with my head, but truly and fully within my heart, to see you, and all women, as equal partners with men, and with all life." He stopped for a moment to catch his breath and consider what to say next. I sat peacefully in tearful witness, softly massaging his feet. He continued, "This made me more human, and a better father to our daughters. I was more able to feel and experience my own life. And for all that, I am grateful."

After several more minutes of pausing to gather his strength and breath, he said, "Second, you confronted me about my alcoholism and insisted and held the belief I could become sober. And I did find recovery. We wouldn't be able to be here now as we are if I hadn't found recovery. For that I am grateful."

"Third, and really the most significant one for me," he said, pausing again for a few moments, breathless with all his talking, "is you helped me to find an authentic and deep sense of spirituality and connection to God. That is what is holding me right now, as I face my own death in this life. And for that, I thank you."

He paused again, catching his breath, then asked me to continue on with my spiritual journey, following my sovereign heart connection to spirit. Then said he hoped I would do research on my lineage and on Guy and do some writing. But most of all, he wanted me to love myself as he loved me. And, going forward after his passing, he wanted me to dance into the rest of my life.

He died the day after Thanksgiving, on November 25, 2005, with our entire family surrounding him in our farmhouse on those five acres of beautiful land, our horses in the pasture holding witness. We were all at his side as he took his very last breath.

Before his passing, Jim and I planned his funeral, with readings and music he loved. Our three daughters read parts of the letters they read to him earlier. Our three sons-in-law read three of his favorite poems. A musician and singer sang his favorite songs of love and of goodbye.

After the ceremony, I led my family in the procession down the aisle out of the church. As Jim requested, the singer was singing the song, 'I Hope You Dance.' Halfway down, I saw Ray, sitting in a pew at the edge of the aisle, weeping. I stopped the procession, leaned over, and embraced him, feeling the wetness of his tears on my already wet face. He embraced me back.

"I love you," I said as I let go of our embrace, looking deeply into his brown eyes, knowing the love and the peace at the funeral would not have been possible without him. "Thank you, Ray."

He nodded in acknowledgment, tears streaming down his face, and responded, "You are welcome, Pam. I love you too."

Each of our three daughters stopped to hug Ray as well.

After the funeral, I crawled into a cave. I just couldn't dance the rest of my life right then.

Ray died less than two years later.

Somehow, I went on with my life, but just barely. I retired from my psychotherapy practice for the time being and tried to focus on being a mother and a grandmother.

I stopped regular meditation and stayed in that cave for quite some time. And raged at God, "How dare you do this to me when I have done every-thing exactly as you asked?! How dare you!!!"

Does this sound familiar?

A part of me refusing, yet yearning, to come home.

Well, you know, caves can be pretty interesting. And provocative.

CHAPTER SIXTEEN

FROM A CAVE TO A MESSAGE IN A LITTER BOX

*"Our lives strung together and joined
by love's flow through time."*

—Ancient Grandmother

For quite some time my life slowed to a crawl. Since I wasn't meditating, I wasn't experiencing contact with Tall Man or the Ancient Grandmother. I was pretty much numb. Stuck grief does this. But somehow Jim provoked me beyond the grave. Because of my promise to him to write about my family and do research on Guy, two experiences arose close together, pulling me out of my numbness.

I decided to go to a writing retreat. The leader of the retreat led us through a meditation. But it was a meditation that ended up taking me on another unbidden, unexpected journey, where I was in two places at the same time.

As I sat at a table with about eight other women, soft music playing throughout our thirty-minute meditation, I found myself taken on a journey to the Far European North, to a cave near the ocean's coast, where I experienced the Ancient Grandmother. But this time, in addition to feeling her expansive eternal love, she spoke in words I could write down.

She summarized my entire life, and our very human journey throughout our lives, in just a few poetic sentences. The Ancient Grandmother said:

Moving. Fluid.
Tears stuck like paste to rocks.
Waiting for warmth to melt,
to flow into caves held in darkness for centuries.

And to flow out,
carrying treasure to the light of day

Oh my dear,
It's been so long I've waited for you,
to listen to the very flow of your heart.

Our lives strung together and joined
by love's flow through time.

In and out
as breath and tide,
moves through space and time,
for love's call home.

I repeated to myself, several times, as I read, "Tears stuck like paste to rocks. Waiting for warmth to melt, to flow into caves held in darkness for centuries. And to flow out, carrying treasure to the light of day."

My own tears were stuck like paste to rocks. Waiting for warmth to melt them, bringing me the gift of homecoming.

But it wasn't just me.

Throughout our human walk for millennia, our ancestors have held unexpressed tears of grief, then passed them down through our common lineage like ghosts. Like my mom's and dad's unexpressed tears at losing the foundation of a loving home. Like Olga, losing her mother at age nine. Like the Sami, having their children, their language, their sense of spirituality, and their homeland, taken from them. Like the Blacks who were taken from their homes in Africa as slaves. Like the Australian Aborigines and the Native Americans. Like the violence perpetrated on Indigenous peoples. That's our human ancestral lineage. It's something we are all holding. And something we need to heal, so we can come home to our soul. To who we truly are. As Tall Man said, to come home to who we truly are, to surrender our small selves to our soul, cannot be bought at any other price.

And as we do this in our own lives, we also heal our ancestral lineage. "Lives strung together and joined by love's flow through time," as Ancient Grandmother conveyed.

I recognized then that unexpressed grief is the foundational emotion fueling fear, leading to anger, then rage, then greed, then false pride, then shame. It's what ultimately fuels the vicious circle we all, all of humanity, need to move beyond.

So how do we do this? I've been working on this all my life.

As Ancient Grandmother conveyed, *"Oh my dear, It's been so long I've waited for you, to listen to the very flow of your heart."*

We open our hearts. And consciously, with awareness, listen to the very flow of our heart. It takes courage. I suppose this may be why the root of the word courage is heart.

And so, I understood then I needed to move into my grief and surrender to my soul. I deeply wanted to come home. And the Ancient Grandmother and Tall Man conveyed the path is through heart, love, surrender, and honoring grief.

I went home from the writing retreat with two commitments. One, I would research and write about my lineage and my history. And two, I would meditate and be aware of my heart, and my grief. The Ancient Grandmother and Tall Man occasionally showed up, always offering loving guidance and words.

Research on my lineage fairly soon involved researching Guy, my mother's cousin, who visited my grandmother Olga after he died. I expected my research to reveal historical facts to share with family, but not much else. I was so wrong.

Guy was my mother's cousin. Olga's sister's son. Mom and Guy were close in age and spent time together as children in Iowa. Just before World War II, Guy signed up for the Army Air Force, the forerunner of our country's Air Force. Before the war broke out, he became a pilot and was shipped off to the Philippines. If you know your history, you know what happened next. It was gut-wrenchingly painful to read the history and all Guy and his fellow soldiers endured.

The day after the Japanese bombing of Pearl Harbor, the Japanese bombed the Philippines and followed up with a full-out invasion. General McArthur, the leader of our country's force in the Pacific, surrendered thousands of American pilots and soldiers, Guy among them, to the Japanese, leaving them with his most famous phrase, "I shall return."

As I read the history of our country's abandonment of Guy and all those soldiers in the Philippines, I felt a haunting similarity with my experience of being abandoned by my own parents and community when I had appendicitis. I felt expendable then. As I read and researched all that took place in the Philippines, I imagined Guy must have felt expendable as well.

Guy walked the brutal sixty-three-mile walk through the sweltering hot Philippine jungles in what is now known as the Bataan Death March. He and his fellow prisoners were beaten, tortured, raped, killed, deprived of food and water, and forced to endure and witness untold horrors committed upon them and their fellow human beings. It is estimated between seven and ten thousand prisoners died along the route. After the war and the full facts were known, the Bataan Death March was declared a Japanese war crime.

But Guy kept on walking—soldiering his way through with many others who also somehow survived the brutality. Guy literally walked his way through hell. Every staggering, sweating, thirsting step—his grit carried him through. He experienced a nightmare many of us, thankfully, will never know.

It was not to end for him when he reached Camp O'Donnell, the Philippine POW Camp. Guy, along with thousands of other American and Philippine prisoners, was held at the POW camp where between twenty to fifty died each day from starvation and illness. Somehow Guy survived. For about two years. Our family knew nothing about the Bataan Death March or the O'Donnell POW camp. Or any of Guy's trials.

Just as the Nazis were faltering in Europe and our country began to pivot attention to the war in the Pacific, the Japanese began to gather their American prisoners in the Philippines with the intent of shipping them to Japan to be used as slaves in the war effort. They put thousands of prisoners on what later became termed "Hell Ships."

Guy was put on the Hell Ship Arisan Maru with nearly eighteen hundred other prisoners. But the Japanese didn't mark the ship as a POW ship, as required under International Law. And as McArthur had just returned to the area four days earlier with the Army, the Navy, and the Army Air Force, our country's military was in full force in the South China Sea the day the Arisan Maru set sail with Guy on board.

The Arisan Maru was torpedoed by our own Navy. Only nine prisoners survived. Guy did not.

At the very same time this happened, half a world away, deep in the middle of the night, my grandmother, Olga, woke shaking and screaming, "Guy is dead! Guy is dead!" She grabbed my grandfather and shook him awake. "Ed! Ed! Wake up! Guy is dead! He is floating in the ocean. He's drowned! Our sailors fired upon his ship. He's dead!"

It was at least eight months before Americans at home were told the truth about the Arisan Maru and what happened to their loved ones. And that our own sailors fired upon them, with most of them dying in the battle as well.

For some time afterwards, Guy visited my grandmother in the middle of the night. Our family tradition, you know. His own mother, in her grief, could not experience him. Grandma said his main concern was to allay his mother's grief so she would know her son lived on and was truly happy and at peace.

The weeks I spent researching reports of the Bataan Death March and the POW camp at O'Donnell, I thought of my own nightmares trudging through a battlefield carrying the soldier over my shoulder. I considered what it would be like to be thirsty and hungry and need to continue walking while someone I knew was being brutally beaten, raped, and left for dead on the side of the road. I read first-person accounts by the very few who survived the sinking of the Arisan Maru. I looked at pictures. I considered what it would be like to tread water in the South China Sea while sharks are circling.

In the midst of my research, I had to carry on with my own life. I had to run my errands, feed the cats, clean litter boxes, go to the grocery store, and everything else it takes to live. But behind all my activity were thoughts of Guy – of his grit and of his desire to return home to the open fields of Iowa, to live a life that had been taken from him that October afternoon in the South China Sea.

After two weeks of grief and tears, such a minimal amount of time compared to the years Guy and his fellow soldiers spent in captivity, on one morning I dragged myself downstairs into the basement to feed my cats and clean their litter boxes. It was an entirely normal daily activity that catapulted me into another consciousness. As I was scooping the boxes clean, shedding tears for all Guy had endured, while picturing him burying the dead bodies of his friends in the concentration camp, recalling my own past life Holocaust flashbacks of doing the same, I felt the physical sensation of a pinprick my right eardrum.

And then I audibly heard a tender but strong male voice say, "Do not weep for me. My life was just as it needed to be."

I stopped scooping the litter and took a deep breath to listen carefully and be aware of the experience. How could this be? Guy saying his life was perfect? When he endured so much brutality and then death in the sea? How?

He began to answer my question – but the answer did not come audibly in single words and sentences, as his first words did, but instead came in a series of connected thoughts and images forming a complete message from some mysterious, loving, and eternal place. It took my breath away. Summarizing as best I can, this is what Guy conveyed:

> *What we humans see as a limited life is a huge, great adventure of our soul spanning many, many lifetimes. I learned to truly love in the Philippines—to care for my fellow humans and to allow them to care for me. I experienced the joy of tenacity, grit, and love. I experienced my love for my family, my love for the community of all people, and my love for life itself. I would not trade one moment of that lifetime for anything. Do not weep for me. Pursue this for yourself. I promise you; it is worth every step of the journey.*

As I sat down on the basement floor, overwhelmed and sobbing with feeling his love, and his message, Guy showed me he forgave the Japanese soldiers, seeing them all as fellow travelers in a confusing and mixed-up world, all searching for relief from fear through acts of war, not knowing until their end that love itself is the final answer.

I was stunned. How could this be? In the midst of the profanity of war and brutality, in the midst of the sixty-three-mile Bataan Death March, the POW camp, and treading water in the shark-infested South China Sea, Guy had found love? And forgiveness? He had done what I have spent my entire life working toward. Hauling the nearly dead soldier over my own shoulder through the dark muddy suicidal battlefield that was my life.

When I meditated later on this experience, I noticed the common core of forgiveness between Guy's message and the message of forgiveness from my Columbine experience. Both advocating for radical forgiveness in the face of brutality and travesty. Not a bypass but advocating for a love beyond anger and fear. And for the courage to face our shadows, our basement bunkers, our grief, and to call ourselves home, to someplace larger and beyond our small, and fearful, personality. To get beyond war. To get beyond the triangle. To get beyond a war we fight with others. And a war we fight within ourselves. To surrender our smaller selves to the soul we truly are.

This is when I pieced things together.

My own life has been a slow walk off the battlefield. Guy, and my past life experiences, were showing me this is our shared human journey. As Tall Man and the Ancient Grandmother also conveyed. We human beings have been walking on battlefields, denying our tears of grief, raging in one way or another, for thousands of years. Bringing about brutal, violent battles with others. And brutal battles within ourselves.

Guy was showing me it's time to walk off the battlefield. With all I'd experienced with Guy, the Ancient Grandmother, and Tall Man, I knew the path forward was to honor my grief and walk into forgiveness. For me specifically, I needed to deeply forgive myself, God, or Universal Love, or whatever name we wish to give it, and also the profanity I saw in life itself. I needed to see the gift in the profane and to heal the rage I felt with Divinity for taking Jim away. Forgiveness seemed to be the pathway to a sense of home.

But how? I had already done so much. I knew any kind of intellectual bypass would not work. That's denial. And it's putting feelings into a shadow basement bunker. I knew, thank you Ray, I needed to have an emotional experience of forgiveness. In present time. And I also knew, thank you Ray, I must feel any fear I have and go forward anyway.

And then, along came a dream. Dreams often provide answers to questions we ask, and often to questions we don't know we need to ask. And so, I say, thank you to dreams. Messages from Spirit itself.

CHAPTER SEVENTEEN

ANCESTORS CALLING

"All over the sky a sacred voice is calling your name."

—Black Elk

I awoke in the middle of the night from the piercing sound of my own screaming.

"Oh, that was just a dream," I said to myself as I let myself drift back into sleep.

And then the dream began again.

I am standing in a large hallway, surrounded by many loving and encouraging friends, facing two large, closed double wood doors. I know these doors open up into the nightmare I just left. My friends are encouraging me with such loving enthusiasm to go back into the dream, but I don't want to. At just the moment I give them a brief consent, the two doors open and before me is an expansive dark night with a cornfield spanning what looks to be hundreds and hundreds of acres. My friends embolden me to leave the hallway and enter again into the nightmare through the double doorway.

I turn and go through the doors, walking into the cornfield. The doors close behind me and I know I am now alone, in a different world, the world of a nightmare. Before me is a muddy path between acres and acres of rows of tall corn. The sky is black and cloudy. A heavy wet wind is blowing. I know a storm is coming.

I realize all over again I backed out of this dream just a moment ago. As I begin to turn around to back out once more, I remember those friends beyond the doorway, relaying to me this dream has an important message. And so I decide to stay, even though I am terrified. I continue walking down the muddy path, further into the darkness of the storm.

About twenty feet in the distance, I see a dark shadow of what looks to be a man walking toward me. And then I again remember the dream and why I woke myself from it screaming just a moment before. This man is going to attack me. I decide again I am going to walk out of the dream. As the man continues walking toward me, I turn around to walk back and out of the dream through those now closed double wooden doors.

As I turn and walk a few steps, I see another large dark shadow of a man standing directly in front of me. He is between me and those doors. And the other dark shadow of a man who was about twenty feet away is now standing next to me. Now there are two of them. They are in communication with each other and planned this attack all along.

The second man is holding a pool cue and is going to impale me. I am sure the first man is going to help him. I know I am outnumbered and out-muscled. I can do nothing. There is no way I can fend this off. This man is going to kill me. But first, he is going to hurt me terribly. I'm going to suffer greatly before dying.

I scream and scream.

I wake up. Again.

Now I've been told, and I believe it's true, a nightmare is an interrupted dream. A caring message from the dream maker in us which was not fully received, and so becomes interrupted, unfinished, and felt as a nightmare.

At the time, I couldn't imagine how this dream could have been in any way a caring message. Unless it was a warning about not walking into a dark cornfield in the middle of the night—which was something I wouldn't do anyway.

I was shaking and in a half-awake, half-asleep state. I knew I could easily slip back to sleep, so I fought it, sitting up in bed, shaking myself further awake for at least two hours, refusing to allow myself to drift back to sleep.

Finally, I decided I could lie down and relax. As my head rested on the pillow, I immediately fell into a hypnogogic state—aware but nearly asleep. I began to hear music. It was a familiar song. I heard it over and over. The music was rhythmic and relaxing, except the message was slightly disturbing. I didn't understand.

A woman was singing about a man she loved for years and years and would love for many more. But he was a man caught in a vice between heaven and earth, more desperate than any man could ever be. And she wanted him to remember the man he was before he became so desperate, before he forgot who he was. If only he would look into her eyes and see love, he would finally find peace.

As I kept hearing the song over and over, I began hearing another voice. It was Ray's. He was talking to me, wanting me to listen particularly to the one line about if only the desperate man would look into his lover's eyes he would see love and would finally be at peace. I laid there and listened to the song and to Ray's soft gravelly voice reassuring me for quite some time.

Later the next day I meditated on this dream. Ray came back again. I became aware the attacking man was the part of me that wanted and tried to suicide so many times, in so many ways, so many years before. It was the part of me desperate and angry with the pains of life itself. I was being urged to deeply forgive myself, to forgive the persecutor in me. To bring that part of me home to my heart. I thought I'd already done this, but apparently, I had further to go.

And just as importantly, I was being urged to forgive God, Universal Love, and Life itself, for not intervening in my trials, for not taking my struggles away. For making me a victim. Apparently, there was a deep part of me wishing for a bypass. Still holding Divinity itself responsible for the consequences of the choices I made. Still holding God responsible for the human pain we all suffer on our learning paths to grow and evolve. Universal Love doesn't work that way. We all need to do our own part for our own healing. Accountability and forgiveness, you know. It's how we learn. And how we become humble. And how we learn to truly love.

I could hear Ray's frequent guidance, "Feel the fear and go forward anyway." I decided to do a dream re-entry. Now, dream re-entry is sort of like a meditation with a plan. The intention is to take on the roles and experience the guidance offered by the characters in the dream. I began by calling in my guides, my higher self, my dream maker, and the Archangels of the Four Directions to hold sacred space, and then I called on Ray. I asked for their help and guidance to understand and to heal from this dream. And then, I re-entered the dream, recalling the felt sense and the images of standing in the dark, stormy, wet, muddy cornfield, with two men next to me wanting to attack, one of them holding a pool cue.

I took on the role of the woman, the victim, just about to be attacked. I could hear Ray's guidance for me to stand with a heart of courage, and to hold a feeling of love. And to look directly into my attacker's eyes. Surrendering to whatever could happen. Surrendering to love itself. I became a witness to all that unfolded.

As I looked directly into the attacker's eyes, I began to see the attacker was Benjamin. I was so shocked it almost pulled me out of the meditation, but somehow, I held steady. I guess after all these years, I needed to forgive him. I thought I had put all that behind me when I became a therapist and went on with my life. Remember, our shadows are unconscious.

I saw all of his pain and anger with life, with love, and with God. All his disappointments. All his rage. I became aware I held the same pain and rage as did Benjamin throughout all my suicidal years. I stood there, holding a loving presence as I gazed into his eyes, seeing the truth of his Divine soul, and also of mine, beyond all the pain and rage. I held this for some time. The heavy, dark, blowing wind began to calm. Benjamin began to soften.

I put my hands together, as in prayer, then bowed to him and said, "I forgive you. And I thank you for all you taught me."

He nodded in acknowledgment, conveying a sense of gratitude. And then disappeared. But what happened next was even more surprising.

I found myself suddenly gazing upon the little girl I was years before as I laid in bed with appendicitis, after giving up my life, asking God to take me home. As I witnessed myself lying there, I noticed I seemed to be dead. My eyes were closed. I was completely still and didn't appear to be breathing. Silent, nearly dead, even to myself, caught in an empty place between heaven and earth, not able to be in either.

I reached my arms out to the little one I was all those years ago and in the present moment of this meditation, pulling her close to my heart. I began to rock her back and forth, slowly and softly saying, as Jim said to me several years before, "Pammie, it will be okay. Know it will all be okay."

After some time of this, I felt her begin to breathe. She finally looked up at me and said, "I've been waiting for you for a long time."

I continued rocking the little one back and forth, as she continued to breathe, more steadily now. And then I became the child, my own little one within me, letting my divine self, my very soul, hold me and rock me. And then somehow, I felt home. And knew I had experienced this place if we can even call it a place, before, but had denied it as such. The Golden Horse meditation. The forgiveness in the Columbine meditation. Meeting Tall Man again in the darkness of the night. The Ancient Grandmother. My experience of Guy. These, and more, were all experiences of coming home to my own soul. It was there all along, within me. Within my very own beating heart.

And then I became aware I was being held and rocked by an ancient lineage of grandmothers, stretching far backward in time. The Ancient Grandmothers were softly singing a song, joined and held by many Ancient Ancestors surrounding us all,

> "May we all know love.
> May we all know peace.
> May we all know we belong."

I was home with my soul. In this life. Here. Now.

I thought about what Ancient Grandmother said at the writing retreat,

> *"Our lives strung together and joined*
> *by love's flow through time.*
>
> *In and out*
> *as breath and tide,*
> *moves through space and time,*
> *for love's call home."*

The Ancient Grandmothers, and all the Ancient Ancestors, were singing to me and to all of us, holding all of humanity with a boundless, Divine love. After some time of this, I heard a gentle chiming telling me the meditation was over. I felt an urging to write something, but I didn't know what. And so I put pen to paper and this is what appeared, a message from the Ancient Grandmother:

Labyrinthine Journey to Soul

You may as well know this at the outset.
Your journey into the labyrinth of your soul
Is painful.
You will bleed tears.

And yes, at times you will need a candle.
Because sometimes the path is dark,
Muddy, and full of snakes and spiders.
I know, I know...

You entered this journey to find your one true love.
You hadn't planned on it being
so painful and full of mud.
But it is.

And you may as well know,
Computers help.
And so does email, google,
and the nightly news on television.
Because at times, you will want diversion and relief.
You will want to pretend you do not know
That you began this journey eons ago

Before time had even started ticking.

You will want to pretend you never
made this decision
To do this muddy and bloody walk into the
labyrinth of your soul.

You will want to pretend you are a victim
of someone else's agenda.
That a decision was made without your consent.
But that's okay.
Denial helps too.

It gives you time to light your candle,
to find your rose,
And listen for the murmurs of your soul far off in the distance
Yet as close to you as your own breathing.
For deep inside, you do know.

You know this place.
You've been here before.
This place where the deepest of love
touches your heart,
Moves through your body,
and touches the world.

Finally, home. Here. In this life. In this present moment. Now. Fighting no more. The war was over.

EPILOGUE

And so, I went on with my life. Quietly. Sharing my spiritual encounters and awarenesses with just a few close friends. Yet finally believing in the truth of my own experiences. Denying them no longer. Owning my own heart. Experiencing a peace I haven't known most of my life.

Of course, my life isn't perfect. There are still times when I experience grief, anger, frustration. That's our human journey. And remember, I'm just a regular person. Life can be difficult and challenging for each of us. But beneath everything, I hold a sound awareness of an enduring love, trusting in the process of life. Knowing there is a purpose and meaning to all we endure and can heal beyond. Knowing of the Divinity in all life. Humans, animals, plants, rocks, dirt, water, sky, sun, planets, stars, and even flies.

Remembering Jim's urging to write, I decided to join a writing group. I planned on writing short vignettes about family history to leave for my children. After several months of attending the group without sharing any writing, I decided it was time. Just before leaving my house to go to the group, without giving any thought to what I was bringing, I grabbed a piece I wrote about Guy years earlier. It was convenient. I was in a hurry and it was the only piece I had copied on paper. But the writing did not include my experiences in the basement while cleaning the litter box. It included only Guy's wartime experience and my grandmother's experience when he came to her after he died.

It turned out to be another sacred synchronicity.

I read it to the group of about ten older women. After listening, they were uncharacteristically silent for several moments. It was clear to me they felt the agony and the love in Guy's story. Then one of the group members shared she had an uncle who died at the Philippine O'Donnell POW Camp. Guy and her uncle, we both decided, must have known each other. I told them of my experience at the litter box in the basement. It was a big step for me to be so open with these experiences, having kept these kinds of things to myself for decades. They urged me to include that part in the writing about Guy.

When I came home, I sat in my comfortable chair, the computer on my lap, and began writing about my experience with Guy at the litter box. And then, suddenly, there was Guy. Very present with me, right there, after all this time, urging me to write about walking off the battlefields of our lives. His story. My story. Our shared human story.

I became aware we humans are an angry, grieving people, lost and searching for home, a sense of our soul, in all the wrong places. Racing to some form of a finish line, some form of material rewards, some form of documentation of our worth. Yes, as my nearly five-year-old little girl noticed all those years before on Mozart Street, surely there is more to life than winning a race against another on a shiny red scooter. And as Tall Man shared, coming home to soul cannot be bought at any price other than walking off the battlefields and surrendering our prideful selves to the very love of our Divine soul.

That's when I began writing the book you are now holding in your hands, sitting in that same comfortable chair where I listened to so many others tell me their stories, I sat with my computer and told you mine.

Guy was there, encouraging me. Within a very short time, so was Jim, soothing my grief at losing him. And then Ray. And then Tall Man and the Ancient Grandmother. All guiding me through the writing, every step of the way.

As I stated earlier, my life is not perfect, but my life is at peace in an ongoing, never-ending journey, in the present moment of eternal time itself. And so I will repeat something I shared earlier. We are never alone. There is not a one of us left out or unworthy. Everyone included. We are all held within an infinite field of love, stretching backward and forward in time and no time. We just need to walk off the battlefield and open our hearts to it. It is there. We are all held and sung to every moment of our days.

> May we all know love.
> May we all know peace.
> May we all know we belong.

In the words of Guy, "Pursue this for yourself. I promise you, it is worth every step of the journey."

Yes.

It surely is.

Amen.

WITH GRATITUDE

My life as it unfolded and the book you are now holding, would not have been possible without the caring presence of many others. Some seen and some unseen. I am so thankful to the following helpers:

My daughters, Melanie, Caitlynn, and Sarah, three Wise Woman. Because of your presence in my life, and my love for each of you, I was able to hold myself accountable to the sacredness of life itself.

Jim, my late husband and soul mate, the Wise Man who held the very ground under my feet, as I trudged through deep and dangerous fields, always holding the truth of "…it will all be okay." I don't think I could have done this life without you. And yes, it has all been okay. And thank you for bringing to me on some mornings the aroma of freshly brewed coffee as I lay in that liminal space between waking and sleeping.

My six grandchildren. You each came into my life and re-introduced me to a fuller awareness of childhood, innocence, joy, and love.

My three sons-in-law. Clearly Wise Men, each of you holding your own expression of grace, wisdom, humor, and authenticity, lovingly partnered with my daughters, although unnamed here, you know who you are.

My mother and father, you did the very best you could in this complicated place we call life. I thank you both for your lessons and for coming to me after you crossed beyond the veil, conveying your forgiveness and your love.

Ray, a truly Wise Man, you went to the wall for me. Always believing in me, always holding hope with true love, courage and wisdom.

Guy W. Iversen, cousin and World War II hero, a man of true grit and grace, who walked through profanity and found the sacred, and brought our family the truth of life beyond death. Thank you for encouraging this writing.

Benjamin, you taught me to trust my own truth and my own voice. I learned never to worship another, to find my truth from deep within. And I learned to deeply forgive.

The four other Wise Men—Jason, John, Dr. Leonard, and Detective Myers. Your names have been changed, but you know who you are. Each of you showed up with just the right support, at just the right moment. You helped restore my faith in humanity itself.

Jennifer, the only woman involved with my lawsuit against Benjamin. You were at my side every step of the way, during every deposition and every interview. I am so grateful for your abiding support.

The two paramedics called to the barn when Gabriel bucked me onto the arena floor. You saved my life. And to all paramedics for all the lives you save every day.

Mr. Raspiller, my ninth-grade biology teacher. You were the first person to help me change the direction of my life. And thank you to all teachers who are truly engaged with mentoring their students. You are not told this frequently enough—you make a difference in your students' lives, and in our world.

The team of nurses and psych techs who surrounded me on one profound day handing me just the right contact information at just the right moment. You were all part of the sacred synchronicity guiding me home. You believed in me and helped me to believe in you.

All the editors and journalists I worked with who guided me and respected my work. You helped me understand how this unusual world of ours works and how to hold myself in it.

Ron and Dave who hired me as a therapist, trusting me and mentoring me with respect and honor. While your names have been changed, you know who you are.

Bill, my husband's alcoholism counselor. Your authentic help and guidance began our family's recovery. Thank you for introducing us to Alcoholics Anonymous, Al-Anon, and the entire Twelve Step network.

All the people in Alcoholics Anonymous and all the Twelve Step programs. You bring recovery into our human community every single day.

The wonderful team of therapists, nurses, techs, and doctors I worked with who showed me more humanity and love than I can convey in words. And to all of those treatment professionals who are now working on the front lines, holding hope, compassion, and guidance for those in the grips of addiction and mental health challenges.

All the patients who trusted me to be their therapist. I learned so much from each of you about love, respect, accountability, and healing.

My small group of Soul Sisters—Debbie Marqui, Cathy Haggerty, Peggy Erday, and Joanne Spence—who, after my husband, were the first to hear of my mystical experiences with Tall Man, Ancient Grandmother, and more. You believed in me.

C. Susan Nunn, my editor, who continued, time after time, to meet with me with patience and wisdom, always willing to trust my own inner voice and guidance.

Annie Bloom, Joanne McElroy, Bill McElroy, Irina Zlatogorova, Lindsay Bates, Abigail Ehrhardt, Cathy Haggerty, Karen Love, Deborah Marqui, Ana Reluzco, Don Thomas, Mel Doerr, Marianne Cirone, Susan Wisehart, Jack Lloyd and Nevenka Radovic, all who took the immense time to read the rough draft of my writing, make comments, and then chose to write an endorsement. Your comments and support have humbled me beyond words.

ABOUT THE AUTHOR

Pam is living the peace and love in her life she always knew was possible. As a mother of three and a grandmother of six, she spends time with her family, especially enjoying playtime with her younger grandchildren, learning about life from all she loves. As a Licensed Clinical Social Worker, Pam spent many years working within the addictions recovery field, working with individuals on later stage recovery, codependency, trauma, grief, and doing Family Intervention Counseling.

She conducts workshops, mentors others, and has a limited private practice. And of course, she writes.

Pam can be reached at BreathingIntoLight@icloud.com.

RECOMMENDED READINGS

Most of the books, authors, and websites mentioned below I am quite familiar with. However, some resources mentioned here I haven't experienced directly, but have either heard about from trusted colleagues or from reading information and reviews. I placed an asterisk next to the authors I particularly recommend. While many of the authors listed have written many more books than noted, if they are on this list, especially if there is an asterisk, I recommend their work.

I particularly recommend you check out the last book on the recommended list about the development of science, The Structure of Scientific Revolutions, by Thomas S. Kuhn. It was written many years ago but the information is important to understand. Kuhn shares how science information changes with research over time, and that it is bound by assumptions that eventually get 'blown away" by new research, dissolving older assumptions, resulting in what he terms a 'paradigm shift.' Our culture is beginning a paradigm shift with current research on quantum fields, creating the potential of integration of science, spirituality, and mysticism.

In putting this list together, I noticed there is an abundance of books and websites encouraging the growth I experienced throughout my life. I found this amazingly hopeful. So it is clear, this list is by far not complete.

Do your own research and find your own path. But remember to engage your heart. Science shows we are all connected in a unified field.

ADDICTION/ALCOHOLISM:

*Beattie, Melody:
Codependent No More: How to Stop Controlling Others and Start Caring for Yourself

Brand, Russell:
Recovery: Freedom from Our Addictions

Burroughs, Augusten:
Dry

Bydlowska, Jowita:
Drunk Mom: A Memoir

Gray, Catherine:
The Unexpected Joy of Being Sober

Hepola, Sarah:
Blackout: Remembering the Things I Drank to Forget

Karpman, Stephen B. M.D.:
A Game Free Life: The Definitive Book on the Drama Triangle and Compassion Triangle

McGovern, George (U.S. Senator for 18 years):
Terry: My Daughter's Life and Death Struggle with Alcoholism

*Rohr, Richard, O.F.M.:
Breathing Under Water: Spirituality and the Twelve Steps

*W., Bill:
Alcoholics Anonymous

Whitaker, Holly:
   Quit Like a Woman: The Radical Choice to Not Drink in a Culture Obsessed with Alcohol

Bridging Physics, Consciousness, and Spirituality:

Antic, Ivan:
   The Physics of Consciousness: In the Quantum Field, Minerals, Plants, Animals and Human Souls

*Arntz, William; Betsy Chasse, Mark Vicente:
   What the Bleep Do We Know!?

*Braden, Gregg:
   The Wisdom Codes: Ancient Words to Rewire Our Brains and Heal Our Hearts; Resilience from the Heart: The Power to Thrive in Life's Extremes

*Currivan, Jude, PhD:
   The Cosmic Hologram: In-formation at the Center of Creation

*Emoto, Masaru:
   The Hidden Messages in Water

*Greene, Brian:
   The Hidden Reality; Until the End of Time: Mind, Matter, and Our Search for Meaning; Light Falls: Space, Time, and an Obsession of Einstein

Kaku, Michio:
   Parallel Worlds: A Journey Through Creation, Higher Dimensions, and the Future of the Cosmos

*Laszlo, Ervin:
   Reconnecting to the Source; The Intelligence of the Cosmos: Why are We Here?; Immortal Mind; Science and the Reenchantment of the Cosmos; Quantum Shift and the Global Brain

*Pert, Candace B., PhD:
   Molecules of Emotion: The Science Behind Mind Body Medicine

*Radin, Dean, PhD:
   Real Magic: Ancient Wisdom, Modern Science, and a Guide to the Secret Power of the Universe; Entangled Minds; The Conscious Universe; Supernormal

*Swimme, Briana Thomas, Mary Evelyn Tucker:
   Journey of the Universe

*Talbot, Michael:
   The Holographic Universe

Wolf, Fred Alan, Ph.D.:
   The Spiritual Universe: One Physicist's Vision of Spirit, Soul, Matter, and Self

Channeled Books:

Schucman, Helen: Foundation for Inner Peace:
   A Course in Miracles

*Selig, Paul:
   I am the Word; The Book of Love and Creation; The Book of Knowing and Worth; The Book of Mastery; The Book of Truth; The Book of Freedom; Beyond the Known: Realization; Alchemy; The Kingdom

Consciousness, Spirituality, Mind/Body/Spirit Connection

*Angelou, Maya:
   I Know Why the Caged Bird Sings; I Wouldn't Take Nothing for My Journey Now; Pocket Maya Angelou Wisdom: Inspirational Quotes and Wise Words from a Legendary Icon; Maya Angelou: Poems

*Byron Katie:
   A Mind at Home with Itself (with Stephen Mitchell); *Loving What is, Revised Edition: Four Questions That Can Change Your Life* (with Stephen Mitchell)

*Chopra, Deepak, M.D.:
   Life After Death: The Burden of Proof; The Book of Secrets; Metahuman: Unleashing Your Infinite Potential

*Chopra, Deepak, Debbie Ford, Marianne Williamson:
   The Shadow Effect: Illuminating the Hidden Power of Your True Self

*Dass, Ram:
   Be Here Now; Words of Wisdom: Quotations from One of the World's Foremost Spiritual Teachers

Dyer, Dr. Wayne W.:
   Wishes Fulfilled: Mastering the Art of Manifesting; The Shift: Taking Your Life from Ambition to Meaning

Ford, Debbie:
   The Dark Side of the Light Chasers: Reclaiming your Power, Creativity, Brilliance, and Dreams; Courage: Igniting Self-Confidence

Kohanov, Linda:
   The Tao of Equus: A Woman's Journey of Healing and Transformation through the Way of the Horse; Riding Between the Worlds: Expanding Our Potential Through the Way of the Horse

Lesser, Elizabeth:
   Cassandra Speaks: When Women are the Storytellers, the Human Story Changes; Broken Open: How Difficult Times Can Help Us Grow; Marrow: A Love Story

*Morter, Sue, Dr. :
   The Energy Codes: The 7-Step System to Awaken Your Spirit, Heal Your Body, and Live Your Best Life

*Prechtel, Martin:
Long Life, Honey in the Heart: A Story of Initiation and Eloquence from the Shores of a Mayan Lake; Secrets of the Talking Jaguar; Memoirs from the Living Heart of a Mayan Village; The Disobedience of the Daughter of the Sun

*Rohr, Richard, O.F.M.:
From Wild Man to Wise Man: Reflections on Male Spirituality; Radical Grace: Hope Against Darkness; The Wisdom Pattern: Order, Disorder, Reorder

*Ruiz, Don Miguel:
The Voice of Knowledge: A Practical Guide to Inner Peace; The Three Questions: How to Discover and Master the Power Within You; Eros: A Return to Unconditional Love (co-authored with Barbara Emrys)

Ruiz, Jr., Don Miguel:
The Mastery of Life: A Toltec Guide to Personal Freedom; The Mastery of Self: A Toltec Guide to Personal Freedom

Shinoda Bolen, Jean, M.D.:
Goddesses in Everywoman: Powerful Archetypes in Women's Lives; Gods in Everyman: Archetypes That Shape Men's Lives

Starwynn, Darren, O.M.D.:
Awakening the Avatar Within

*Swimme, Brian:
Spiritual Ecology: The Cry of the Earth; Journey of the Universe (co-written with Mary Evelyn Tucker)

*Tolle, Eckhart:
A New Earth; The Power of Now: A Guide to Spiritual Enlightenment; Oneness With All Life; Stillness Speaks

*Watts, Alan:

The Ego and the Universe: Alan Watts on Becoming Who You Really Are; Out of Your Mind: Tricksters, Interdependence, and the Cosmic Game of Hide and Seek

*Williamson, Marianne:

Tears to Triumph: The Spiritual Journey from Suffering to Enlightenment; A Return to Love: Reflections on the Principles of A Course in Miracles; A Woman's Worth; Everyday Grace: Having Hope, Finding Forgiveness, and Making Miracles

Dreams

*Aizenstat, Stephen, Ph.D.:

Dream Tending: Awakening to the Healing Power of Dreams

*Mellick, Jill:

The Art of Dreaming: Tools for Creative Dream Work

*Moss, Robert:

Growing Big Dreams: Manifesting Your Heart's Desires Through Twelve Secrets of the Imagination; Dreaming the Soul Back Home: Shamanic Dreaming for Healing; Active Dreaming: Journeying Beyond Self-Limitation to a Life of Wild Freedom; Conscious Dreaming: A Spiritual Path for Everyday Life; Dreamgates: Exploring the Worlds of Soul, Imagination, and Life Beyond Death; The Secret History of Dreaming

*Villoldo, Alberto, Ph.D.:

Courageous Dreaming: How Shamans Dream the World into Being

Forgiveness:

*Frankl, Viktor E., M.D., PhD:

Man's Search for Meaning

*Jampolsky, Gerald G., M.D.:
    Forgiveness: The Greatest Healer of All

Pratt, Katherine Schwarzenegger:
    The Gift of Forgiveness: Inspiring Stories from Those Who Have Overcome the Unforgivable

*Smedes, Louis B.:
    Forgive and Forget: Healing the Hurts We Don't Deserve

Tipping, Colin:
    Radical Forgiveness: A Revolutionary Five Stage Process to Heal Relationships, Let Go of Anger and Blame, Find Peace in Any Situation

*Tutu, Desmond and Mpho Tuto:
    The Book of Forgiving: The Fourfold Path for Healing Ourselves and Our World

Grief:

Cacciatore, Joanne PhD:
    Bearing the Unbearable: Love, Loss, and the Heartbreaking Path of Grief

Didion, Joan:
    The Year of Magical Thinking

*Martin Prechtel:
    The Smell of Rain on Dust: Grief and Praise

*Moody, Raymond Jr. MD, Dianne Arcangel:
    Life After Loss: Conquering Grief and Finding Hope

Rando, Therese A.:
    How to Go On Living When Someone You Love Dies

Van Praagh, James:

Healing Grief: Reclaiming Life After Any Loss

Meditation

*Dass, Ram:

Journey of Awakening: A Meditators Guidebook

*Dyer, Dr. Wayne W.:

Living the Wisdom of the Tao: The Complete Tao Te Ching and Affirmations

*Hanson, Rick, PhD.:

Neurodharma: New Science, Ancient Wisdom, and Seven Practices of the Highest Happiness; Hardwiring Happiness; Resilient (written with Forest Hanson); Buddha's Brain (written with Richard Mendius, M.D.), Buddha's Brain; Just One Thing

*Rohr, Richard, O.F.M.:

Daily Meditations

*Ruiz, Don Miguel:

The Circle of Fire: Inspiration and Guided Meditations for Living in Love and Happiness

*Thich Nhat Hanh:

Living Buddha, Living Christ; The Miracle of Mindfulness; Peace is Every Step: The Path of Mindfulness in Everyday Life; Being Peace; True Love: A Practice for Awakening the Heart

Mysticism:

*Bourgeault, Cynthia:

Love is Stronger than Death: The Mystical Union of Two Souls; The Wisdom Jesus; Centering Prayer and Inner Awakening

*Dossey, Larry, M.D.:

One Mind; Prayer Is Good Medicine; Recovering the Soul; The Power of Premonitions

*Fox, Matthew, PhD.:

Julian of Norwich: Wisdom in a Time of Pandemic and Beyond; The Coming of the Cosmic Christ; The Hidden Spirituality of Men; One River, Many Wells: Wisdom Springing from Global Faiths; Order of the Sacred Earth: An Intergenerational Vision of Love and Action

*Freke, Timothy:

The Mystery Experience: A Revolutionary Approach to Spiritual Awakening; The Wisdom of the Christian Mystics

*Rohr, Richard, O.F.M:

What the Mystics Know; The Universal Christ; Everything Belongs; Immortal Diamond; Divine Dance; The Naked Now: Learning to See as the Mystics See; The Wisdom Pattern: Order, Disorder, Reorder

Van Praagh, James:

Adventures of the Soul: Journeys Through the Physical and Spiritual Dimensions

Near-Death Experiences:

*Alexander, Eban, M.D.:

Proof of Heaven: A Neurosurgeon's Journey into the Afterlife; The Map of Heaven: How Science, Religion, and Ordinary People Are Proving the Afterlife; Living in a Mindful Universe: A Neurosurgeon's Journey into the Heart of Consciousness

*Greyson, Bruce, M.D.:

After: A Doctor Explores What Near-Death Experiences Reveal about Life and Beyond

*Moody, Raymond, M.D.:

Life After Life: The Bestselling Original Investigation That Revealed Near Death Experiences; Glimpses of Eternity: Sharing loved one's Passage From This Life to the Next; God is Bigger than the Bible

*Moorjani, Anita:

Dying to be Me: My Journey from Cancer, to Near Death, to True Healing; What if This is Heaven?: How Our Cultural Myths Prevent Us from Experiencing Heaven on Earth

Past Lives, Soul Retrieval

Botkin, Allan L., Craig Hogan:

Induced After Death Communication

*Dyer, Dr. Wayne W. and Dee Garnes:

Memories of Heaven: Children's Astounding Recollections of the Time Before They Came to Earth

*Moody, Raymond A., MD:

Life After Life; Glimpses of Eternity: An Investigation into Shared Death Experiences;

*Ingerman, Sandra:

Speaking with Nature: Awakening to the Deep Wisdom of the Earth; The Book of Ceremony: Shamanic Wisdom for Invoking the Sacred in Everyday Life; Walking in the Light: The Everyday Empowerment of a Shamanic Life; Soul Retrieval: Mending the Fragmented Self

Villoldo, Alberto, Ph.D:

Soul Retrieval: Mending the Past and Healing the Future; Healing States: A Journey into the World of Spiritual Healing and Shamanism (with Stanley Krippner, Ph.D.); Soul Journeying: Shamanic Tools for Finding Your Destiny and Recovering Your Spirit

*Weiss, Brian, M.D.:

Through Time into Healing: Discovering the Power of Regression Therapy to Erase Trauma and Transform Mind, Body, and Relationships; Messages from the Masters: Tapping into the Power of Love; Miracles Happen: The Transformational Healing Power of Past-Life Memories; Only Love is Real: The Story of Soulmates Reunited; Same Soul, Many Bodies: Discover the Healing Power of Future Lives Through Progression Therapy; Mirrors of Time: Using Regression for Physical, Emotional, and Spiritual Healing

*Wisehart, Susan:

Soul Visioning: Clear the Past, Create Your Future

Science:

*Kuhn, Thomas S.:

The Structure of Scientific Revolutions

Websites:

Retreat, Research, and Education Websites:

A.R.E.—Edgar Cayce's Association for Research and Enlightenment: edgarcayce.org

A.R.E. is a non-profit organization founded upon the psychic readings of Edgar Cayce and dedicated to creating profound personal change in body, mind, and spirit. The A.R.E. has an affiliation with Atlantic University in Virginia.

Buffalo Dreaming Lodge, Utah: https://buffalodreaminglodge.com

Center for Action and Contemplation: cac.org

This is a non-profit educational organization founded by Richard Rohr to foster the Christian path of transformation. They offer meditations, trainings, and educational programs intended to integrate contemplation with action in the world.

Esalen Institute, Big Sur, California:
esalen.org

Esalen is a non-profit organization to foster the transformation of humankind. They work with individuals and institutions integrating the body, mind, heart, spirit, and community in a nurturing relationship with the environment.

HeartMath Institute—California:
heartmath.org

This is a non-profit organization dedicated to opening the heart of humanity, with a plethora of research, trainings, and events.

IANDS—International Association for Near Death Studies, Inc.—North Carolina:
iands.org

IANDS is a non-profit organization devoted to promoting research, education, and support around near-death and similar experiences.

Institute of Noetic Sciences (IONS) California:
https://noetic.org

IONS is a research and retreat center focused on the intersection of science and consciousness.

Monroe Institute—Virginia:
www.monroeinstitute.org

The Monroe Institute is a non-profit educational and research institute, offering numerous programs and recordings, dedicated to exploring human consciousness.

Omega Institute—New York:
omega.org

"Omega is a global community that awakens the best in the human spirit."

Sacred Acoustics:

sacredacoustics.com

This site has information and recordings to enhance brain wave states intended to foster brainwave rhythms leading from normal waking awareness to those associated with altered states of consciousness.

Addiction:

Research and Information Websites:

asam.org

American Society of Addiction Medicine—a professional medical society founded in 1954 representing over 7,000 physicians and clinicians in the field of addiction.

cdc.gov

Particular articles relevant to alcohol and drug addiction:

—About Drugs and Addiction in Persons Who Inject Drugs/ July 19, 2018

—Alcohol and Substance Use

ncbi.nlm.nih.gov

NCBI—"The National Center for Biotechnology Information advances science and health by providing access to biomedical and genomic information."

NIDA.NIH.GOV

National Institute on Drug Abuse — This is "the lead federal agency supporting scientific research on drug use and its consequences."

psychiatry.org

American Psychiatric Association—article: "What is Addiction?

recoveryanswers.org

Recovery Research Institute of Massachusetts General Hospital, affiliated with Harvard Medical School samhsa.gov

Substance Abuse and Mental Health Services Administration (a Treatment Referral Routing Service) 1-800-662-HELP (4357); text: 435748 (HELP4U)

"SAMHSA's mission is to reduce the impact of substance abuse and mental illness on America's communities."

Addiction Support and Recovery Websites:

aa.org

—Alcoholics Anonymous site—A fellowship and recovery program for those who are having problems with their alcohol use.

al-anon.org

—-A fellowship and recovery program for those who are concerned about someone with a drinking or drug problem.

ca.org

—-Cocaine Anonymous—a fellowship and recovery program for those having problems with cocaine.

coda.org

—-A fellowship and recovery program for those who may be codependent.

emotionsanonymous.org

—-A fellowship and recovery program centered around support and help handling emotions.

gamblersanonymous.org

—-A fellowship and recovery program for those having problems with compulsive gambling.

na.org

—-Narcotics Anonymous—a fellowship and recovery program for those struggling with addiction to narcotics.

<u>oa.org</u>

—-Overeaters Anonymous—a fellowship and recovery program for those having a difficult relationship with food and eating.

<u>saa-recovery.org</u>

—-Sex Addicts Anonymous is a Twelve Step Program fostering recovery from sexual addiction.

<u>smartrecovery.org</u>

—-This is a non-Twelve Step recovery program offering a variety of tools to foster recovery from addiction.